Mixed Methods
Design in Evaluation

Evaluation in Practice Series

**Christina A. Christie and Marvin C. Alkin,
Series Editors**

Mixed Methods Design in Evaluation

Donna M. Mertens
Gallaudet University

Los Angeles | London | New Delhi
Singapore | Washington DC | Melbourne

FOR INFORMATION:

SAGE Publications, Inc.
2455 Teller Road
Thousand Oaks, California 91320
E-mail: order@sagepub.com

SAGE Publications Ltd.
1 Oliver's Yard
55 City Road
London EC1Y 1SP
United Kingdom

SAGE Publications India Pvt. Ltd.
B 1/I 1 Mohan Cooperative Industrial Area
Mathura Road, New Delhi 110 044
India

SAGE Publications Asia-Pacific Pte. Ltd.
3 Church Street
#10-04 Samsung Hub
Singapore 049483

Acquisitions Editor: Helen Salmon
Editorial Assistant: Chelsea Neve
Production Editor: Kelly DeRosa
Copy Editor: Mark Bast
Typesetter: C&M Digitals (P) Ltd.
Proofreader: Lawrence W. Baker
Indexer: Mary Mortensen
Cover Designer: Candice Harman
Marketing Manager: Susannah Goldes

Printed in the United States of America

Library of Congress Cataloging-in-Publication Data

Names: Mertens, Donna M., author.

Title: Mixed methods design in evaluation / Donna M. Mertens.

Description: Los Angeles : SAGE, 2018. | Series: Evaluation in practice series | Includes bibliographical references and index.

Identifiers: LCCN 2017004455 | ISBN 9781506330655 (pbk. : alk. paper)

Subjects: LCSH: Mixed methods research. | Social sciences—Research—Methodology.

Classification: LCC H62 .M423166 2018 | DDC 001.4/2—dc23
LC record available at https://lccn.loc.gov/2017004455

This book is printed on acid-free paper.

MIX
Paper from
responsible sources
FSC® C014174
www.fsc.org

17 18 19 20 21 10 9 8 7 6 5 4 3 2 1

Brief Contents

Detailed Contents

Sara Miller McCune founded SAGE Publishing in 1965 to support the dissemination of usable knowledge and educate a global community. SAGE publishes more than 1000 journals and over 800 new books each year, spanning a wide range of subject areas. Our growing selection of library products includes archives, data, case studies and video. SAGE remains majority owned by our founder and after her lifetime will become owned by a charitable trust that secures the company's continued independence.

Los Angeles | London | New Delhi | Singapore | Washington DC | Melbourne

Volume Editors'
Introduction

Conducting an evaluation is a complex endeavor, one that requires technical training in research methodology and, arguably more importantly, an understanding of the theoretical, methodological, and practical issues that are specific to evaluation. While the field has a leading peer-reviewed journal, *The American Journal of Evaluation*, and many texts on the topic, there are few shorter, practically focused publications that address issues specific to evaluation, and none do so as an organized series. This series offers readers the opportunity to delve into a specific evaluation issue or topic with more depth and complexity than what is provided in a general textbook on evaluation, but in a form that is more concise than books published on specific evaluation topics. The literature lacks a focused, dedicated publication that offers an understanding of a particular evaluation issue and then provides a discussion of how an understanding of that topic can influence practice.

The *Evaluation in Practice* series is intended to serve that purpose. It has as its focus two audiences: (a) students and faculty in courses in program and policy evaluation and (b) professionals working as evaluators. For the former, the books in this series might serve as supplemental texts in an evaluation course, providing students with an in-depth discussion of specific topics and issues and resources for both formal and independent professional learning. They provide extended discussions of how these issues and topics are connected to practice. Such information helps students and future practitioners to make better choices in their evaluation work.

The books may be of particular assistance in the various programs that offer graduate courses in program evaluation. The primary problems instructors encounter in teaching an evaluation course concern how to give students a sense of the ways in which evaluation is actually practiced. The proposed series was intended as a resource to allow instructors to delve deeply into issues that are important to evaluation with focused topic-driven books on both introductory and advanced evaluation issues.

Evaluation practitioners may also independently benefit from each book in the series. This information can inform practitioners' own work, suggesting ways in which they may bring focus, conscious choices, and compromise to improve the nature of their evaluations.

The first book in the series, *Mixed Methods Design in Evaluation* by Donna Mertens, helps to fill one of the niches in the evaluation literature by providing a concise discussion of mixed methods in a manner that enhances the possibility of improving evaluation practice. Readers are invited to explore the various approaches to mixed methods use in evaluation through examples and discussions. As the use of mixed methods gains popularity, this text is an indispensable guide for expanding the reader's methodological capacity.

In every chapter, readers are challenged to reflect on the assumptions and philosophical paradigms that influence methodological decisions. To conduct quality mixed methods evaluations, practitioners must have much more than just a mastery of quantitative and qualitative methods. They must also have a willingness and capacity to see and make sense of the world in different ways and from diverse perspectives. Casting a discussion on methodology within a theoretical framework may not be helpful to all readers. Nonetheless, the concepts encompassed within that discussion can be quite valuable. Mertens ambitiously weaves together methodologies, philosophical paradigms, and theoretical approaches unique to evaluation, and thus guides readers towards a more holistic approach.

In this text, Mertens also analyzes 29 published papers that demonstrate how a mixed methods approach has been previously used. Drawing on her years of experience as the editor of the *Journal of Mixed Methods Research*, Mertens features published papers that benefit from the mixing of methods. Each chapter highlights papers on a different topic of interest to evaluators, including: evaluation of interventions, developing evaluation instrumentation, policy evaluation, and the systematic review of evaluations. She begins by summarizing each paper. While not all papers are exemplars of mixed methods research, Mertens helps readers consider the problems and offers advice on how to conduct a similar evaluation. Mertens concludes with prompts that engage the reader in thinking about how mixed methods can improve social inquiry. These prompts create an opportunity to engage in self-reflection or can be used to guide discussion amongst colleagues and classmates.

Throughout her career, Mertens has been an advocate for the practice of evaluation to address social inequities. As a faculty member at Gallaudet University, she taught research methods to Deaf and hard-of-hearing students. This experience influenced her belief that evaluators should be inclusive and draw on local context and knowledge. Mertens shares her approach to evaluation by including a wide ranging yet concise chapter on the use of mixed methods in evaluations that align with the following approaches: gender responsive, Indigenous, universal design, developmental, needs assessment, visual spatial analysis, arts based, and conflict zones. By doing so, Mertens demonstrates how to conduct quality mixed methods evaluations while maintaining reverence for the local context and culture.

Typically, methodology training tends to focus on either quantitative or qualitative methods. However, the complexity of social science research often demands a broader and more reflective approach. While there are some exceptional primary texts, there are limited options for educators who seek to instill an interest in and capacity for the use of mixed methods in evaluation. Evaluation texts rarely offer a comprehensive discussion of methods, let alone mixed methods. For example, *Program Evaluation: Methods and Case Studies* (8th edition) by Emil Posavac details how to use quantitative and qualitative methods separately, however scarcely mentions integrating them to enrich evaluation findings. Similarly, Rossi, Lipsey, and Freeman in *Evaluation: A Systematic Approach* (7th edition) focus their methods discussion on experimental and quasi-experimental approaches. While they outline the essentials of researching social programs, the text does not identify and discuss mixed methods as a distinct methodology. Furthermore, methodology textbooks typically default to either quantitative or qualitative methods but rarely demonstrate how to best mix methods. There are some excellent mixed methods textbooks, such as Creswell and Plano-Clark's *Designing and Conducting Mixed Methods Research;* however, they offer few examples of its application in evaluation.

Mertens's text supplies an essential companion to existing sources on evaluation methodology.

By addressing mixed methods as a distinct methodology, Mertens has crafted a text that will benefit evaluation students, emerging practitioners, and established evaluators eager to improve their practice. She gives readers the tools to make informed methodological decisions by first helping them understand the different epistemological, ontological, and theoretical assumptions underlying every decision. However, the discussion of these assumptions is not removed from the practical nature of evaluation work. By integrating the discussion of *how* and *why* we make certain decisions with case studies of past evaluations, Mertens reveals the complications and opportunities with mixing methods. While many evaluators understand the importance of weaving together quantitative and qualitative methods, most learned about them separately. This text helps evaluators move past entrenched methodological divides and supports them in reimagining the methodological choices they make.

Alana Kinarsky, Marvin C. Alkin,
and Christine A. Christie
Volume Editors

Preface

I had the privilege of serving as the editor for the *Journal of Mixed Methods Research* for 5 years; this afforded me the opportunity to read manuscripts from all over the world that purportedly addressed the journal's purpose, that is, to publish "ground-breaking and seminal work in the field of mixed methods research." Of course, not all manuscripts are accepted; however, in my experience, the primary reason for rejection was because the authors had not contributed to advancing thinking about mixed methods theoretically or methodologically.

The purpose of this book is to share groundbreaking and seminal work on the design of mixed methods evaluation studies through the use of various philosophical frames associated with methodological advances in the design of mixed methods evaluations. To this end, I explore the meaning of mixed methods evaluation, its evolution over the last few decades, and the dominant philosophical frameworks influencing thought and practice about the design of mixed methods evaluations. The majority of the book is of a practical nature guiding the reader's thinking about the design of mixed methods evaluations through the use of illustrative examples and explanations for further applications.

INTENDED AUDIENCE ●

The book focuses on mixed methods designs, hence, you will not find specific guidance on how to develop a survey or how to analyze data statistically or thematically. I make assumptions that readers are knowledgeable about quantitative and qualitative design options and are reading this book to learn about how those design options can be applied in the conduct of mixed methods studies. Thus, the intended audience ranges from the beginning evaluation student through the practiced professional. Beginning evaluation students need to have been exposed to the quantitative and qualitative methods that appear in introductory evaluation textbooks. For their benefit, I have included definitions of common terminology used in evaluation that appear in bold throughout the text. More advanced evaluation students will benefit from the use of this book because it will guide them in the creative use of evaluation design options in a variety of settings. Practicing evaluators who either received training primarily in quantitative or qualitative methods can use the book to see the possibilities for adding another component to their studies when appropriate. For evaluators who have come to mixed methods intuitively, without formal mixed methods training, this book will provide the instruction and examples of more sophisticated applications of mixed methods studies in order to more effectively address complex contexts in evaluation.

● ORGANIZATION OF THE BOOK

Each chapter begins with an advance organization feature that lists the content of the chapter. The first chapter provides an overview of the use of mixed methods in evaluation and the evolution of the theory and practice of mixed methods in this field. The dominant philosophical frameworks that are influencing thinking in evaluation are introduced and used to inform readers about the influence of their philosophical assumptions on design decisions in evaluation. The next four chapters provide in-depth examples and guidance for functions that evaluators commonly perform: evaluation of the effectiveness of interventions, development of instruments, systematic reviews, and policy evaluations. The sixth chapter provides guidance and examples of specific evaluation approaches that are often required in specific contexts, including gender-responsive evaluations, Indigenous evaluations, universal design evaluations, developmental evaluation, needs assessment, visual spatial analysis, arts-based evaluations, and evaluations in conflict zones. For each type of evaluation, an explanation is provided about the relevance of mixed methods for that type. Sample studies are then provided that are reflective of the various philosophical frames evaluators use. This allows the reader to see the influence of the philosophical assumptions on methodological choices as well as to see the practical application of those assumptions in a real study. A final chapter provides ideas about the challenges facing mixed methods evaluators in the future.

PEDAGOGICAL FEATURES   ●

As mentioned previously, each chapter includes an explanation of mixed methods designs situated in different philosophical frameworks used in the field of evaluation. Terminology necessary for understanding the evaluation type is provided in bold with definitions in the text. The explanations then are followed by sample studies that are summarized with an emphasis on the mixed methods design features and analyzed to illustrate the benefits that the use of mixed methods provided in the evaluation. A subsequent section provides specific steps for the design of that type of evaluation. Finally, readers are provided with an opportunity to extend their thinking through application exercises. Additional resources related to mixed methods evaluation are provided in an appendix.

Acknowledgments

My experience in mixed methods evaluation can be traced back to my first evaluation position that I held at the University of Kentucky College of Medicine. I was trained in quantitative methods in graduate school, but I intuitively knew that the use of only quantitative methods was not allowing me to gain a thorough understanding of the experiences of incoming medical students. Fortunately for me, this was the beginning of the period in evaluation history fondly (or not so fondly) remembered as the "paradigm wars." What it meant for me was that Egon Guba and Yvonna Lincoln were fighting valiantly for the inclusion of qualitative methods in evaluation, despite opposition from some evaluation thought leaders. I acknowledge the insights into the use of qualitative methods and then the placement of methods decisions into philosophical frameworks that Lincoln and Guba contributed as being foundational for my understanding not only of qualitative methods but to begin my glimmerings of understanding of combining quantitative and qualitative methods.

My motivation to pursue the meaning of mixing methods was exponentially increased when I took a position as a faculty member at Gallaudet University. Gallaudet is the only university in the world that has a mission to serve the Deaf and hard-of-hearing communities. I chose to go there because my previous positions had allowed me to do evaluations on stakeholder groups without immersion in the communities affected by the programs. I keenly felt this lack of community connection; therefore, I sought a place where I could do evaluations with members of a marginalized community. When I arrived at Gallaudet, I thought I was equipped to share my expertise in quantitative and qualitative methods with the students so we could do studies together. As I worked with the Deaf community, I became aware of the amazing cultural knowledge they shared with each other, a knowledge that, as I came to understand, was necessary in order to do respectful evaluations together. The synergy that evolved in my relationships with Deaf community members created a transformation in my thinking about methodology so that it would not only be inclusive of quantitative and qualitative approaches but also reflective of the cultural complexity in the context in which I was working.

I am a methodologist at heart; therefore, I wrote and spoke about the developments in methodologies that emerged from my work with the Deaf community. Members of other marginalized communities contacted me and asked me to work with them in the development of appropriate methodologies that would incorporate their cultural concerns. An international group of scholars interested in mixed methods contacted me about presenting at a mixed methods conference at Cambridge University. The rest they might say is history. I became immersed in the mixed methods community, contributed to the establishment of the Mixed Methods International Research Association, and served as the editor of the *Journal of Mixed Methods Research*. I want to acknowledge those leaders in mixed methods who support the advancement of thinking about this approach, especially Jose Francisco Molina, Nancy Gerber, Michael Fetters, Sharlene Hesse-Biber, Pat Bazeley, Jennifer Greene, and John Creswell.

I also want to thank the SAGE staff who are supportive of me and this project, especially Helen Salmon, acquisitions editor; Chelsea Neve, editorial assistant; and Kelly DeRosa, production editor. I appreciate the input from the series editors, Marvin Alkin and Tina Christie, for their willingness to undertake guidance for authors in this series. I thank the reviewers of early versions of this book for their helpful feedback: Leah C. Neubauer, Northwestern University Feinberg School of Medicine; Jori N. Hall, University of Georgia; Sanjay K. Pandey, George Washington University; Amanda S. Birnbaum, Montclair State University; Sebastian Galindo-Gonzalez, University of Florida; Kathleen Norris, Plymouth State University; and Kelly L. Wester, University of North Carolina at Greensboro. And I want to acknowledge the wondrous influence of my sons, Jeffrey and Nathan, because they keep me grounded and help me understand that we do this work for a better future.

About the Author

 **Donna M. Mertens** is professor emerita at Gallaudet University in Washington, DC. She taught research methods and program evaluation to Deaf and hearing students at the MA and PhD levels for over 30 years. Her research and evaluation work includes studies on such topics as transformative mixed methods approaches that can contribute to improvement of environmental justice in Korea, economic development and child health in Indigenous communities in Guatemala, reducing violence and improving quality of life in Chile, improvement of special education services in many international settings, enhancing the educational experiences of students with disabilities, preventing sexual abuse in residential schools for Deaf students, improving access to the court systems for Deaf and hard-of-hearing people, and improving the preparation of teachers of the Deaf through appropriate use of instructional technology. Her research focuses on improving methods of inquiry by integrating the perspectives of those who have experienced oppression in our society. She draws on the writings of feminists, racial and ethnic minorities, people with disabilities, and Indigenous peoples who have addressed the issues of power and oppression and their implications for research methodology.

Dr. Mertens has made numerous presentations at the meetings of the Mixed Methods International Research Association, American Evaluation Association, Association for College Educators of the Deaf and Hard of Hearing, International Sociological Association, Australasian Evaluation Society, American Psychological Association, African Evaluation Association, Canadian Evaluation Society, Visitors Studies Association, and other organizations that explore these themes. She served as president and board member of the American Evaluation

Association from 1997 to 2002 and as a member of the Board of Trustees for the International Organization for Cooperation in Evaluation, 2002–2003. She was editor of the *Journal of Mixed Methods Research* from 2009 to 2014. She served as a visiting professor at La Universidad del Valle in Guatemala and a Fulbright specialist in Santiago, Chile, in 2016.

Her publications include four edited volumes, *Indigenous Pathways to Social Research* (coedited with Fiona Cram and Bagele Chilisa, 2013), *Handbook of Social Research Ethics* (coedited with Pauline Ginsberg, 2009), *Creative Ideas for Teaching Evaluation* (1989), and *Research and Inequality* (coedited with Carole Truman and Beth Humphries, 2000), and several authored books, including *Research and Evaluation in Education and Psychology* (4th ed., 2015), *Program Evaluation: A Comprehensive Guide* (with Amy Wilson, 2012), *Transformative Research and Evaluation* (2009), *Research and Evaluation Methods in Special Education* (coauthored with John McLaughlin, 2004), and *Parents and Their Deaf Children* (coauthored with Kay Meadow-Orlans and Marilyn Sass Lehrer, 2003). She also publishes many chapters and articles in edited volumes, encyclopedias, handbooks, and journals, such as *Journal of Mixed Methods Research*, *Qualitative Social Work*, *Educational Researcher*, *International Journal of Mixed Methods Research*, *New Directions for Program Evaluation*, *American Journal of Evaluation*, *American Annals of the Deaf*, *Studies in Educational Evaluation*, and *Educational Evaluation and Policy Analysis*.

1

Mixed Methods in Evaluation: History and Progress

A range of analytic methods is needed, and often several methods—including quantitative and qualitative approaches—should be used simultaneously. (American Evaluation Association, 2013, p. 6)

Sometimes a single method is not sufficient to accurately measure an activity or outcome because the thing being measured is complex and/or the data method/source does not yield data reliable or accurate enough. Employing multiple methods (sometimes called "triangulation") helps increase the accuracy of the measurement and the certainty of your conclusions when the various methods yield similar results. (U.S. Department of Health and Human Services, Centers for Disease Control and Prevention, 2011, p. 63)

In This Chapter

- The scholarship behind methodological choices
- Definitions of mixed methods in evaluation

- Increased interest in and demand for mixed methods evaluations
- Overview of mixed methods frameworks and philosophical assumptions
- Criteria for judging quality of mixed methods studies

● HISTORY OF EVALUATION AND MIXED METHODS

The beginning of evaluation as a practice, not as a profession, is as old as the first human who decided what was safe to eat and what was not. In the United States, the roots of professional evaluation can be traced back to the 1800s when the government required inspectors to evaluate publicly funded programs such as prisons, hospitals, schools, and orphanages (Stufflebeam, Madaus, & Kellaghan, 2000). However, a formal recognition of the profession of evaluation in the United States is generally acknowledged to have occurred in the 1960s with the mandate for evaluation of programs funded under the Great Society initiatives and the War on Poverty (e.g., the Manpower Development and Training Act, Head Start for Early Childhood Services, and the Elementary and Secondary Education Act) (Shadish & Luellen, 2005). Evaluation in Europe formally emerged in the 1970s and was reinforced by the establishment of the European Structural Fund in 2004. In the rest of North America, South America, Africa, Asia, Australia, and island nations, evaluation has become more prominent over the past decades because of demands by domestic and international agencies, governments, foundations, and businesses. Throughout this long history, the evaluation world has been characterized by the use of many different methods. In my lifetime, I witnessed the early years of evaluation when quantitative methods dominated, followed by a period in which qualitative methods were contested and then came into acceptance, and, at first in unofficial ways and then more formally, the emergence of mixed methods.

The history of the use of mixed methods can also be traced back to the 1800s. Hesse-Biber (2010) reported that mixed methods, that is, the use of both quantitative and qualitative techniques, were used in the 1850s in studies of poverty in families in Europe (Le Play, 1855). W. E. B. Du Bois (1899) argued for the use of both statistical and observational data; he applied this approach in his landmark study *The Philadelphia Negro*. Campbell and Fiske (1959) contributed to mixed methods with their multitrait, multimethod matrix that recommended the use of several methods (some quantitative, some qualitative) to measure each of several traits in order to strengthen the validity of research conclusions. "Many evaluators intuitively came to the conclusion that evaluations on complex social programs could be enhanced by the use of multiple methods; hence the combination of both quantitative and qualitative data in the same study is nothing new" (Mertens & Hesse-Biber, 2013, p. 1). Despite evidence of the use of both quantitative and qualitative methods in the past, it was only in the late 1980s and early 1990s that mixed methods research was recognized as a "distinct and self-conscious strategy" with attention being given to how to effectively combine these approaches (Maxwell, 2015, p. 1).

SCOPE OF THIS BOOK

Formal recognition of mixed methods as an important area for discussion in the evaluation community was influenced by Greene and Caracelli's (1997) publication in a volume of *New Directions for Evaluation* on that topic that discussed the role mixed methods approaches can play in evaluation. This volume began an important discussion that is expanded on in this book, the purpose of which is to elucidate mixed methods as a distinct and self-conscious strategy in evaluation to bring greater understanding to what it means to mix methods in order to strengthen the credibility of evaluation findings. Rather than covering all aspects of mixed methods in evaluation, this book focuses on the variations of mixed methods designs and their implications for data collection and use. Evaluators are asked to evaluate many things— for example, programs, projects, policies, needs, contexts, public relations campaigns, services, organizations, and systems; evaluators use the term **evaluand** to refer to the object of the evaluation. This book explores the applicability of the use of mixed methods for this full range of evaluands.

DIFFERENTIATING MIXED METHODS RESEARCH AND MIXED METHODS EVALUATION

Given the youthful status of discussions about the meaning of mixed methods, it should come as no surprise that there are differences of opinion on the definition of **mixed methods**. For the moment, a generic definition of mixed methods research presented by Creswell and Plano Clark (2007) can be used as a starting point for discussions about the meaning of mixed methods: "MM research is a research design with philosophical assumptions as well as methods of inquiry. . . . Its central premise is that the use of quantitative and qualitative approaches, in combination, provides a better understanding of research problems than either approach alone" (p. 5). Johnson, Onwuegbuzie, and Turner (2007) offer the following definition of mixed methods:

> Mixed methods research is the type of research in which a researcher or team of researchers combines elements of qualitative and quantitative research approaches (e.g., use of qualitative and quantitative viewpoints, data collection, analysis, inference techniques) for the purposes of breadth and depth of understandings and corroboration. (p. 123)

The key characteristics present in most definitions of mixed methods research are the inclusion of both quantitative and qualitative strategies at different levels of the study and the integration of thinking resulting from the use of both types of strategies.

Whereas research and evaluation share much of the same territory in terms of methods of inquiry, the purpose of the inquiry and the political context of evaluation stand out as important differentiating characteristics between research and evaluation (Mathison, 2014). Evaluations are generally conducted for the purpose of informing decision making about the value, merit, or worth of an evaluand. Evaluations are conducted in contexts of limited resources and so involve competing value systems that are political in nature; hence, evaluators must be attentive to the different perspectives and values of their relevant constituencies or stakeholders in the language of evaluation. **Stakeholders** are people who have a stake in the evaluation; they can be influenced positively or negatively by the evaluation process and findings.

Given the overlap between research and evaluation, it is no surprise that definitions of mixed methods evaluation borrow many of the concepts from the mixed methods research community and extend the definitions to include the purpose of evaluations and the political context in which evaluation resides (Mertens & Tarsilla, 2015). Mixed methods evaluation includes the use of

> both quantitative and qualitative data collection and data analysis techniques to answer a particular question or set of questions in evaluations. It is important to understand that mixed methods is not just about (mixing and combining) methods.

The use of any given method or set of methods in an evaluation is also tightly linked to specific epistemologies, methodologies (theoretical perspectives), and axiological assumptions, as well as being connected to particular stakeholder perspectives (Giddings, 2006; Greene, 2007; Hesse-Biber, 2010). (cited in Mertens & Hesse-Biber, 2013, pp. 5–6)

This definition of mixed methods in evaluation acknowledges the grounding of evaluation questions in specific philosophical assumptions to guide thinking about ethical practice, the nature of knowledge, and the nature of reality. Evaluators function in a world with multiple paradigms associated with different philosophical assumptions. These assumptions lead to different stances in terms of methodologies; for example,

> those methodologies that hold up the importance of studying the "lived experience" of individuals (interpretive methodologies); those methodologies that privilege the importance of hypothesis testing and causality as the most important goal of social inquiry (positivist and post-positivist methodologies); those methodologies that stress issues of power and control and social justice (transformative, feminist, and critical methodologies). (Mertens & Hesse-Biber, 2013, p. 6)

Mixed methods can be used within any of these methodological frameworks. The way they are used will be influenced by the assumptions that constitute the evaluator's methodological stance. Further discussion of the different paradigms functioning in the evaluation world and the implications for the use of mixed methods are discussed in a subsequent section of this chapter.

INCREASED INTEREST IN AND DEMAND ●
FOR MIXED METHODS EVALUATIONS

Given the use of mixed methods over such a prolonged time, what rationale can there be for the growth of professional interest in and literature on this topic in evaluation? As noted previously, it is only recently that mixed methods has become a "distinct and self-conscious strategy" (Maxwell, 2015, p. 1). The increased interest in and demand for mixed methods in evaluations can be illustrated by the rapid growth in professional developments on the topic, as well as by growing awareness in the evaluation community of the need to address issues of complexity.

Professional Developments: Publications and Organizations

Important strides were made in the publication of books and journals on the topic of mixed methods over the last decades. In the same year that Greene and Caracelli (1997) published their *New Directions for Evaluation* on mixed methods, the National Science Foundation published the *User-Friendly Handbook for Mixed Methods Evaluation* (Frechtling & Sharp, 1997). A first edition of the *Handbook of Mixed Methods in Social and Behavioral Research* was published in 2003, with a second edition in 2010 (Tashakkori & Teddlie). A second *New Directions for Evaluation* was published in 2013 on increasing the credibility of evidence in evaluation through the use of mixed methods (Mertens & Hesse-Biber, 2013). The peer-reviewed journal *Journal of Mixed Methods Research* was launched in 2007. Oxford University Press also published a handbook on mixed methods edited by Hesse-Biber and Johnson (2015).

Developments also occurred in organizations related to mixed methods. For example, both the American Educational Research Association and the American Evaluation Association established special/topical interest groups on mixed methods in 2009 and 2010, respectively. The American Evaluation Association (2013) prepared *An Evaluation Roadmap for a More Effective Government* that included the sentence that opened this chapter. The purpose of the roadmap was to provide guidance for the federal government on how to improve effectiveness and efficiency of services by outlining steps to strengthen the practice of evaluation throughout the life cycle of programs. The roadmap emphasizes the importance of using more than one method. In 2013, an international organization, the Mixed Methods International Research Association (MMIRA), was formally established. Annual conferences have been held since 2005 in the United Kingdom and the United States (with regional conferences being held on other continents) that focus on mixed methods and provide the network of interested researchers and evaluators that created the MMIRA.

● COMPLEXITY IN EVALUATION CONTEXTS AND THE ROLE OF MIXED METHODS

As noted earlier, evaluators have intuitively used mixed methods, possibly because they sensed that the programs, policies, products, systems, and organizations they were asked to evaluate were complex and that use of a single approach or type of data collection would not capture that complexity. The concept of "wicked problems" was introduced by urban planners Rittel and Webber in 1973, a concept that has relevance for evaluators because of the complex contexts in which they work. This description of **wicked problems** provides a rationale for why evaluators are interested in this concept and why this interest is associated with increased use of mixed methods:

> Wicked problems [are] those that involve multiple interacting systems, are replete with social and institutional uncertainties, and for which only imperfect knowledge about their nature and solutions exists. Hence, they [Rittel and Webber] argue that there are no completely right solutions to this type of problem; only better and worse solutions that are in part determined by how the problem is understood. Levin, Cashore, Bernstein, and Auld (2012) added the concept of super wicked problems distinguished by these additional characteristics: problems for which time is running out, there is no central authority, the persons trying to solve the problem are also causing it, and policies to address them discount the future. Methodologically, Camillus (2008) claims that wicked problems cannot be resolved by traditional processes of analyzing vast amounts of data or more sophisticated statistical analyses. Examples of wicked problems include climate change, terrorism and conflict, social inequities, health care, educational access, and poverty. (Mertens, 2015a, p. 3)

Mixed methods are particularly appropriate for addressing these wicked problems and other problems that are couched in complex contexts because they allow evaluators to have a common language to discuss methodology with colleagues, to address the needs of diverse stakeholders who can be accommodated by using a variety of methods, and to provide information for policymakers about the nature of problems and solutions in a more nuanced way (Gomez, 2014). Thinking from a mixed methods mind-set opens the door to asking more complex evaluation questions, such as these:

- How can we understand the context and experiences of diverse communities in culturally appropriate ways, especially for those who are displaced or from low-income households?

- How can strategies be developed and implemented that address the human and environmental implications of this wicked problem?

- How can mixed methods be used to capture the complexities inherent in moving forward to a more resilient and healthy path of growth and development?" (Mertens, 2015a, p. 4)

Recent advances in integrating complexity theory in evaluation have provided the scholarship necessary to examine how evaluators can systematically address issues of complexity (Bamberger, Vaessen, & Raimondo, 2016; Institute of Medicine of the National Academies, 2014; Patton, 2011). However, I want to start with a caveat: Not all evaluations take place in complex contexts, and not all evaluations require the use of mixed methods. Patton (2011) distinguished between three types of evaluation situations: simple, complicated, and complex (see Table 1.1). This distinction should not be read as a guide to decisions about whether to use mixed methods. Mixed methods can be useful in many contexts, but I would argue that the more complex the context, the greater likelihood that mixed methods will be a wise choice for the evaluator.

Patton (2011) argues that the distinctions presented in Table 1.1 are important because evaluators are often called on to conduct evaluations

Table 1.1   Levels of Complexity

| Level of Complexity | Characteristics | | Example |
	Certainty of Solution	Agreement on Solution	
Simple	Yes	Yes	Seatbelts reduce traffic fatalities.
Complicated	Either a high degree of uncertainty OR a high degree of disagreement		Prevention of teenage pregnancy; solutions are certain (abstinence, birth control, sterilization), but disagreements are high about implications of solutions.
Complex	No	No	Climate change, prevention of violence

Note: Table constructed by Mertens for this text based on Patton (2011).

that support cause-and-effect claims. These claims are easier to support in simple contexts, less so in complicated contexts, and incredibly difficult in complex contexts. Thus, the degree of complexity does have implications for the type of evaluations conducted.

In simple contexts, evaluators can ask questions such as Did the intervention work? or What is the evidence that the intervention caused the outcomes? It might be possible to use a single method to obtain answers to these questions. However, as intimated in the example of a simple context in Table 1.1, using a single method might not obtain insights into human factors such as resistance to participation in a recommended (or even legally required) practice. In complicated contexts, the use of mixed methods might be more often recognized as being important. Extending the example of preventing teenage pregnancy included in Table 1.1, the technical solutions are listed. It could be possible to quantify the increased use of birth control and correlate it with a decrease in teenage pregnancy. However, qualitative data might also be necessary to identify the different value systems that are relevant when addressing this problem, the perspectives about teenage pregnancy, and the need for a more comprehensive program approach to engage young women (and men) in alternative activities (other than having unprotected sex). In the example of prevention of violence, mixed methods are needed to understand the context in which the violence occurs, the cultural and political factors supporting the violence, the options viewed as acceptable to communities to prevent violence, and the willingness of community members to engage in the identified activities. With problems that are complex, like preventing violence, there are no clear solutions, hence, methodologies need to be used that allow for ongoing data gathering and use to enhance the probability of success.

Raimondo, Bamberger, and Vaessen (2016) add to the implications of complexity theory for the use of mixed methods in evaluation by their identification of five sources of complexity that evaluators encounter:

1. *Context*. Evaluations are conducted in real-life contexts with "historical economic, political, sociocultural, administrative, ecological, and legal contextual factors that influence the course of an intervention" (p. xxxvii). The systems are interconnected and can change at different rates.

2. *Evaluand*. What is the intervention, and what is it trying to achieve? Interventions can vary in terms of their origins, size, scope, design, and levels they are expected to influence.

3. *Human factors.* Many actors are involved in most interventions; the actors may come with differences in values and assumptions about the nature of the problem and the options for solutions. Mixed methods use allows for the documentation of the influence of human factors and provides a basis for addressing values and assumptions with data-based evidence.

4. *Making causal claims.* Evaluators are often expected to answer a question: Did it work? As indicated in the previous section, cause and effect is not necessarily a linear process because of the contextual and human factors just specified. It is possible that the original conceptualization of the problem and solutions will change radically as a response to improved understanding made possible by mixed methods evaluations.

5. *Constraints and opportunities.* Evaluators always work with constraints and opportunities in many forms, such as time and resources, access to stakeholders, and acceptance of evaluation as a part of organizational learning. Mixed methods can improve responsiveness to information needs by various stakeholder groups in ways that they consider to be appropriate.

The importance of understanding how to use mixed methods in evaluation in the context of complexity is clearly stated by Raimondo et al. (2016):

> No single evaluation method is able to fully address all dimensions of complexity. Consequently, it is almost always necessary to use a mixed methods design that combines the strengths of a number of so-called quantitative and qualitative methods. Moreover, while no established evaluation approach is fully equipped on its own to deal with complexity, existing established approaches can be the building blocks for evaluation designs tackling complexity. In many cases, these designs may need to be enhanced with more novel approaches for data collection and analysis. (p. xxxix)

Complexity Theory

What does complexity theory tell us that is useful in this discussion of mixed methods? Patton (2011) identified six concepts derived from **complexity theory** with relevance for evaluators and the use of mixed methods. Although he discusses these concepts in the context of development evaluation, they have broader applicability in our discussion of mixed methods in evaluation.

- The first concept is nonlinearity, that is, change is not necessarily a linear process; unanticipated, critical events can be the trigger for observed changes. The use of mixed methods can provide insights from quantitative indicators that create a qualitative shift in an organization, program, or system.

- The second concept is emergence, that is, individuals may act alone or in small groups, but interaction among individuals and groups results in the emergence of new conditions that can go beyond what was intended. Mixed methods can document the formation and dissolution of groups and the emergence of understandings related to problems, processes, and outcomes.

- The third concept is adaptive, that is, through interactions, individuals and organizations adapt to exposure of new knowledge, practices, relationships, resources, or other elements they encounter. Mixed methods can be used to identify the new elements as well as to document the adaptive (or maladaptive) response to these elements.

- The fourth concept is uncertainty, that is, particularly with complex contexts, uncertainty exists with regard to the nature of the problem(s), potential solutions, and responsiveness of stakeholders to these conditions. Mixed methods allow for the collection of data in ways that make visible areas of uncertainty and differences in values and perceptions that can lead to increased insights needed for progress.

- The fifth concept is dynamical, that is, systems are dynamic in the sense that the various parts change in interaction with each other; these changes can be rapid in nature. Mixed methods allow for inclusion of approaches that can provide rapid feedback when necessary and that can track changes and their implications.

- The sixth concept is coevolutionary, that is, active agents (organization and evaluator) evolve together; the evaluation is not seen as separate and apart from the innovation, rather, the evaluation evolves as the innovation evolves. Mixed methods can provide the qualitative and quantitative data to track the evolutionary process, as well as the use of the evaluation in this process.

Based on the advances in understandings of wicked problems and complexity theory, agencies that fund evaluations are increasing their support for mixed methods evaluations. For example, the Office of Behavioral and Social Science Research of the National Institutes of Health supports the use of mixed methods and recognizes that researchers and evaluators need specific guidance in the preparation of proposals that use mixed methods. Their interest in this topic was operationalized by the preparation of a guide to best practices in the use of mixed methods in the social sciences (Creswell, Klassen, Plano Clark, & Smith, 2011).

Funding agencies' interest in mixed methods also emanates from a sense of frustration that interventions, in many cases, do not have the desired effects; positive and negative unintended consequences are missed; or the data available are not sufficient to support claims of effectiveness (Bamberger, Tarsilla, & Hesse-Biber, 2016). With an increasingly competitive funding climate, evaluators are motivated to propose studies that are methodologically innovative, making mixed methods an apt choice. However, simply including both quantitative and qualitative data collection strategies does not a mixed methods study make. Hence, there is the need to explore developments in the understanding of how to design mixed methods in complex contexts for evaluators.

● CONCEPTUAL FRAMEWORK: PARADIGMS AND BRANCHES OF EVALUATION

You might think that an evaluation begins when an evaluand is identified, but multiple factors influence the conceptualization of the object of the evaluation. Two critical factors are the political context in which evaluators operate and evaluators' philosophical assumptions that guide their thinking. It has long been acknowledged that evaluation exists in a political context by virtue of the need to appropriately identify problems and solutions in a context of resource scarcity. The politics of evaluation are complicated by the presence of diverse stakeholders. Recall that having multiple stakeholders with different information needs, power positions, and backgrounds is often why evaluators choose to use mixed methods. The second factor, which is now discussed at some length, is the philosophical framework (or paradigm) that constitutes an evaluator's worldview.

PHILOSOPHICAL FRAMES FOR MIXED METHODS EVALUATION

As mentioned previously, the evaluation community enjoys (or suffers from, depending on who you ask) a plethora of **paradigms**, that is, a set of philosophical assumptions commensurate with each other that guide thinking and decision making in evaluation work. Thomas Kuhn (1962) published an influential book, *The Structure of Scientific Revolution*,[1] in which he used the concept of paradigm shifts to describe how changing assumptions lead to decisions about the appropriateness of specific research methods. Guba and Lincoln (1989, 2005) adapted the concept of paradigms and extended their meaning to include four sets of philosophical assumptions that characterize a person's worldview. The four sets of assumptions include:

- Axiology—the nature of ethics and values

- Ontology—the nature of reality

- Epistemology—the nature of knowledge and the relationship between the evaluator and stakeholders

- Methodology—the nature of systematic inquiry

Three of the paradigms Guba and Lincoln identified are present in the evaluation world: positivism/postpositivism, constructivism, and pragmatism. Mertens (2015b) added a fourth paradigm, that is, transformative, to provide a framework for evaluations that explicitly address issues of social justice and human rights.[2] The assumptions of these paradigms are briefly displayed in Table 1.2. Dialectical pluralism was put forth by Greene and Hall (2010) and Johnson and Stefurak (2013) as a metaparadigmatic stance that allows for dialogue across paradigms in mixed methods studies. These four paradigms and dialectical pluralism provide the framing for the content of each

---

[1] Personal confession: I read Kuhn's book when I was an undergraduate; it was my gateway into the philosophy of science.

[2] Some Indigenous authors have proposed a fifth paradigm: Indigenous paradigm (Chilisa, 2012; Cram, 2016; Cram & Phillips, 2012; S. Wilson, 2008). I include examples of mixed methods designs situated in the Indigenous paradigm in Chapter 6.

chapter in this book. The chapters are organized by type of evaluations typically conducted. Within each chapter, guidelines and examples illustrate the meaning and use of mixed methods for evaluators who identify primarily with one of the paradigms or with dialectical pluralism as a philosophical stance.

I base my argument for the usefulness of paradigms as a conceptual framing for understanding mixed methods and the different ways they are used in the evaluation field on an observation made by Shadish (1998). He noted that many of the fundamental arguments about appropriateness of methods are not really about methods. Rather, most debates in evaluation are "about epistemology and ontology, about what assumptions we make when we construct knowledge, about the nature of many fundamental concepts that we use in our work like causation, generalization and truth" (p. 3). Mathison (2014) adds: "The inquirers' role in both evaluation and research is dependent on epistemological assumptions and the particular skills most central to a particular paradigm" (p. 44).

● CONNECTING PARADIGMS WITH THE FIELD OF EVALUATION

Alkin (2013) and Christie's work on theoretical lenses in evaluation is a significant contribution toward understanding the different positions from which evaluators conduct their work. In this text, I extend their initial work in this area to make an explicit connection between philosophical paradigms and evaluation theories. They organized evaluation theories into three branches of a metaphorical tree, labeled Methods, Use, and Values. Mertens and Wilson (2012) added a fourth branch: Social Justice. Theoretical approaches and evaluators appeared on the branches of the Christie and Alkin (2013) tree in alignment with their emphasis of different values and approaches.

The **Methods branch** represents the positivist and postpositivist paradigm and contains those evaluators who emphasize the use of research methods in the form of techniques used to conduct the evaluations. Christie and Alkin (2013) note that "applied research depends on well-designed experimental studies and other controls" (p. 18). The Methods branch is not limited to evaluators who advocate for the use of randomized controlled trials (RCTs); however, it is on this branch that evaluators are found who place priority on the use of RCTs as the most desirable method with sufficient rigor to achieve credible results (Mertens & Tarsilla, 2015; White, 2013b).

Table 1.2 Philosophical Assumptions Associated With Major Paradigms

Basic Beliefs	Postpositivism	Constructivism	Transformative	Pragmatic
Axiology (nature of ethical behavior)	Respect privacy; informed consent; minimize harm (beneficence); justice/equal opportunity	Balanced representation of views; raise participants' awareness; community rapport	Respect for cultural norms; beneficence is defined in terms of the promotion of human rights and increase in social justice; reciprocity	Gain knowledge in pursuit of desired ends as influenced by the researcher's values and politics
Ontology (nature of reality)	One reality, knowable within a specified level of probability	Multiple, socially constructed realities	Rejects cultural relativism; recognizes that various versions of reality are based on social positioning; conscious recognition of consequences of privileging versions of reality	Asserts that there is a single reality and that all individuals have their own unique interpretation of reality
Epistemology (nature of knowledge; relation between knower and would-be known)	Objectivity is important; the researcher manipulates and observes in a dispassionate, objective manner	Interactive link between researcher and participants; values are made explicit; created findings	Interactive link between researcher and participants; knowledge is socially and historically situated; need to address issues of power and trust	Relationships in research are determined by what the researcher deems as appropriate to that particular study
Methodology (approach to systematic inquiry)	Quantitative (primarily); interventionist; decontextualized	Qualitative (primarily); hermeneutical; dialectical; contextual factors are described	Qualitative (dialogic), but quantitative and mixed methods can be used; contextual and historical factors are described, especially as they relate to oppression	Match methods to specific questions and purposes of research; mixed methods can be used as researcher works back and forth between various approaches

Sources: Mertens (2015b, p. 11). Adapted from Guba & Lincoln (1989, 2005) and Morgan (2007).

The **Use branch** theorists noted that even with the most rigorous methods, evaluations would not be worth doing if no one used their findings. They prioritize the need to "assist key program stakeholders in program decision making" (Christie & Alkin, 2013, p. 40) and share "an explicit concern for the ways in which evaluation information will be used and focus specifically on those who will use the information" (p. 13). Mertens and Tarsilla (2015) extend the logic of assisting key stakeholders to include evaluators who see the "importance of identifying the intended users and designing studies that would be viewed as credible by that constituency" (p. 431).

According to Christie and Alkin (2013),

> the **Values branch** theorists maintain that placing value on the subject of the evaluation, that is, the evaluand, is essential to the evaluation process. They identify two types of theorists on this branch: those who prioritize values and subjective meaning (more closely aligned with the constructivist paradigm) and theorists who prioritize values with a secondary concern for methods (more closely aligned with postpositivists). The Values branch theorists emphasize the importance of context and multiple stakeholders' construction of reality as the pathway to creating knowledge that is credible. (Mertens & Tarsilla, 2015, p. 431)

Evaluation theorists on the **Social Justice branch** represent the voices of marginalized groups in society and their advocates, the need to explicitly address issues of power, and the design of evaluations to support social transformation in the interest of supporting human rights (Mertens & Wilson, 2012). The four paradigms discussed previously align with these branches of evaluation in the following way:

Paradigms	Branches
Positivism/Postpositivism	Methods
Constructivist	Values
Pragmatism	Use
Transformative	Social Justice
Metaparadigm	Dialectical Pluralism

Sources: Mertens & Tarsilla, 2015, p. 433; adapted from Mertens & Wilson, 2012.

Postpositivism and the Methods Branch

Positivism and **postpositivism** are based in empiricism, a way of knowing that depends on reception of information through our five senses (Howell, 2013). Positivists, who emerged in the 17th century, held the ontological assumption that an external reality exists and that we can measure it. (See Table 1.2 for the assumptions associated with this paradigm.) Postpositivists challenged this concept of reality, holding that an external reality does exist, but we can only know it probabilistically because of limitations of human consciousness. Because much of the work evaluators do involves delving into human consciousness to discern the complexities in social situations, I focus Methods branch discussions and examples of evaluations on the postpositivist paradigm. To accumulate knowledge about reality, evaluators who align themselves with the postpositivist paradigm test hypotheses through the conduct of experiments that include the quantitative measurement of variables, as well as through the use of other dominant quantitative designs. The goal of controlled experiments is to eliminate as many competing explanations as possible to support an **attributional claim of cause and effect**, that is, the claim that an intervention caused the outcomes measured. Given the evaluation question Did it work?, White (2013b) states that "a randomized control trial (RCT) is very likely to be the best available method for addressing this attribution question if it is feasible" (p. 61).

Given the philosophical assumptions associated with postpositivism and the advocacy for RCT evaluation designs, you might wonder, how does mixed methods fit into this space? White (2013a) discusses one limitation of using only an RCT as being able to answer a single question: What difference did the intervention make? However, he advocates for the use of mixed methods when he continues his description of evaluation designs:

A high quality impact evaluation will answer a broader range of evaluation questions of a more process nature, both to inform design and implementation of the program being evaluated and for external validity. Mixed methods combine the counterfactual analysis from an RCT with factual analysis with the use of quantitative and qualitative data to analyze the causal chain, drawing on approaches from a range of disciplines. The factual analysis will address such issues as the quality of implementation, targeting, barriers to participation, or adoption by intended beneficiaries. (pp. 61–62)

Thus, the door is opened to mixed methods when the evaluation seeks to answer multiple questions, including those about the impact of the program. The use of mixed methods allows the evaluator to answer questions about the context, recruitment, causes of the problems, quality of implementation, barriers to adoption or participation, and reasons for success or failure. The use of mixed methods under the Methods branch can take several forms; the examples provided in subsequent chapters illustrate these different applications of mixed methods in the Methods branch.

Constructivist Paradigm and the Values Branch

When the **constructivist paradigm** entered the world of evaluation in the 1980s, it was not greeted with open arms by the entire professional community (Mertens & Tarsilla, 2015). This was because of differences at the philosophical level between postpositivists (who represented the dominant paradigm at the time) and constructivists. The differences of greatest import were their ontological, epistemological, and methodological assumptions. Constructivists did not hold that there was one reality out in the world waiting to be measured within a certain range of probable accuracy. Rather, they viewed reality as being socially constructed and thought multiple social realities could be constructed by different stakeholders. Their epistemological assumption commensurate with their ontological assumption is that the evaluator needs to be interactive with the stakeholders, building relationships that allow for the construction of reality to develop, rather than being distant from the stakeholders to avoid bias, as postpositivists held. The constructivists' ontological and epistemological assumptions led to the methodological assumption that qualitative approaches were needed to support respectful relationships between evaluators and stakeholders and to reflect the multiple realities that emerged in the process of conducting an evaluation.

Despite the constructivists' emphasis on the use of qualitative methods, historically, the door has been and continues to be open to the use of mixed methods within the Values branch of evaluation. Guba and Lincoln opened the door to the use of mixed methods back in 1989 when they wrote that quantitative data could be included in a primarily qualitative study. Denzin (2012) also supports the use of mixed methods rooted in the constructivist paradigm, Values branch of evaluation because it gives evaluators an "opportunity to assess the interpretive, contextual level of experience where meaning is created and provides a roadmap to address social justice" (cited in Mertens & Tarsilla, 2015, p. 435). Constructivists would agree with Denzin on the ability to gain insight into the interpretive, contextual level of experience; however, not all constructivists would agree that their paradigm is the framework for conducting social justice work (Merriam & Tisdell, 2016). Many constructivists hold the assumption that their work should be interpretive and descriptive but not necessarily activist. Hence, it is possible to use a constructivist framework to do social justice–focused evaluations, but evaluations conducted within this paradigmatic framework need not focus on social justice.

As evaluators are often called on to collect data that can support causal claims (i.e., the intervention caused the change in specified outcomes), discussions in the evaluation community about the concept of causality and which paradigm allows causal claims to be made were particularly heated. This argument is ongoing in the evaluation community; the postpositivists' claim that RCTs are the best way to establish a cause-and-effect link are addressed further in Chapter 2. Constructivist evaluators also present arguments that qualitative methods are well-suited to support causal claims. Hesse-Biber (2013) suggests that situating an RCT within a constructivist framework can provide evidence that strongly supports causal claims. Maxwell (2012) argues that "causal explanations in the social sciences depend on the in-depth understanding of meanings, contexts, and processes that qualitative research can provide" (p. 655). He also adds that the use of mixed methods in primarily qualitative studies can provide insights into causal relationships that would be even stronger than those permitted by the use of one methodology alone. The use of mixed methods under the Values branch can take several forms; the variety of approaches to mixed methods in the Values branch is illustrated by examples in subsequent chapters.

Pragmatism and the Use Branch

In response to criticisms from philosophers of science that quantitative and qualitative research rest on different epistemological foundations and thus are incompatible and cannot be integrated (see discussion in Johnson, Onwuegbuzie, & Turner 2007; Tashakkori & Teddlie, 2003, 2012), mixed methods proponents have adopted the philosophy (and research practice) of pragmatism. **Pragmatism** "is a philosophy rooted in common sense and dedicated to the transformation of culture, to the resolution of the conflicts that divide us" (Sleeper, 1986, in Maxcy, 2003, p. 4), thus approving of the use of the formulation or combination of evaluation methods that best meet the needs of the evaluation questions and, by extension, of society.

Teddlie and Tashakkori (2009) argue that the understanding of reality is provisional and ever changing and equal value should be given to both objective and subjective knowledge. Different methods, techniques, and procedures, which ought to be flexibly tailored to the purposes of each epistemological query, can lead to a more balanced and complete view of social phenomena by drawing on the strengths of both approaches and increasing the internal and external validity of findings (Dures, Morris, Gleeson, & Rumsey, 2010).

Pragmatism, as used in the mixed methods community, has not been free of controversy that emanates from its definition as espoused by Dewey (1920, 1938) and the definitions that underlie its use to support a "what-works" or expediency approach (Denscombe, 2008; Denzin, 2012; Hall, 2013). A **"what works"** definition of pragmatism is reflected when evaluators hold that the evaluation questions or funding requirements drive the methods choices, without critical reflection on the philosophical assumptions that guide thinking. Hall (2013) offers an explanation of Dewey's pragmatism in a way that enhances our understanding of the conduct of mixed methods studies. Dewey's pragmatism does not support a dualism between objectivity and subjectivity, thus opening the door for a mixed methods approach to problem solving. Dewey recognized the importance of contextual sensitivity and the need to understand the nature of problems not as initially presented but rather through the use of systematic inquiry to understand the conditions, causes, and characteristics of a problem from multiple perspectives. "Pragmatically, mixed methods are used with the understanding that they are being utilized intelligently to attend to a specific problem, and to provide information that will help to make evaluative judgements" (Hall, 2013, p. 19). "Pragmatism expands the role of credibility beyond the examinations of methodological rigor to include continuous reflections on evaluation practices and the consequences they have in the lives of people" (Hall, 2013, p. 21).

Transformative Paradigm and the Social Justice Branch

The **transformative paradigm** emerged because of concerns raised by members of marginalized communities and their advocates that evaluation was not accurately representing their experiences, nor was it adequately contributing to the improvement of their living conditions (Mertens, 2015b; Mertens & Tarsilla, 2015; Mertens & Wilson, 2012). The impetus came from marginalized communities who saw a great deal of evaluation being done "on" them, yet they noted that "little has changed in the quality of the lives of people who are poor and/or discriminated against based on race/ethnicity, disability, deafness, gender, Indigeneity and other relevant dimensions of diversity" (Cram & Mertens, 2015, p. 94). Whereas issues of human rights and social justice can be addressed in other evaluation branches, evaluators who situate themselves in the Social Justice branch hold the assumption that social justice and human rights are the quintessential values that must be supported in their work. The transformative paradigm guides thinking about the design of evaluations that address "issues of power inequities, the impact of privilege and the consequences of these for achieving social justice" (Mertens & Wilson, 2012, p. 163).

The use of mixed methods designs in evaluation rooted in the Social Justice branch allows for the capture of different realities in their complexity from the view of stakeholders' lived experiences. Mixed methods also supports the use of culturally responsive strategies that are needed to respectfully engage with a diverse set of stakeholders. In addition, mixed methods can facilitate responsiveness to different information needs of stakeholders who hold varying levels of power within the context, thus increasing the possible use of findings for transformative purposes. The combination of quantitative and qualitative strategies and data provides multiple opportunities for use of data by different stakeholders throughout the course of the evaluation. The transformative lens in evaluation can also be used in combination with various critical theories such as feminist theory, critical theory, disability rights theory, deafness rights theory, and critical race theory, a practice that leads to asking different kinds of questions about cultural and structural supports for systemic discrimination. The understandings that result from this approach provide support for structural and systemic changes that can reduce discrimination and oppression and increase social justice.

Dialectical Pluralism and Mixed Methods Evaluation

Johnson and Schoonenboom (2015) describe **dialectical pluralism** (DP) as a metaparadigm and process philosophy:

DP views reality as plural and uses dialectical, dialogical, and hermeneutical approaches to knowledge construction. Using DP and its "both/and" logic, and its attempt to produce new creative syntheses, researchers on heterogeneous teams can better dialogue with qualitative and mixed methods approaches, concepts, paradigms, methodologies, and methods to improve their intervention research studies. The concept of reflexivity is utilized but is expanded when it is a component of DP. (p. 16)

An evaluator who works from a stance of DP is more likely to work with a team of evaluators with a mixture of philosophical paradigms. The mixed methods DP evaluator's role is to provide a respectful forum where multiple voices can be brought into decisions about the evaluation questions and study design as well as in the data collection, analysis, interpretation, and use phases of the study. The both/and logic means that adherents of different evaluation branches need to be included in order to get an accurate picture of complex phenomena (Johnson & Schoonenboom, 2015). Different forms of evidence from different sources and methods need to be brought into dialogue with each other and compared and combined so that the sum is greater than the parts.

Johnson (2012) further described the processes associated with a DP approach as follows:

- Dialectically and dialogically listen, carefully and thoughtfully, to different paradigms, disciplines, theories, and stakeholder and participant perspectives.

- Combine important ideas from competing paradigms and values into a new workable whole for each research study or program evaluation.

- State and "pack" the approach with stakeholders' and researchers' epistemological and social/political values to set the socially constructed standards and guide the research. This includes the valued ends one hopes for and the valued means for getting there.

- Try to reach at least some agreement among different researchers/ practitioners on valued ends and means.

- Facilitate understanding, dissemination, and use of research findings (locally and more broadly).

- Continually, formatively evaluate and improve the outcomes of the research and use process to have local and larger societal impacts.

Although DP evaluations adhere to the assumptions of the Methods branch for RCTs, the Values branch for qualitative data collection, and the Use and Social Justice branches when appropriate, there is an important distinction to be made regarding their ontological and epistemological assumptions. The DP ontological assumption holds that reality is plural (in keeping with the Values branch) and uses a dialectical/dialogical/hermeneutical epistemology—in other words, a great deal of discussion and critical reflection. This is needed in order to conduct high-quality mixed methods evaluations.

Important Caveats and an Alternate Metaphor

Any of the paradigms aligned with their evaluation branches can be used for evaluations that use mixed methods. However, the approach to the use of mixed methods will vary depending on the philosophical framework and evaluation branch that is dominant in an evaluation context. This is not meant to suggest that evaluators in the Methods branch, for example, cannot address social justice issues through the use of mixed methods. They certainly can and do. However, members of marginalized communities have expressed dissatisfaction with evaluations that have been conducted in their communities because of a lack of responsiveness to issues of culture and power. Hence, the transformative paradigm emerged as a response to these voices.

Evaluators did live through a period known as the "paradigm wars," during which postpositivists and constructivists argued with each other about which methods were best. The characterization of the evaluation field as being organized by paradigms and branches is not meant to fan the flames of the paradigm wars again. Nor is it meant to suggest that the boundaries between paradigms and between branches are rigid. The boundaries for both are permeable. This is in keeping with Christie and Alkin's (2013) characterization of the branches of the theory tree. They state, "The three tree branches are not meant to be viewed as independent from one another but rather have been drawn to reflect a relational quality between them" (p. 13). The branches and paradigms indicate differences in assumptions that reveal differences in emphasis and practice. Yet there is overlap among the branches and paradigms in terms of the methods used and the intent of the evaluations. I hope that

Figure 1.1 The Global Conveyor Belt
http://oceanservice.noaa.gov/education/kits/currents/06conveyor2.html

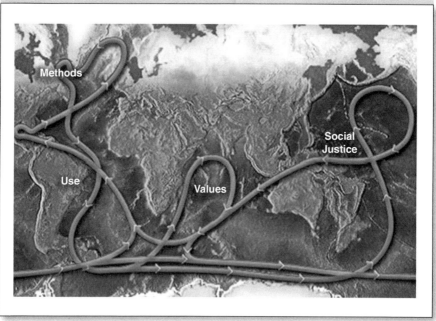

Source: NOAA (2015).

the emergence of mixed methods as an approach to be taken seriously will bring about a scholarly détente and allow for conversations across paradigms and branches. To this end, I offer a different metaphor for the field of evaluation, that is, the Global Conveyor Belt.

According to the National Oceanic and Atmospheric Administration (NOAA, 2015), winds drive ocean currents in the upper 100 meters of the surface. There are 17 major surface currents, some of which may be familiar to you, such as the Gulf Stream, the Canary Current, the Humboldt Current, and the Equatorial Current. There are also ocean currents that flow thousands of meters below the surface; this body of currents is called the Global Conveyor Belt. The deep ocean currents are created when very cold sea water gets saltier and sinks; surface water that is warmer and less salty rushes in to replace the sinking water. This process of moving and mixing means that water from all the surface currents eventually becomes part of the Global Conveyor Belt. If we envision the branches of evaluation as the surface currents and the Global Conveyer Belt as the exchange and integration of ideas from the branches, then we can see that this metaphor allows for opportunities to enrich understandings of how to do better evaluations. This metaphor was first introduced in *Program Evaluation Theory and Practice* (Mertens & Wilson, 2012); it will be used to link together the work of the mixed methods community across paradigms and branches of evaluation herein. As you read the examples of mixed methods studies for each paradigm/branch presented in the chapters of this book, you might occasionally scratch your head and say, Why is this an example of this branch and not another branch? It will be at moments like this that the evaluation global conveyer belt is in evidence.

OVERVIEW OF MIXED METHODS ● APPROACHES AND PURPOSES

The U.S. Department of Health and Human Services Centers for Disease Control and Prevention (2011) provides this overview of **mixed methods** designs:

Table 1.3   Mixed Methods Designs

Design	Process
Concurrent QUAN + QUAL	The quantitative and qualitative parts of the study occur simultaneously.
Sequential QUAN -> QUAL QUAL -> QUAN	The quantitative portion occurs first and is followed by the qualitative portion, or the opposite strategy is used.
Embedded QUAN(qual) QUAL(quan)	The evaluation is primarily quantitative with a less dominant qualitative part, or the opposite strategy is used.
Multistage, phase, or cyclical	The evaluation occurs in multiple phases, with each phase including QUAN, QUAL, concurrent, sequential, or embedded designs.
Multiple methods	Separate studies are conducted that use quantitative or qualitative approaches and then they are integrated.

Note: Morse (1999) suggested the use of QUAN, QUAL, arrows, and plus signs to describe mixed methods designs. This table uses an adaptation of that system.

Mixed data collection refers to gathering both quantitative and qualitative data. Mixed methods can be used **sequentially**, when one method is used to prepare for the use of another, or **concurrently**. An example of sequential use of mixed methods is when focus groups (qualitative) are used to develop a survey instrument (quantitative), and then personal interviews (qualitative and quantitative) are conducted to investigate issues that arose during coding or interpretation of survey data. An example of concurrent use of mixed methods would be using focus groups or open-ended personal interviews to help affirm the response validity of a quantitative survey. (p. 63)

The simplest way to think about mixed methods design is as depicted in the previous quotation, that is, using both quantitative and qualitative methods, either sequentially or concurrently. However, more sophisticated mixed methods designs have been developed by evaluators seeking to address the issues of complexity and context.

Examples of these types of designs are presented in each chapter to illustrate how an evaluator can depict a mixed methods approach. A list of the main sample studies is included in Table 1.4.

Table 1.4   Sample Mixed Methods Studies

Study	Design	Evaluand
2.1 Peterson et al. (2013)	Multiphase sequential MM RCT	Program to increase exercise and medicine adherence in New York
2.2 Catallo, Jack, Ciliska, & MacMillan (2013)	Two-phase sequential explanatory mixed methods	Disclosure of intimate partner violence in Canada
2.3 Midgley, Ansaldo, & Target (2014)	RCT with qualitative interviews	Effect of treating depression in adolescents in the United Kingdom
2.4 Jones et al. (2014)	Transformative multistage MM design with RCT	Treatment for women who use drugs in the Republic of Georgia
2.5 Hall & Howard (2008)	Dialectical pluralism (DP) MM design with RCT	Health screening for women in Australia
3.1 Clarke et al. (2011)	Methods branch concurrent MM design	Instrument development for mental health in the United Kingdom

Study	Design	Evaluand
3.2 Crede & Borrego (2013)	Instrument development constructivist	Graduate engineering student retention in the US
3.3 Daigneault & Jacob (2014)	Multistage MM instrument development pragmatic	Measuring stakeholder participation in evaluations in Australia
3.4 Ungar & Liebenberg (2011)	Instrument development transformative	Youth resilience in 11 countries
3.5 de-la-Cueva-Ariza et al. (2014)	DP instrument development	Patient satisfaction with nursing care in Spain
4.1 Iregbu (2008)	Methods concurrent MM time series policy	Policy to remove lead paint from homes in Baltimore
4.2 Beletsky et al. (2015)	Methods embedded quantitative qualitative policy	Policy change to decriminalize drug use in Mexico
4.3 Hunt, Moloney, & Fazio (2011)	Values policy Large-scale qualitative studies	Drug use by youth in San Francisco, Rotterdam, and Hong Kong
4.4 Veitch et al. (2012)	Use policy	Australia disability services
4.5 Todrys, Amon, Malembeka, & Clayton (2011)	Transformative policy	Zambia prison HIV and TB prevention and treatment
4.6 Hoddinott, Britten, & Pill (2010)	DP policy	Breastfeeding in Scotland
5.1 Thomas et al. (2004)	Methods systematic review	Increasing healthy eating in children in the United Kingdom
5.2 Archibald, Radil, Zhang, & Hanson (2015)	Value qualitatively dominant systematic review	Mixed methods articles published in qualitative journals
5.3 Edwards, Noyes, Lowes, Spencer, & Gregory (2014)	Use MM systematic review	Children with diabetes in school
5.4 Everson-Hock et al. (2013)	Transformative MM systematic review	Diet and exercise to prevent diabetes in the United Kingdom

(Continued)

Table 1.4   (Continued)

Study	Design	Evaluand
5.5 Petrosino, Turpin-Petrosino, Hollis-Peel, & Lavenberg (2013)	DP systematic review	Scared Straight in the United States: preventing juvenile delinquency
6.1 Ackerly (2012)	Gender analysis	Funding program for women in Asia and the Pacific
6.2 Cram et al. (2015)	Indigenous evaluation	Secondary school for Maori boys in New Zealand
6.3 Improve Group (2013)	Universal design evaluation	Support services for people with disabilities, mental illness, and chronic health conditions in Minnesota
6.4 Hargreaves et al. (2013)	Developmental evaluation	Obesity reduction in the United States
6.5 Jacklin and Kinoshameg (2008)	Needs assessment	Health needs in Aboriginal community, Lake Huron, Ontario
6.6 Knigge & Cope (2006)	Visual spatial analysis and ethnography	Community gardens as economic and political empowerment in New York
6.7 Shannon-Baker (2015a)	Arts-based evaluation	Study-abroad program; US students in South America
6.8 Maphosa (2013)	Conflict zones evaluation	Peacebuilding initiative in Burundi

● CRITERIA TO JUDGE QUALITY IN MIXED METHODS EVALUATION DESIGN

Criteria to judge quality in mixed methods evaluation designs are discussed here in generic terms; because of the diversity of contexts and types of evaluations, no one set of criteria are going to fit all mixed methods evaluation designs. The general criteria for mixed methods designs in evaluation are useful to provide guidance for you to assess strengths and weaknesses of the studies used as examples in this book.

Consider the following criteria:

- Be explicit about the mixed methods design being used.

- Determine that the study does use both quantitative and qualitative data (and other forms of data as appropriate).

- Follow criteria available for judging quantitative studies and qualitative studies (Mertens, 2015b). For example, different criteria would be used to assess the quality of a randomized controlled trial than for a survey or an ethnographic case study.

- Examine the points at which qualitative and quantitative methods are integrated in the study. Note how this is done and how the integration results in a stronger study than would be possible for one approach alone.

- Situate the work within existing literature about mixed methods approaches and indicate how this approach expands understandings methodologically.

- Examine the philosophical framing claimed for the study and determine the extent to which the study reflects the assumptions of the chosen framework.

The National Institutes of Health developed a checklist that identifies these elements and others for mixed methods proposals submitted for funding. (See https://obssr-archive.od.nih.gov/scientific_areas/methodology/mixed_methods_research/pdf/Best_Practices_for_Mixed_Methods_Research.pdf) (Creswell et al., 2011). This checklist is useful but does not address the quality of specific approaches used in a mixed methods design.

SUMMARY AND MOVING FORWARD: OVERVIEW OF THIS BOOK

This introductory chapter has acquainted you with developments in mixed methods in the evaluation community. Chapters 2 through 5 are organized by evaluation types:

- Evaluation of an intervention
- Instrument development
- Policy evaluation
- Systematic reviews

I chose these four because they encompass the major types of evaluations that are commonly conducted. Within each chapter, you will find examples of mixed methods evaluations that have been conducted using the frameworks of the Methods branch, Use branch, Values branch, Social Justice branch, and dialectical pluralism. For each of these examples, I provide a summary of their methods and highlight the benefits that the use of mixed methods provide. I also provide guidance for the design of a mixed methods evaluation rooted in each of these branches.

In Chapter 6, I provide examples of mixed methods studies that address specific contexts of evaluation that are providing innovative mixed methods designs. These include mixed methods designs that use gender analysis; Indigenous frameworks; universal design for people with disabilities, mental illness, or chronic health conditions; needs assessment; visual spatial analysis; arts-based evaluations; evaluations in conflict zones; and evaluations that use a developmental approach. The final chapter provides a synthesis of issues related to mixed methods in evaluation and explores pathways to the future.

2

Mixed Methods Designs to Evaluate Interventions

All impact evaluations should adopt a theory-based design employing mixed methods. (White, 2013, p. 36)

Mixed methods not only enhance the understanding of the poverty and social impacts of a reform but create space for participation by local stakeholders. (World Bank, 2012, p. 20)

In This Chapter

- Overview of mixed methods and experimental designs
- Experimental mixed methods designs from the Methods branch
- Experimental mixed methods designs from the Values branch
- Experimental mixed methods designs from the Use branch
- Experimental mixed methods designs from the Social Justice branch
- Experimental mixed methods designs from dialectical pluralism

● EVALUATING INTERVENTIONS

Scriven (1980) framed the prototypical questions for evaluators as Is x good, bad, or indifferent? How good is x? And is x better than y? What these questions share is a focus on the effect of an intervention x (as compared to an intervention y). As simple as these questions appear, the complexities of answering them are manifest in multiple ways. For example, what criteria are used to define good, bad, indifferent, and better? Who decides on those criteria? If x turns out to be bad or indifferent, what are the reasons for that? These are the complexities evaluators encounter when they are hired to conduct an evaluation to determine the effectiveness of an intervention.

● METHODS BRANCH: MIXED METHODS AND EXPERIMENTAL DESIGNS TO TEST INTERVENTION EFFECTIVENESS

In the Methods branch, emphasis is placed on the rigor of the methodology primarily as defined by the postpositivist paradigm. MM designs within this branch are typically characterized as quantitatively driven MM designs, meaning that the collection of quantitative data is dominant with qualitative data being used as a secondary strategy. For the quantitative part of a Methods branch mixed methods study, clarification of some terminology is needed. I assume readers know the basic terminology for experimental and quasi-experimental designs such as **independent variable** (the intervention), **dependent variable** (the outcome or impact expected to change based on experiencing the intervention), **experimental group** (the group that gets the intervention), and **control group** (the group that does not get the intervention).

Mixed methods designs come in many varieties (Mertens, 2015b). For Methods branch evaluators, the **randomized controlled trial (RCT)** is considered to be the "true" experimental design and is characterized by having an experimental and a control group (sometimes there are more than two groups) with participants randomly selected from a population and then randomly assigned to one of the groups, with an equal chance of being included in either group. **Quasi-experimental** designs are similar to experimental designs, except that the evaluator is unable to randomly assign participants to the groups. This can include naturally occurring groups that are used for comparison purposes. Other designs that fit into this branch include **regression discontinuity designs** and **time series designs**. Regression discontinuity is used when random assignment is not possible and quantitative data are available for the purpose of creating groups with specific characteristics. The evaluators create comparison groups by using a quantitative measure to divide the participants into two groups, one group that scores high on a chosen measure and the other one low. An intervention is implemented for the low group and the evaluator compares their postintervention performance, especially at the cutoff point used to divide the high and low groups. If there is an increase in the scores of the low group at the cutoff point, then this would be indicative of an effective intervention. The **time series design** is used by gathering data from one group with several measures of the dependent variable taken at specific intervals to establish baseline. The intervention is then introduced and is followed by measurements of the dependent variable again to demonstrate the effect of the intervention. Finally, there are **quantitative nonexperimental designs** such as pre-then posttest designs or retrospective pretest designs.

Evaluators combine these Methods branch, quantitatively dominant designs with qualitative designs to create a mixed methods study. The first example of a Method branch mixed methods study illustrates the use of an RCT with a qualitative portion and a pilot study prior to the RCT. A summary of this study is presented as Sample Study 2.1. You might notice that this study is situated between the disciplines of research and evaluation in that the research focus is on implementation of a treatment to increase patient adherence to prescribed exercise and medication regimes. The evaluation focus is on determining what the intervention should be and on the effectiveness of the intervention.

Sample Study 2.1: Methods Branch

Sequential mixed methods design: How to get people with chronic disease to exercise and take their medications (Peterson et al., 2013).

Problem: How to motivate people with chronic disease to make long-term behavior change? Three high-risk clinical groups were identified: people with coronary artery disease with low activity levels, people with asthma who also had low activity levels, and African Americans with hypertension who did not take their medicine as prescribed.

Evaluand: The intervention included a combination of strategies to enhance positive affect and self-affirmation. Participants in the experimental group were asked to sign a behavioral contract for activity/adherence and were given a disease-specific education book. They were introduced to the practices of enhancing positive affect and self-affirmation. The positive affect was induced

(Continued)

(Continued)

by asking the participants to begin each day by thinking of some small thing that makes them happy and to enjoy those thoughts. To induce self-affirmation, the participants were told to think of a moment they felt proud of themselves and to remember that thought when it seemed difficult to adhere to the exercise or medication regime. They were also given a workbook on staying positive. They received a phone call every two months following the intervention for a total period of 12 months. They were sent gifts two weeks prior to each follow-up visit, given positive affect and self-affirmation reinforcement, and were reminded by their entries in the Staying Positive Workbook. The control group participants signed the activity/adherence contract and got a disease-specific education book.

Design: Multiphase sequential mixed methods design with three phases. A qualitative phase was used to explore values, a pilot phase was used to develop the intervention, and a randomized controlled trial (RCT) phase was used to determine the effectiveness of the intervention.

Sample: Three groups, as specified in the problem section, were used from the New York Presbyterian Hospital–Weill Cornell Medical Center. During the qualitative phase, 60 participants were used from each group. For the pilot phase, a total of 131 people participated (44 cardiac patients, 40 people with asthma, and 47 people with hypertension). For the RCT, 379 people were randomly assigned to the experimental group and 377 to the control group.

Data collection: Phase 1: structured, open-ended interviews. Phase 2: questionnaires pre- and postintervention and interviews; weekly team meetings. Phase 3: Several quantitative measures were used, such as the Morisky Medication Adherence scale, the Paffenberger Physical Activity and Exercise Index, the Positive and Negative Affect Schedule, and the electronic pill monitor.

Data analysis: There is no discussion of the qualitative data analysis strategies. This is a weakness of the study because evaluators should describe their analysis strategies for both quantitative and qualitative data. The evaluators described the use of descriptive statistics and logistical regression analyses with the quantitative data.

Results: Participants in the cardiac and hypertension experimental groups were significantly more likely than control participants to achieve successful behavior change over 12 months. There were no significant differences in the asthma group between experimental and control groups.

Benefits of using MM: The qualitative phase findings were used to create culturally relevant informational workbooks for each disease category. They integrated quotations from participants' qualitative interviews into the workbooks to increase the relevance for the population. The qualitative findings were also used to develop the pilot intervention and to refine recruitment strategies. The intervention was refined based on results of ongoing data collection (both quantitative and qualitative) and through weekly team meetings in which they reflected on possible changes.

To learn how to develop a mixed methods design for a study that includes an RCT and qualitative methods in the development, piloting, and assessment of an intervention, it is useful to diagram the design itself. Figure 2.1 illustrates a mixed methods design as it was applied in the Peterson et al. (2013) study.

Figure 2.1   Methods Branch Sequential Mixed Methods Design: Qualitative, Pilot, RCT

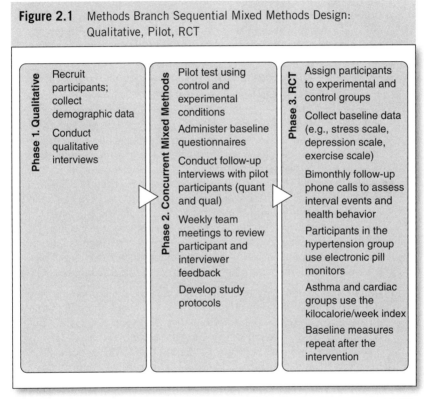

Note: Figure constructed by Mertens for this text based on Peterson et al. (2013).

Guidance for Methods Branch Sequential Mixed Methods Design for Development and Implementation of an Intervention

1. Mixed methods designs can continue over several phases. Give consideration to several cycles of data collection as a way to address the need for continuous data. Note that in the Peterson et al. (2013) mixed methods design, quantitative and qualitative data were collected in each of the three phases; however, one approach dominated in each phase.

(Continued)

(Continued)

2. Evaluators designing an MM Methods branch study begin with a mental model that focuses on a quantitative assessment of program effectiveness. This means they often consider the use of control or experimental groups as a major part of the design. However, they also consider how qualitative data can be used to inform the development of the intervention. We see this in the Peterson et al. (2013) study in Phase 1 where qualitative methods dominated, with quantitative methods being used only for collecting demographic information. The main method of data collection in phase one of Peterson et al.'s (2013) study was interviewing.

3. A second phase of a Methods branch MM program intervention study might include the use of both qualitative and quantitative data as part of a pilot testing of the intervention. This is what we see in Phase 2 of the Peterson et al. (2013) study where qualitative and quantitative data were both used to examine the quality of the implementation, the intervention itself, and the measurements used for outcomes. The evaluators in the Peterson et al. (2013) study used an RCT design in the pilot testing of the intervention and also used regular team meetings to analyze and apply the findings from the pilot test. In this phase, the evaluators adhered to the postpositivist paradigm and Methods branch by focusing on an existing reality through the use of standardized quantitative measures designed to avoid potential bias that might occur because of interactions with the participants.

4. A field testing of the intervention might reflect a more quantitatively dominant part of the design as was seen in Phase 3 of the Peterson et al. (2013) study in which quantitative methods dominated but qualitative data were collected by interviewing participants during the implementation period. Peterson et al. (2013) used an RCT design with multiple quantitative measures in a pre- and posttest design. The evaluation in this phase reflects the postpositivist paradigm and Methods branch for reasons given in Item 3.

5. Also note that the sampling plan will probably change for each phase of the mixed methods design, with smaller samples selected for Phase 1 and 2 and a larger sample for the final phase.

6. Evaluators need to make plans for the analysis of both quantitative and qualitative data in their studies. Peterson et al.'s (2013) study provided a detailed explanation of their quantitative data analysis, but they did not provide information about their qualitative data analysis; hence, this is a weakness in this study.

7. Evaluators should also include in the design plans how the data will be used in each phase of the study. In Peterson et al. (2013), the data from each phase were used to inform the actions taken in subsequent phases, thus allowing for the integration of quantitative and qualitative data throughout the study.

Extending Your Thinking

Methods Branch Sequential Mixed Methods Design Application

1. Using the scenario provided here, design a sequential mixed methods design for the development and implementation of an intervention that follows the philosophical assumptions of the postpositivist paradigm and the Methods branch in evaluation.

Scenario: In the United States, police officers encounter especially challenging situations when a person who is acting erratically comes to their attention, especially if the person seems to be suffering from mental illness. In some cities, law enforcement agencies are training police to be mindful and centered and to calm themselves through meditation. The officers are trained how to deescalate a situation and calm things down. However, not everyone thinks this is a good idea. A second school of thought thinks that police training should be more aggressive, emphasizing accuracy with weapons and strategies of attack. Design a multiphase mixed methods study that includes the use of an RCT in order to evaluate a new program in a metropolitan area that wants to compare these two approaches.

2. Using an example from your own evaluation work, design a sequential mixed methods study for the development and implementation of an intervention that follows the philosophical assumptions of the postpositivist paradigm and the Methods branch in evaluation.

VALUES BRANCH: QUALITATIVELY DOMINANT RCT MIXED METHODS DESIGN

Hesse-Biber (2013) provides food for thought on the kinds of evaluation questions that are possible when using a constructivist framing for a mixed methods study that includes an RCT. Such questions include the following:

- *Cultural responsiveness.* How well does the intervention respond to the culture and context of the target population?

- *Inclusion.* To what extent does the target population reflect the range of diversity with regard to the overall goals of the project? Who is left out? Why?

- *Ethics.* To what extent is ethical practice (e.g., cultural responsiveness, attention to power inequities) built into the recruitment and evaluation process? How well does the target population understand what they are consenting to?

- *Acceptance of design.* To what extent do participants accept the outcomes of randomization? Are participants willing to be randomized? (Adapted from Mertens & Tarsilla, 2015, p. 435)

Catallo, Jack, Ciliska, and MacMillan (2013) developed an evaluation of an intervention related to the decision process used by women about whether to disclose intimate partner violence in an emergency room visit that used grounded theory as the primary methodology. They integrated their grounded theory work with an RCT that compared the effectiveness of two approaches emergency room staff used with women who presented injuries in the emergency room. Because the RCT was already in progress when the grounded theory portion of the study was planned, the evaluators were not able to follow all the guidance provided by Hesse-Biber (2013). Nevertheless, they were able to provide insights that were viewed as useful by emergency personnel regarding a woman's decision to disclose or not disclose.

Sample Study 2.2: Values Branch

Two-phase sequential explanatory mixed methods study that combined a grounded theory approach with an RCT: Identifying intimate partner violence in emergency room visits (Catallo et al., 2013).

Problem: Some women who suffer intimate partner violence choose to disclose that this is the source of their injuries and some choose not to disclose. This study was needed to understand the decision processes women use to decide whether to disclose the source of their injury.

Evaluand: The evaluand was the type of process used to screen women when they came into an emergency room. The two treatments were screening for intimate partner violence as compared to usual care in reducing violence and improving life quality.

Design: Two-phase sequential explanatory mixed methods study that combined a grounded theory approach with an RCT. The RCT was a multisite study underway when the qualitative portion of the study was implemented. The qualitative portion of the study used a grounded theory approach (see Figure 2.2).

Sample: For the quantitative part of the study, 1,182 women participated from three emergency department sites in Canada. The qualitative phase included 19 women who had been in the quantitative phase, 18 of whom reported intimate partner violence. "Theoretical sampling and saturation guided sampling and data collection for the grounded theory phase. . . . Continuous comparison is a key element of grounded theory where comparisons are made between the developing theory and the raw data until no new findings or views emerge regarding a concept or category" (p. 4).

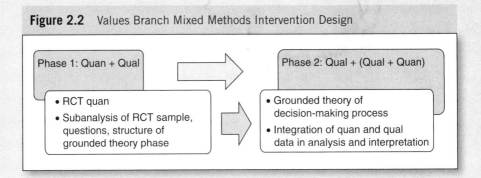

Figure 2.2   Values Branch Mixed Methods Intervention Design

Phase 1: Quan + Qual

- RCT quan
- Subanalysis of RCT sample, questions, structure of grounded theory phase

Phase 2: Qual + (Qual + Quan)

- Grounded theory of decision-making process
- Integration of quan and qual data in analysis and interpretation

Data collection: Quantitative data were collected using two instruments: the Composite Abuse Scale and the Woman Abuse Scale Tool. The qualitative data were collected through interviews; 50 interviews were completed with the 19 women. Constant comparison was used in the qualitative data collection. The evaluators began by interviewing four women and developing codes based on their interviews. They then continued to interview additional women, using a constant comparison approach to determine the status of their theory as it developed.

Data analysis: Quantitative data were analyzed to determine the rate of disclosure from the screening instruments and to the emergency room staff. In the qualitative portion, the data were collected and analyzed simultaneously, as is common in grounded theory approaches. The data from each interview were compared against the set of codes that had emerged from earlier interviews until the evaluators reached a point of **saturation** in theory development (i.e., no new concepts or categories were emerging). In the end they had over 100 different intimate partner violence disclosure events in their database. The analytic procedure involved developing the codes, refining the codes, grouping codes into clusters, and then labeling their clusters as concepts. The concepts were then organized into categories as the basis for building theory.

Results: Only 1.9% of the women disclosed in the emergency room that their injuries were the result of intimate partner violence. The grounded theory analysis revealed three processes involved in their decision to disclose or not disclose: "deciding how and when to seek emergency care, evaluating how well they trusted emergency department health care providers, and establishing a personal readiness to disclose" (p. 7). Women were reticent to disclose the violence because they did not want social services to investigate their home life and possibly take their children away, and because they feared retribution from the partner who perpetrated the violence.

Benefits of using MM: The study benefited by using the quantitative findings to inform the development of an interview guide for the qualitative part of the study and in developing preliminary codes during analysis. The quantitative data were also used to establish criteria and strategies for selecting participants and development of initial research questions in the qualitative portion. The quantitative portion left the evaluators wondering why women did not

(Continued)

(Continued)

disclose intimate partner violence in emergency rooms. The quantitative data were integrated into the qualitative data by dividing women into high, medium, and low categories of violence exposure and by type of abuse experienced. This yielded useful insights such as women in the high category of exposure were most concerned about being judged by health professionals if they disclosed, and women in the emotional abuse category found it hardest to recognize that they were in an abusive relationship.

Guidance for Designing an Intervention Study in the Values Branch That Includes an RCT

1. Begin the study by formulating questions about the context, populations, culture, values, and diversity where the evaluation will take place. For example, consider questions that ask about factors that influence decision making or bases for discrimination in a specific context.

2. Determine the qualitative approach most appropriate for the evaluation questions (e.g., phenomenology, ethnography, grounded theory, case study).

3. Conduct contextual analysis to understand the history, language, culture, values, and diversity in the stakeholders' communities.

4. Use qualitative methods to examine recruitment strategies that are inclusive and culturally appropriate and yield the desired targeted sample for the study.

5. Use data collection methods that are culturally appropriate for inclusion of the full range of stakeholders.

6. Include the voices of participants and experts in the design and pilot testing of an intervention.

7. Be mindful of the participants' acceptance of design issues such as randomized selection and assignment to groups. Include data collection methods to investigate participants' willingness to be part of an experimental or control group.

8. Follow standard procedures for RCT design such as identifying comparison groups, randomization strategies for assigning participants to groups, and quantitative measures (often quantitative measures are administered pre- and postintervention). Collect quantitative data for the RCT portion of the study while collecting qualitative data during the implementation of the treatment.

9. Integrate the findings of the quantitative and qualitative portions of the study throughout to inform decisions about recruitment, design of the intervention, and interpretation of the results (adapted from Hesse-Biber, 2013).

Extending Your Thinking

Values Branch Qualitative Dominant With an RCT Design Application

1. The use of a mixed methods design with a dominant qualitative portion in the Catallo et al. (2013) study was limited by the introduction of the grounded theory portion after the RCT portion of the study was completed. Develop a design for this study using the assumption that you can plan the quantitative and qualitative parts of the study together, that is, before the RCT is underway. What would that design look like? What would be the benefits of using such a design in terms of the quality of the intervention, recruitment of participants, and inclusion of diversity?

2. Examine different qualitative approaches, such as case study, ethnography, phenomenology, or grounded theory. How would you suggest integrating an RCT into an evaluation that used one of these qualitative methodologies as the primary portion of the study?

USE BRANCH: RANDOMIZED CONTROLLED TRIAL WITH QUALITATIVE METHODS

The use of RCTs in mixed methods in the Use branch is similar to that described in the Methods branch section in this chapter. Evaluators who work from a pragmatic paradigmatic stance note that the RCT can only indicate if a treatment is effective. It cannot account for the level of treatment effectiveness, nor can it provide insights as to whether the treatment was implemented as planned without having an additional component of qualitative data collection. For example, RCTs are designed to control for effects of participant dropouts by random assignment to conditions; they cannot explain the processes that lead individuals to decide to drop out. Use branch evaluators argue that different methods are right for answering different questions; therefore, to answer questions mentioned in this paragraph, qualitative data are useful. Midgley et al. (2014) provide a description of a mixed methods design framed from the pragmatic paradigm's assumptions in order to provide information useful for those who provide therapy for adolescents who suffer from depression. The published article on this study describes the design; they do not provide results of the study.

Sample Study 2.3: Use Branch

Randomized controlled trial with qualitative methods in Use branch: Treatment of adolescent depression (Midgley et al., 2014).

Problem: The incidence of depression in adolescents in the United Kingdom is very high and is associated with an increased risk of suicide and/or additional public health costs.

Intervention: Psychoanalytic and cognitive behavioral therapy (CBT) for adolescents suffering from depression in the United Kingdom.

Design: The RCT part of the study will compare individual CBT and short-term psychoanalytic psychotherapy, systemic family therapy and child dynamic psychotherapy with each other and with treatment as usual with children and young people with moderate to severe depression over three time periods. The qualitative data will be collected at the start of treatment, the end of treatment, and 1 year after the end of treatment. This mixed methods design is multiphase with the quantitative part being dominant in the early part of the study and the qualitative part being embedded in the design just prior to, during, and after the intervention is implemented.

Sample: 540 young people from the United Kingdom have been chosen for inclusion in the quantitative study; they all suffer from moderate to severe depression. The qualitative sample will consist of 77 of those families, purposefully selected to represent the three treatment conditions and to include those who were successful, dropped out, or relapsed.

Data collection: The RCT started 2 years before the qualitative part of the study. Standardized psychometric measures of depression were used. An interview guide was developed based on expectations of therapy. The pretreatment interview was conducted with young people and their parents and focused on the circumstances that brought them to the therapy center. The two later interviews will be conducted with all the families in one geographic region (London) and will focus on what was positive and negative about the therapy they received. A sample of therapists will also be interviewed at Time Point 2. The qualitative data will also be collected on certain subgroups, such as young people who dropped out of therapy, those who seemed to be successful in therapy, and those who relapsed by the 1-year follow-up period.

Data analysis: Quantitative data will be analyzed using traditional statistical analysis strategies. Qualitative data on young people's experiences will be analyzed using qualitative analytic strategies. The qualitative data on expectations of therapy will be converted into quantitative data to look at correlations between expectations and outcomes. Quantitative and qualitative data for the dropout group will be integrated to get an understanding of the factors that influenced their decisions.

Results: No results are available for this study at this time. The authors report that they plan to analyze the qualitative data using themes, such as emotions (e.g., anger or fear); therapy as relationship; and developing new capacities. They will explore the relationship between the expectations that the youth had before therapy started with their motivation to engage in the treatment for the prescribed length of time.

Benefits of using MM: "Such a mixed-methods approach, we have argued, has several advantages. The 'triangulation' of the findings combines quantitative outcome data about the effectiveness of treatment with a deeper understanding of the therapeutic process and mechanisms of change that lead to such outcomes. The collection of in-depth interview data alongside the battery of standardized outcome measures will shed light on important questions around the factors facilitating or hindering the young people's engagement and retention in therapy, including dropout and treatment failure. This way we can go beyond a set of predefined outcomes to include unexpected broader social, cultural, and contextual factors to build a more complex reality-based model of adolescent depression and process of change inside and outside the therapy" (Midgley et al., 2014, p. 135).

Extending Your Thinking

Use Branch RCT Mixed Methods Design Application

1. Imagine that you have been hired to do an evaluation in an organization that says it wants to do an RCT to test the effectiveness of a new intervention. It does not seem to be aware of the limited nature of the types of questions RCTs can answer. How would you persuade the organization to consider using a Use branch mixed methods that combines RCT with qualitative data collection to answer a broader range of questions?

2. Design an RCT with a qualitative component that aligns with the Use branch for an evaluand you are familiar with from your workplace, your experience, an article in the newspaper, or a scholarly article. What makes this design different from the RCT with a qualitative component that might be designed under the Methods or Values branches?

● SOCIAL JUSTICE BRANCH: MIXED METHODS WITH RCT AND QUALITATIVE DESIGNS

It is possible to use an RCT in the Social Justice branch of evaluation; however, there are differences in the approach as compared to Methods branch RCTs because of the explicit concerns with being culturally responsive, addressing power issues, and avoiding denial of treatment as much as possible. Jones et al. (2014) conducted a cyclical transformative MM study using an RCT as part of the design to evaluate the effectiveness of a treatment program for women who inject drugs in the Republic of Georgia.

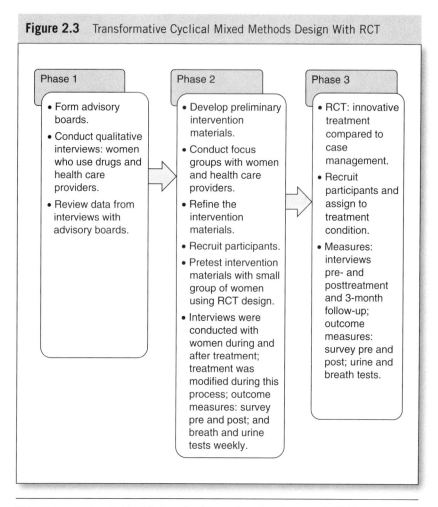

Figure 2.3   Transformative Cyclical Mixed Methods Design With RCT

Phase 1	Phase 2	Phase 3
• Form advisory boards. • Conduct qualitative interviews: women who use drugs and health care providers. • Review data from interviews with advisory boards.	• Develop preliminary intervention materials. • Conduct focus groups with women and health care providers. • Refine the intervention materials. • Recruit participants. • Pretest intervention materials with small group of women using RCT design. • Interviews were conducted with women during and after treatment; treatment was modified during this process; outcome measures: survey pre and post; and breath and urine tests weekly.	• RCT: innovative treatment compared to case management. • Recruit participants and assign to treatment condition. • Measures: interviews pre- and posttreatment and 3-month follow-up; outcome measures: survey pre and post; urine and breath tests.

Note: Figure constructed by Mertens for this text based on Jones et al. (2014).

Sample Study 2.4: Social Justice Branch

Transformative cyclical MM design with RCT: Treating women who inject drugs (Jones et al., 2014).

Problem: In the Republic of Georgia, women who inject drugs are marginalized, stigmatized, and discriminated against; few publicly funded treatment programs are available for them.

Intervention: A woman-centered, woman-specific treatment program for women who inject drugs was developed based on a combination of a reinforcement-based treatment and a women's co-op model.

Design: Transformative mixed methods cyclical design with RCT (see Figure 2.3). Qualitative data were collected in the first stage, a pilot RCT design was used in Phase 2 that allowed for adaption and refinement of the treatment, and a small-scale RCT was used in Phase 3.

Sample: The sampling strategy involved referrals from the advisory boards and snowball sampling. The design included three cycles: 55 women and 35 health providers were interviewed; 15 women and 12 health providers participated in focus groups; 20 women participated in a pilot RCT; the final RCT was conducted with 128 women. Participants for the two RCTs were recruited from venues where women who use drugs typically congregate.

Data collection: The evaluators established two advisory boards, one community based and one consisting of beneficiaries of the program. To gain an understanding of the cultural meaning of drug use in the Republic of Georgia, the evaluators conducted interviews with drug-using women that concentrated on their understandings of the health risks, patterns of use, connection of drug use with risky behaviors such as HIV, and treatment needs and experiences. They also interviewed health care providers who worked in the drug treatment system to obtain understandings of barriers, stigma, quality of treatment resources, and their knowledge of treatment. The advisory boards reviewed the data from the interviews. These data were used to formulate questions for four focus groups: two with drug-using women and two with providers. The focus groups were specifically used in the development of the initial woman-focused, culturally sensitive treatment. The evaluators pilot tested it with women who used drugs, using both interviews and an outcome measure: risk behavior assessment that includes questions about demographics, drug use, health knowledge, sexual practices, and victimization. The instrument was translated from English to Georgian, backtranslated, and then reviewed by Georgian staff for cultural appropriateness and accuracy. Following the pilot, the treatment was revised and a small-scale RCT was conducted, comparing two groups: one

(Continued)

(Continued)

with the woman-focused, culturally sensitive treatment and one with traditional case management. Interview data and the outcome measure data were collected posttreatment and in a 3-month follow-up. Urine testing and breath analysis were also conducted in the pre- and posttreatment period.

Data analysis: Qualitative data were analyzed by means of content and thematic analysis completed by two independent coders. They used NVivo to search the text for themes and used the themes to form subcategories and categories. The qualitative findings were converted into tables, and visual displays showed word frequency and connection mapping of thematic results. Urine tests were analyzed as dichotomous variables: yes for positive drugs in the system and no for no drugs. The survey and biological outcome measures data "were examined with generalized estimating equations (GEE) models, with the between-subjects effect of intervention condition, the within-subjects effect of assessment time point, and their interaction, with biological assay for illicit drugs assumed to be a binary variable following a binomial distribution, and the needs assessment assumed to be a count variable following a Poisson distribution" (p. 9).

Results: The women's interview data revealed high levels of guilt and shame, unsafe injection and sexual practices, cultural norms that discouraged the use of condoms, emotional abuse, desire for a safe person to talk with, and infrequent use of treatment services because of lack of access and fear of repercussions from others in their lives. The health care provider interviews revealed that they viewed women who used drugs as failures as mothers and wives and were unaware of any treatments specifically for women. Quantitative and qualitative data collected during Phases 1 and 2 were used to refine the treatment materials by cyclically applying the treatment and refining it based on participant responses. The RCT small-scale study revealed a positive and statistically significant change from baseline to end of treatment on both the survey responses (indicating decreased needs) and urine screening (indicating less use of drugs).

Benefits of using MM: The combination of the quantitative and qualitative data from the first and second stage were used to bring focus to the development of the treatment to ensure that it reflected Georgian culture "so that it used the language of the culture, so that its content and processes were understandable to the treatment population, and its goals were consistent with the goals of women entering the treatment" (p. 7). Engagement with the advisory boards in the framing of the study and interpretation and use of data provided a number of advantages. The boards were knowledgeable about the stigma and barriers to treatment, thus contributing to the quality of the data collected and its use in designing and refining the treatment. They also formed a sustainable network of organizations that treat women who use drugs, something that was nonexistent before the study.

Guidance for Designing a Transformative Cyclical Mixed Methods Evaluation of an Intervention

1. Evaluations of interventions in the Social Justice branch begin with an acknowledgement of the marginalization and discrimination and the increased risks associated with that condition that exist for particular groups.

2. There is also a recognition that problems are rooted in social norms and cultural environments that support an oppressive status quo through asymmetric power relations and restrictions on life chances for the marginalized group. Contextual factors, such as economic problems, also contribute to sustaining oppression.

3. Theoretical frameworks are often used in social justice MM evaluations such as critical theory, critical race theory, feminist theory, Indigenous theory, disability rights theory, and deafness rights theory (Mertens & Wilson, 2012).

4. Evaluators have a responsibility to contribute to understanding the cultural and contextual factors as a means to supporting the development of interventions that are responsive to the norms and contextual factors that serve as barriers to members of marginalized communities having their rights respected.

5. Social justice MM designs need to include mechanisms for inclusion of marginalized and powerful voices in ways that give legitimate opportunity for participation in the evaluation, recognizing that inequities in terms of power and supportive accommodations need to be addressed. Use of advisory boards is one means to include diverse stakeholders. Boards' roles need to be active and allow for safe expression of experiences and reactions. In the Jones et al. (2014) study, the community advisory board "aided the investigative team in identifying and establishing a presence in several cities in Georgia, . . . provided input and feedback on the development of interview guides, . . . and provided input, guidance, and feedback on the interpretation of the interviews" (p. 4). The beneficiary advisory group also provided insights regarding their experiences with drugs and treatment (e.g., reporting being harassed by police), assisted with interpretation of data and recruitment of participants, and provided commentary on the intervention materials.

6. The use of a cyclical design to make continuous improvement to an intervention is common in social justice MM intervention designs. This allows for data to be used to develop a more culturally responsive intervention.

Extending Your Thinking

Social Justice Mixed Methods Design Application

1. What groups experience discrimination in your community? What is the basis of the discrimination (e.g., race/ethnicity, gender, economic class, religion, disability status, deafness, age)? What are the consequences of the discrimination in terms of denial of human rights and quality of life? Select a marginalized community and a problem that they experience. How would you begin the design of a social justice MM transformative cyclical design to evaluate an intervention? How would you incorporate RCT into the design?

2. Children in displaced families in Nepal live along the riverbanks in makeshift camps in Kathmandu. They do not attend school regularly. How would you determine the nature of the barriers that prevent their attendance and identify factors of resilience in the communities along the riverbank? How would you proceed to design a social justice transformative MM cyclical evaluation for an intervention that is culturally responsive to this community's needs?

● DIALECTICAL PLURALISM: MIXED METHODS FOR INTERVENTION EVALUATIONS

Dialectical pluralism (DP) preserves the assumptions of the Methods, Values, Use, and Social Justice branches when designing MM evaluations for interventions. From the Methods branch, evaluators hold that experimental and quasi-experimental designs are best to test for effectiveness because an RCT can establish causal relationship when there is a treatment and control group, random assignment to groups, and, if possible, blinding to conditions (Johnson & Schoonenboom, 2015). However, RCTs have limitations such as the individual's understanding of the measurement instruments or within-group variation. Additional qualitative data can provide insights missing from the RCT design; hence DP supports the use of mixed methods designs. The qualitative component is planned and conducted to reflect the philosophical assumptions of the Values, Use, or Social Justice branches.

To accommodate different views from different paradigms and bring them into dialogue with each other, Johnson and Schoonenboom (2015) recommend the use of teams in evaluations because evaluators make many decisions including decisions about the paradigm(s), constructs to be examined, measurement, forms of data collection, research design, data analysis, and the interpretations and conclusions that the research team draws. To the extent that team members' and participants' (e.g., practitioners, subjects, stakeholders) knowledge and voices are heard and considered and are used to inform the research purpose, questions, and design (from beginning to end), more valid research results can be obtained. Furthermore, when a deliberative democratic process for decision making among different kinds of experts (e.g., methods choices, paradigms to use) is used (i.e., through thoughtful discussion and democratic vote) the decisions will be more easily accepted by all research team members and any audiences represented on the team.

The mixed methods researcher role in such interventions is to facilitate an interactive process of dialoguing with difference, managing the team through easy and hard times, and helping to move the process from planning to conduct, to completion, to dissemination, to utilization of results. (p. 3)

The use of an evaluation team is not absolutely necessary for conducting a DP evaluation if the evaluator is sufficiently knowledgeable and skilled with quantitative and qualitative approaches and the associated philosophical assumptions.

Hall and Howard (2008) conducted a DP evaluation in Australia of interventions related to testing for the human papillomavirus (HPV) that included a team and lead evaluators well versed in postpositivist and constructivist philosophical paradigms. Hall and Howard (2008) discuss the strategies they used to maintain balance in their work across paradigms. They originally started their study as quantitative only, but the results of the quantitative findings convinced them that they were not able to answer important questions that needed qualitative data:

Our study was originally designed from the foundation that we would be able to find the objective (independent) truth about women's screening preferences by carefully eliciting their values, which are objectified or already present within them. . . . Observations made during the face-to-face interviews encouraged us to ask whether this epistemological stance alone answered our research question: Which abnormal Pap smear management option do women prefer and value? Although we were able to elicit women's preferences and values, we were not able to consider why they were selecting their chosen answers and how that made sense to them in the broader context of their lives. (pp. 261–262)

Sample Study 2.5: Dialectical Pluralism

RCT with qualitative component in a synergistic relationship: Testing for HPV (Hall & Howard, 2008).

Problem: HPV is found in virtually all cervical cancer diagnoses. Testing for HPV has the potential to identify women most at risk for developing cervical cancer.

Intervention: Three levels of intervention that would direct future diagnostic tests and management for women who had an abnormal Pap smear: "(a) conventional triage management with a repeat Pap smear at 6 months after the index abnormal smear; (b) an immediate HPV triage test; or (c) a decision aid arm, where women could choose between conventional repeat Pap smear triage or HPV triage" (p. 256).

Design: RCT and qualitative components of equal weight.

Sample: Thirty-two women participated in the qualitative part of the study; they were purposefully selected using criterion sampling. Random sampling from the women in the RCT was used to select women for the quantitative data collection. An extreme or deviant case sampling strategy was used when the quantitative and qualitative data were integrated.

Data collection: Qualitative interviews were conducted 1 and 12 months after the triage test.

1. The authors noted that the data collection took place in the field. In the Improving the Management of Abnormal Pap Smears Quality of Life (IMAP QOL) study, they conducted interviews in the field in New South Wales and Queensland, Australia. Interviews were conducted in urban and rural settings, and locations included people's homes, farms, cafes, parks, and family planning clinics. The interviews were conducted in locations chosen by the participants.

2. Data were gathered by multiple sources, including observation and interviews. Interviews were the main method of data collection, and this was supplemented with observations, field notes, and the quantitative methods.

3. The interviews were unstructured, and the interviewer used an open-ended interviewer guide.

Quantitative data collection included a ranking exercise to determine women's preference for a particular state of health. This ranking exercise was used to calculate a quantitative indicator of value or well-being and to assess quality of life (QOL). Women also completed a multiattribute utility instrument with five dimensions: self-care, mobility, usual activities, anxiety/depression, and pain/discomfort. A third quantitative measure was a standard gamble (SG) instrument designed to measure valuing of chronic health status.

The evaluators and their partners developed a collaborative relationship enhanced by having regular meetings where they could discuss project goals and differing methodological points of view. They met formally and informally and had an ongoing relationship, so trust was already part of the context. They worked to be respectful of different professional perspectives and to work toward the bigger mixed methods agenda for the study.

Data analysis: The qualitative data were thematically coded to reveal the women's values and experiences with the triage methods. The team of evaluators met regularly and conducted the qualitative data analysis on an ongoing basis, using the results of this analysis to connect to variables from the quantitative data. They quantitized the qualitative data by calculating frequency of occurrence of codes. Extreme or deviant cases in the quantitative findings were identified by their quantitative data and these were matched with their qualitative data to gain understanding of the nature of their experiences. This was also done with qualitative data that was exceptional; it was aligned with its quantitative data to get better insights.

Results: Quantitative and qualitative data revealed three patterns of how women responded to the interventions. Some women had high QOL scores throughout the study and were optimistic about their situation; others had low values at the beginning that increased over time, and they reported negative reactions at the outset and improved over time. A third group of women had low QOL scores throughout the study and reported that they always expected the worst.

Benefits of using MM: "We adopted qualitative methods and thus a mixed methods research design in the IMAP QOL study after observing a number of contextual and process-related issues that qualitative approaches could best record and analyze. The data we gathered from women's final quantitative answers were not adequately capturing the dilemmas and issues they faced in reaching their final choices. To understand the depth and logic of their decision making, we needed to facilitate and systematically record women's relating of their experiences. Mixing the two approaches would further enable us to consider the direct relationship between women's preferences and their contextual frame of reference" (p. 258).

Guidance for Designing a Dialectical Pluralism Mixed Methods Evaluation of an Intervention

1. If the quantitative portion of a DP study includes an RCT, then use an RCT design as specified in the Methods branch. Evaluators who adopt a dialectical pluralism stance adhere to the postpositivist methodological assumption that the RCT is the best way to establish cause-and-effect and thus demonstrate the effectiveness of a treatment. Hence, a dialectical pluralism mixed methods design may include an RCT with a treatment and control group, random assignment to conditions, and, if possible, some form of blinding of the evaluators to the conditions of each group. Adherents of dialectical pluralism also recognize that RCTs are inherently limited in terms of external validity because of the required control of extraneous factors built into strong experimental designs. If conducted appropriately, an RCT will generalize to the population from which the sample is drawn, but it cannot be generalized to diverse populations outside the scope of the random sampling pool. Such limitations can be overcome by repeating the experiments with other populations and in different contexts. Another limitation is the use of group averages to determine treatment effectiveness, leaving a void in understanding of effectiveness at the individual level.

2. Add a qualitative component. To obtain knowledge about individual effects and understand the mechanisms that drive the observed effects, dialectical pluralism evaluators recommend the inclusion of qualitative methods in studies, thus setting up a mixed methods study design. Such designs can also provide evidence of unintended consequences of the treatment and mediating factors in effects that might be missed by a single RCT design.

3. Establish a team of evaluators that represent different paradigms and develop a process for working together. Set ground rules for interacting that allow evaluators from different philosophical stances to express their ideas and for all to be heard respectfully. Ensure that input is obtained throughout the process of the evaluation to influence the development of the mixed methods design that has integrity for the different team members.

4. Include mixed methods leadership. Ensure that the team includes an evaluator with expertise in mixed methods in order to facilitate the interactive processes and ensure the integration of methods and findings. Support the development of warranted conclusions that have withstood the test of multiple and varied stakeholders' reflective dialogues.

5. Before beginning the RCT, conduct contextual analysis to determine the fit of the program for the intended beneficiaries. Make decisions about data collection instruments inclusive of both quantitative and qualitative strategies. Engage with diverse stakeholders to establish buy-in to the evaluation.

6. During the RCT, collect qualitative and quantitative data (as appropriate) related to the participants' acceptance of the treatment and the experiences of the control group. Also, collect data to document the integrity of the implementation of the treatment. Consider adding case studies to obtain more in-depth understandings of the process and experiences of participants. Such case studies can collect both quantitative and qualitative data about the processes and experiences (e.g., dosage, reach, fidelity of implementation).

7. After the RCT, collect data to document the meaning the intervention had for participants and their experiences with the qualitative and quantitative data collection strategies used (adapted from Johnson, 2015; Johnson & Schoonenboom, 2015; Johnson & Stefurak, 2013).

Extending Your Thinking

Dialectical Pluralism and Intervention Design Application

1. You have been hired as part of an evaluation team that includes evaluators from the Methods and Values branch of evaluation. There appears to be dissension among the team members about the value of using mixed methods, for each camp thinks their approach is best. What strategies would you employ to engage the team members in constructive dialogue to consider the use of mixed methods, using a stance of dialectical pluralism?

2. Design a mixed methods evaluation using the dialectical pluralism framework for a project you are currently working on or look in the newspaper to find an article about a controversial treatment (e.g., reduction of violence, implementation of a new educational program).

3. Look at an evaluation study report that claims to have used a stance of dialectical pluralism. Analyze the methods used to identify what characterizes that study as dialectical pluralism.

SUMMARY AND MOVING FORWARD

Evaluators frequently are asked to conduct evaluations to determine if something works. In this chapter, you have seen five framings for mixed methods design in evaluation that can be used in these circumstances. Each example illustrates how the evaluator's philosophical stance influences methodological decisions. In the Methods branch, the primary focus is on the use of RCTs as a means to answer the effect/impact questions, with qualitative methods being used to inform the development of the intervention. In the Values branch, more emphasis is put on the use of qualitative methods as a way to come to a deeper understanding of the phenomenon under study, with an RCT being used in conjunction with ongoing qualitative data collection. In the Use branch, evaluators work from the evaluation questions to determine which methods are appropriate to answer each evaluation question and how the evaluation processes and results can influence decision making. In the Social Justice branch, evaluators spend more effort trying to gather quantitative and qualitative data about the context, participants, other stakeholders, culture, and power relations to inform the development of an intervention. The focus is on a culturally responsive set of strategies for evaluating the nature of the problem and the intervention, with an intent for action to follow the evaluation. In DP, a team approach is more common with quantitative expertise being brought to bear for an RCT part of the study and qualitative expertise for the qualitative part of the study. The key characteristic for DP is bringing the quantitative and qualitative experts/data into conversation with each other to leverage the added knowledge gained by using a mixed methods approach.

In the next chapter, we look at another important purpose evaluators are often called on to fulfill: instrument development. Evaluators can develop instruments in a program effectiveness evaluation as well, but I treat this as a separate purpose for the use of mixed methods in evaluation because of the complexity of the process of instrument development and the ubiquity of the need for evaluators to engage in this activity.

3

Mixed Methods Evaluation Designs for Instrument Development

Our study's weighting between quantitative and qualitative phases enabled a more thorough understanding of a complex phenomenon like IPV [interpersonal violence] disclosure in emergency departments that would not have occurred using a RCT alone. (Catallo et al., 2013, p. 9)

The use of qualitative research methods prior to designing and administering a survey will help ensure a more valid survey, open the researcher up to new hypotheses to test, provide a means of exploring mixed analysis techniques, and further review and revise the survey. (Crede & Borrego, 2013, p. 75)

In This Chapter

- Overview of mixed methods and instrument development
- Mixed methods designs for instrument development from the Methods branch

- Mixed methods designs for instrument development from the Values branch

- Mixed methods designs for instrument development from the Use branch

- Mixed methods designs for instrument development from the Social Justice branch

- Mixed methods designs for instrument development from dialectical pluralism

---

● INSTRUMENT DEVELOPMENT

Data collection is an important part of any evaluation. The development of data collection instruments can occur as part of a larger evaluation. However, instrument development can also be a standalone endeavor. Either way, evaluators are typically involved in the development or adaptation of instruments for data collection purposes. Hence, this chapter is dedicated to the explanation of different approaches to development of instruments for data collection as viewed through the various philosophical stances and evaluation branches.

Data sources are commonly divided into primary and secondary (Mertens, 2015b). **Primary data sources** include such sources as people interviewed, surveyed, or tested; documents produced as part of the evaluation study (e.g., student portfolios or art projects); and geographic information system mapping that occurs during the study. **Secondary sources** include data existing before the study is designed and created for purposes other than the evaluation, such as administrative records, websites, published or unpublished studies, and extant data bases. The focus of this chapter is on the development of primary data collection instruments such as questionnaires, surveys, checklists, interview guides, and observation guides.

Guidance for the development of instruments can be found in most major research and evaluation textbooks (see Mertens, 2015b; Mertens & Wilson, 2012). However, the guidance rarely extends to how to use a mixed methods design for instrument development. The type of mixed methods designs used for instrument development differ based on the branch of the evaluation theory tree in which evaluators situate themselves. As in Chapter 2 on evaluations of interventions, this chapter looks at designs of mixed methods studies for instrument development for the four branches of evaluation—methods, use, values, and social justice—and dialectical pluralism (DP). Study examples of the use of mixed methods to develop quantitative instruments for all four branches and DP are presented. An additional example of mixed methods to develop a qualitative instrument is presented under the Values branch. The use of mixed methods for this purpose is less common, but the example provides insight into how mixed methods can be used for this purpose. Perhaps it will stimulate others to consider this approach.

METHODS BRANCH: MIXED METHODS AND INSTRUMENT DEVELOPMENT

As mentioned, one of the most common uses of mixed methods is in the process of developing data collection instruments. This can take the form of using a qualitative stage to get ideas for what should be included in an instrument, followed by a quantitative stage to establish the instrument's psychometric qualities. It could also take the form of a quantitative stage of development first, followed by a qualitative stage to explore the applicability of the instrument in diverse cultural contexts. Or it could take a multistage form with several iterations of qualitative and quantitative cycles to inform refinement of instruments.

Clarke et al. (2011) used a concurrent mixed methods design, collecting quantitative and qualitative data simultaneously to establish the psychometric properties of a scale to measure mental well-being in adolescents and to get insights into the adolescents' perceptions of the scale items. See Sample Study 3.1 for details of the Clarke et al. (2011) study.

Sample Study 3.1: Methods Branch

Concurrent mixed methods design for instrument development: Measuring mental health in adolescents (Clarke et al., 2011).

Problem: Mental health issues in adolescents are traumatic and can have far-reaching consequences in terms of quality and longevity of life and social costs. In the United Kingdom, the National Institute for Health and Clinical Excellence established the prevention of emotional and behavioral problems and promotion of mental and emotional health as a priority. The evaluators in this study identified a problem because of a lack of validated measures of mental illness and health in childhood and adolescence.

Evaluand: The evaluators validated the Warwick-Edinburgh Mental Well-Being Scale (WEMWBS) with adolescents in England and Scotland.

(Continued)

(Continued)

Design: The evaluators used a concurrent mixed methods design.

Sample: The sample for the quantitative portion of the study consisted of 1,650 students ages 9 to 11 in England and ages 13 to 16 in Scotland. The sampling strategy for this portion of the study was as follows: "Six schools (three each from two cities, one in Scotland and one in England) were selected to reflect variation by geographical location, socioeconomic deprivation (based on pro-portion of children in receipt of free school meals) and educational attainment (proportion of children achieving 5+ GCSE grades A–C (England)/5+ awards at SCQF Level 4 (Scotland)" (p. 3). A random sample of 12% of these students were asked to take the measure twice to establish reliability. The evaluators also conducted 12 focus groups with 40 students ages 13–14 and 40 who were ages 15–16. They were members of the same cohort (who were not included in the 1,650 students used to establish the measure's psychometric properties). The focus groups were conducted in same-sex, same-age groups, two in each of the schools in the larger sample.

Data collection: The WEMWBS was administered to the quantitative sample during lesson times. The focus group participants completed the measurement instrument and then discussed their reactions to the instrument in groups of six to eight students for approximately an hour.

Data analysis: Descriptive statistics and multiple linear regression analysis were conducted on the quantitative data to compare responses by sociodemo-graphic characteristics. Psychometric statistics were calculated to obtain the validity and reliability information on the instrument. Confirmatory factor analy-sis was done to test the factor structure of the instrument. Qualitative data were coded based on the protocol used in the focus groups. The codes were combined into themes and the themes were compared to see if there were differences by gender, location, or age.

Results: The Cronbach alpha was high (.87) with a 95% confidence interval of .85–.88, and the test-retest reliability was moderately high (.66), with a 95% confidence interval of .59–.72, indicating an acceptable level of reliability. Validity was judged to be high based on correlations with other measures of similar constructs. The factor analysis demonstrated one underlying factor. The qualitative data indicated that the participants generally found the scale "simple, short, and easy to complete" (p. 6). However, they also indicated that some of the items were redundant and some were embarrassing, and they also suggested new items that could be added to the scale.

Benefits of using MM: The instrument developers concluded that they had produced a valid and reliable instrument for this age group. Because of the concurrent mixed methods design, the qualitative findings were not used to make changes to the instrument. The authors stated that they did not see the benefit of making changes based on the qualitative findings because they did not want to lose the continuity with the adult version of this instrument that had been previously validated.

Guidance for Designing an Instrument Development Study in the Methods Branch

1. The first step to develop an instrument, whether using mixed methods or not, is to conduct a comprehensive literature review to determine the current status of instruments in existence related to the concept of interest and/or to identify the full scope of literature about the concept of interest in order to develop items for an instrument. In the Clarke et al. (2011) study, the investigators examined the literature, not to identify the full scope of literature related to the concept but to identify measures already in use to measure mental health in the United Kingdom. Their review of literature revealed that there was no scale validated "to monitor teenage population mental wellbeing and to evaluate interventions and programmes targeted to this age group" (p. 488).

2. A common mixed methods design used to develop instruments in the Methods branch is the sequential mixed methods design where the scope of the concept is determined using qualitative methods, including literature review and interviews with relevant stakeholders. This is followed by the use of quantitative methods to test the quality of the instrument using standard psychometric analysis strategies. This quantitative stage of the study can be combined with the concurrent use of qualitative methods to determine problems with administration or interpretation of meaning in the items. Use of a concurrent mixed methods design is a bit unusual for the purpose of instrument development because it does not allow for the modification of the instrument based on findings from one portion of the study or the other. However, evaluators can use this design to establish psychometric properties of instruments and to understand the perceptions of the people who complete the measure about the measure itself. This is the design Clarke et al. (2011) chose to establish the validity and reliability of the instrument in their study.

3. In the quantitative portion of a mixed methods study to develop an instrument, the procedures mirror practice in instrument development without the mixed methods component in that the concern is with calculating the reliability and validity coefficients from a defined population.

4. The addition of a qualitative portion in mixed methods allows for the investigation of problems with administration and problematic content either because of difficulties in understanding the meaning or perceptions of relevance or comprehensiveness of the items.

5. If evaluators are examining an instrument validated on one population for use with another population, they will have access to the established psychometric properties established for the original population. However, this may contribute to a reluctance to change items in the scale because it would have implications for the established reliability and validity estimates.

Extending Your Thinking

Mixed Methods Design Instrument
Development in the Methods Branch

1. Race relations can be harmonious or they can be contentious. A community service agency wants an instrument to measure the quality of race relations that is reliable and valid and perceived by the intended respondents as containing appropriate content. They also want to be sure that it is easy for people to complete. Design a concurrent MM study to develop such an instrument. What are the advantages and limitations of using this MM design for this purpose?

2. Instead of using a concurrent MM design for designing an instrument, what would the design look like if it was sequential or multistage MM design? How would that change what the evaluator does?

● VALUES BRANCH: INSTRUMENT DEVELOPMENT WITH QUALITATIVE APPROACH DOMINANT

In both the Methods and the Values branch, development of an instrument to collect quantitative data includes mixed methods in the form of literature review, stakeholder input, and establishment of psychometric properties such as reliability and validity. When the instrument development mixed methods study comes from the Values branch, the literature review and stakeholder input take on increased presence in the study with an aim to obtain improved understanding of complex cultural and linguistic issues present in the diverse stakeholder community, as well as to increase the breadth of items to reflect the experiences of the stakeholders in all its diversity and complexity. Literature review is treated as a qualitative data collection strategy, that is, document review and the results of the document review are used to enrich understanding of the construct to be measured by the instrument when it is developed. If an **ethnographic methodology** is used as the qualitative part of the study, then the evaluator will spend time observing in naturalistic settings, interviewing stakeholders formally and informally, and interacting with stakeholders multiple times over the course of the instrument development to ensure he or she is capturing the complexity of the concept in culturally responsive ways. The interaction with stakeholders (intended targeted population and experts) continues through the piloting of the instrument; this is followed by larger-scale testing of the instrument to establish reliability and validity.

Mixed methods designs can also be used to develop qualitative data collection instruments (e.g., interview guides or observation guides). This is less commonly done by evaluators, but the approach represents a potential area of growth for mixed methods design. Hence, I include Sample Study 3.3 (Phillips, Dwan, Hepworth, Pearce, & Hall, 2014) that demonstrates the use of a mixed methods design to develop a qualitative evaluation strategy.

Crede and Borrego (2013) used an ethnographic methodology as the primary approach in the design of a quantitative survey instrument to determine factors that influence retention in graduate engineering programs. They began with a literature review and then collected ethnographic data over a 9-month period as the beginning point for their instrument development. The design and process of their study are presented in Sample Study 3.2.

Sample Study 3.2: Values Branch

Quantitative instrument development with qualitatively dominant approach: Retention of graduate engineering students (Crede & Borrego, 2013).

Problem: In the United States, the preparation of graduate-level science and engineering students is viewed as necessary to maintain a technological edge to foster innovation and a workforce able to contribute to the national economy. The graduation rate from doctoral-level engineering programs is lower for U.S. students than for international students.

Evaluand: Graduate school experience in three engineering research groups.

Design: Sequential exploratory mixed methods with extensive ethnography. The evaluators conducted an ethnographic study for 9 months before they developed an instrument to measure factors that influence retention in engineering graduate school.

Sample: The qualitative sample came from three research groups from two engineering departments at a large public university. Electrical engineers were the most frequent (n = 20 from six countries) and aerospace engineering was the smallest group (n = 4 from China and the United States); 12 students came from a multidisciplinary program in aerospace and electrical engineering. These students were from the United States and India. The quantitative sample came from four universities: a large public university in the Midwest,

(Continued)

(Continued)

a historically black university in the East, a large private university in the West, and a large public university in the East.

Data collection: The qualitative data collection consisted of an extensive literature review followed by 9 months of ethnographic observations and interviews that focused on the student experience in terms of language and culture. Ethnographic data collection included formal (20 semistructured interviews) and informal interviews, lengthy periods of observation, and participation in most research group activities. The quantitative data collection involved the use of a survey based on the results of the qualitative data collection. The students and experts in graduate engineering education were involved with the evaluation team members by reviewing drafts and commenting on clarity of language and survey items. The draft instrument was piloted with 50 graduate engineering students. The evaluators revised the survey based on the results of the draft administration results and an additional review by an expert in engineering education and a small group of students who had participated in the ethnographic part of the study. The administration of the final survey was distributed online to students at four universities across the United States and was completed by 837 students (18.5% response rate).

Data analysis: In the qualitative analysis, themes that arose in the literature on graduate student retention were combined with themes that emerged from qualitative analysis of the ethnographic data. The quantitative analysis consisted of calculation of an internal consistency index (Cronbach alpha), an indicator of validity.

Results: The qualitative themes that emerged from the analysis included international diversity; expectations of students and faculty; climate in terms of acceptance, belonging, and competitiveness; organizational support from experienced students, resources, and advisors; individual preferences such as belief about the importance of the work and values of diversity and teamwork; and feeling valued in terms of the research group. These themes formed the basis of the survey the evaluators developed; the survey consisted of items related to the graduate school experience that were measured using a five point Likert-type scale. The final survey had seven subscales, with Cronbach alpha values that ranged from .86 to .63.

Benefits of using MM: The survey was developed based on the ethnographic data. At several points during the quantitative testing of the survey, the evaluators included qualitative data collection in the form of review with students and experts. The internal consistency was improved after the expert review resulted in rewording of several questions and the addition of several items related to student development (learning). The ethnographic data helped the evaluators create an instrument reflective of the concept of international diversity in engineering graduate research groups.

Phillips et al. (2014) used a qualitatively dominant mixed methods design to develop qualitative data-gathering instruments and strategies that could be used to evaluate small, community-based organizations. They were interested in the development of qualitative instruments and strategies as well as in maximizing the trustworthiness and authenticity of them. These are criteria from the constructivist paradigm that are often used in qualitative studies that parallel the concept of validity in the postpositivist paradigm.

Sample Study 3.3: Values Branch

Values branch mixed methods design for development of qualitative instruments and strategies for data collection: Community-based health care organizations in Australia (Philips et al., 2014).

Problem: Limited evaluations have been conducted to assess the quality of health care delivered by small, community-based organizations. The staff providing the services have limited time to engage in evaluation activities because of time constraints and other pressures.

Evaluand/instrument and strategies: The Qualitative Rapid Appraisal Rigorous Analysis (Q-RARA) is a set of qualitative instruments and strategies designed specifically for evaluating small, community-based health care organizations. The Q-RARA is predominantly qualitative with a small component of quantitative data being collected. It was developed to study nurses in general practice in Australia.

Design: Qualitatively dominant Values branch concurrent mixed methods design. The design combined the use of a constructivist version of rapid appraisal (Nyanzi, Manneh, & Walraven, 2007) and qualitative mixed methods designs. The evaluators "chose to work within an interpretive theoretical perspective involving extensive analytic input from researchers by choosing to locate the study within the nurses' work environments, and to interpret their actions, positions and the meanings they gave to their roles" (p. 561). Data were collected concurrently and combined at the stage of analysis.

Sample: Data were collected from "25 practices that varied in size, organizational structure and geographic location across two Australian states" (p. 561). The sample included doctors, nurses, and practice managers, although the authors do not tell us the specific number of people in the sample.

Data collection: The qualitative data collection strategies included using in-depth interviews with nurses, doctors, and practice managers; structured observations and unstructured observations of nurses' activities;

(Continued)

(Continued)

photographs of nurse-identified worksites; floor plans; and field notes. Quantitative data collection included a questionnaire that summarized staff numbers and working hours and a social scan. Social scanning "included the collection of publicly available census and health service provision data to describe the socio-geographic setting of each practice" (p. 561). The data were collected by a single evaluator at each site for a period of one day in order to minimize disruption of the provision of services.

Data analysis: The evaluation team analyzed the data to determine the quality and rigor of the data produced and to determine the capacity of the Q-RARA to adequately reflect the stakeholders' views of the trustworthiness and authenticity of the data produced by this set of instruments and strategies. Lincoln and Guba (1985) proposed that "trustworthy data are credible, transferable, dependable, and confirmable. Data should also be assessed for authenticity, a domain that includes fairness, and educative, ontological, tactical, and catalytic authenticity" (p. 567). The evaluators analyzed the data related to trustworthiness by comparing their processes and findings against the criteria defined by Lincoln and Guba, especially regarding the credibility of the data. Credibility was determined by ascertaining the extent to which prolonged engagement and persistent observation were possible in the form of determining the access to the backstage of general practice that the evaluators were permitted in each setting. In addition, peer debriefing was conducted by means of the senior member of the team reviewing the field notes and reflections of each site visit to provide feedback as a peer to the evaluators who collected the data. The evaluation team met fortnightly to offer opportunities for critical reflection (i.e., progressive subjectivity: a process designed to allow for the evaluators to become aware of any biases they hold, become aware of identify shifts in their understandings throughout the study, and examine ways to avoid the influence of their own biases in the data collection). Member checks were conducted to share and check the findings and interpretations with the participants by providing summaries of the findings for verification. The authors also posted deidentified findings on a website for practicing nurses to obtain feedback. Transferability was determined by analyzing the extent to which background information was provided in each case to provide sufficient information for readers to make a judgment about the transferable nature of the findings to their own setting. Dependability, that is, the stability of the study procedures and methods over time, was assessed through multiple meetings over the course of the study with multiple stakeholders to review the process and document any changes. The final trustworthiness criterion is confirmability, or the documentation that the findings are grounded in data. A confirmability audit was conducted that linked all case summaries, analysis documents, and non-public documents to deidentified codes for each participant/site.

Authenticity is also multifaceted. Fairness, the extent to which diverse stakeholder perspectives are included and used in the formulation of recommendations, was determined by analyzing the range of participants and documenting their involvement in the formulation of recommendations. Ontological authenticity, that is, the extent to which stakeholders' understanding of reality is improved or expanded, was assessed by documenting the inclusion of diverse perspectives that might not have been broadly known. Educative authenticity, that is, the extent to which stakeholders develop a better understanding of the perspectives of other stakeholders, was determined by analyzing the process used to distribute the findings to diverse audiences. Catalytic authenticity, that is, the extent to which participation in the evaluation and exposure to the findings elicits action and change, was determined by analyzing changes in policies and practices. Tactical authenticity, that is, the extent to which stakeholders feel empowered by having participated in the evaluation, was determined by documenting future uptake of the study recommendations by participants.

Results: The Q-RARA was judged to be trustworthy because, even though prolonged engagement was precluded by the one-day timeframe of data collection, the evaluators were granted access to observe the participants in meetings, on their rounds, and as they moved across the spaces in the practice in each of the settings. Persistent observation was also not possible; however, the evaluators did repeat their observations of specific phenomenon throughout the day at each site. The peer debriefing between the evaluators in the field and the senior member of the team resulted in clarification of the interview process and questions. The process of progressive subjectivity resulted in challenges to assumptions evaluators had made during the study. Member checks resulted in feedback on specific topics. Transferability was viewed as sufficient because of the extensive background information included for each case site. Dependability was also viewed as sufficient because of the documentation of changes that occurred in procedures and protocols. Evidence of confirmability revealed that links could be made between all the data collection documents and their data with the sites in which the data were collected. The instruments and procedures were viewed as fair because many diverse stakeholders were included and their advice was used to develop the recommendations. Ontological authenticity was deemed to be acceptable because of the differences in perspectives revealed, particularly with regard to the less recognized role of nurses as educators. Educative authenticity was supported by the increased understanding by doctors of the multiple roles played by nurses. Catalytic authenticity was judged to be strong because "the national body responsible for preparing doctors for general practice has now funded trials of practice nurses training general practice registrars" (p. 569). Tactical authenticity was also judged to be strong because the findings were adopted by the chief nurse in the Department of Health and Ageing, and additional funding has been provided to support the role of nurses as educators.

Benefits of using MM: The authors noted that prior evaluations of this type of organization have relied on collection of data by means of quantitative measures or single qualitative methods such as interviews or focus groups. "Single method studies do not capture the richness and variety of organizational functioning, the ways that staff members interact and use their time, and the impact of the spatial environment of the organization on their work" (p. 559). The use of a mixed methods design resulted in an approach that included primarily qualitative instruments and strategies, with some quantitative data collection, that was

(Continued)

(Continued)

well received by the participants, particularly by the practice nurses who felt that their work was validly portrayed and evaluated. They appreciated the nondisruptive nature of the data collection. The use of this mixed methods approach permitted the collection of a range of data, inclusion of a multidisciplinary team, and use of an iterative approach to data analysis that "allowed us to engage in a dialogue with the data and produce authentic and trustworthy findings" (p. 572).

Guidance for Designing a Mixed Methods Instrument Development Study in the Values Branch

1. Conduct a comprehensive literature review to determine what is already known about the phenomenon under study.

2. Plan a qualitative study such as an ethnographic approach or a multimethod qualitative strategy that includes purposeful sampling criteria based on established criteria for relevant stakeholder groups, being inclusive of diversity in the population.

3. Use qualitative data collection methods that include observation, formal and informal interviews, and document reviews that focus on the cultural considerations relevant to the phenomenon you want to measure.

4. If the primary focus is on the development of a quantitative instrument, involve stakeholders in the interpretation of the qualitative data and its use to formulate an instrument that is responsive to the data already collected. Disaggregate both quantitative and qualitative data by dimensions of diversity relevant in that context (e.g., international and domestic students). If the primary focus of the study is to test the quality of qualitative instruments and procedures, consider use of the methods used in the Phillips et al. (2014) study that used Lincoln and Guba's (1985) framework for assessing trustworthiness and authenticity.

5. Pilot test the instrument with a representative quantitative sample for a quantitative instrument and with a qualitative sample for a qualitative instrument.

6. Involve experts and other stakeholders to review the results of the pilot test; make revisions of the instrument.

7. Conduct a larger-scale quantitative study with the instrument to establish reliability and validity for a quantitative instrument. Conduct a follow-up study for a qualitative instrument to determine its sustained trustworthiness and authenticity.

Extending Your Thinking

Values Branch Instrument Development

1. The Centers for Disease Control and Prevention has a program to prevent sexually based violence that focuses on working with men to address cultural perceptions of masculinity and healthy relationships between men and women (as well as between men and men and women and women). Design an instrument development evaluation using qualitative methods as the primary method combined with a quantitative strategy to establish reliability and validity. How does the sensitivity of the concept influence your design? How does the challenge to cultural norms that support oppression of women or vulnerable partners influence the design? How would you change the design if you were developing a qualitative instrument?

2. What measurements are you using in your evaluation work? How could these measurements be improved by using a qualitative phase as a basis for revision? Design a Values branch MM evaluation to improve the measurement instrument you use.

USE BRANCH: MULTIPHASE INSTRUMENT DEVELOPMENT

Instrument development has largely been the purview of quantitative evaluators who use statistical calculations to demonstrate the reliability and validity of the instruments. However, evaluators in the Use branch point out that many questions cannot be answered by quantitative data alone that are pertinent to establishing the quality of measurement instruments. Hence, they recommend the use of mixed methods to answer a wider range of questions related to the validation of inferences that can be drawn from the results based on quantitative instruments. Combining strategies such as factor analysis and cognitive interviewing can provide the evaluator with greater confidence about construct validity.

Sample Study 3.4: Use Branch

Multiphase instrument development: Measuring participation by stakeholders in evaluations (Daigneault & Jacob, 2014).

Problem: Evaluations sometimes claim to be participatory but do not proffer evidence that supports the extent or nature of the participation by stakeholders.

(Continued)

(Continued)

Evaluand: Participatory Evaluation Measurement Instrument (PEMI). This purpose of this instrument is to measure stakeholder participation in evaluations.

Design: Multistage MM instrument development in the Use branch. The authors noted that their initial plan was to conduct a quantitative study, but they obtained qualitative data unexpectedly in the form of open-ended comments and informal e-mail correspondence that turned the study into a mixed methods study. Thus, the first stage of the study is a concurrent MM design with quantitative and qualitative data being collected simultaneously. Then the authors extended the study to include a second stage that included revision of the instrument and collection of additional quantitative data for validation purposes.

Sample: For the quantitative portion of the study, they used a purposive sampling strategy to select 40 evaluation studies that displayed various levels of stakeholder participation from peer-reviewed journals published between 1985 and 2010.

Data collection: The authors developed an instrument, the Participatory Evaluation Measurement Instrument, based on a review of literature on stakeholder participation and a framework on participation developed by Cousins and Whitmore (1998). Their instrument contained items about the extent and nature of participation using a 5-point scale. As a quantitative validation of the PEMI, the evaluators used the PEMI to assess the degree of participation exhibited in 40 articles that were screened to represent participatory approaches to evaluation. The intention of the first stage was to collect quantitative data that could be used to establish the interrater reliability using Cohen's *kappa* and the intraclass correlation coefficient. The evaluators shared the results of their application of the PEMI with the authors of the 40 studies by means of an online survey.

> The online survey had two sections. The first section focused on questions relative to the PEMI. Respondents had to check boxes about types of participants, steps in which they were involved, and their level of control on the evaluation process. On the next page of the online survey, 5-point indices were automatically generated from respondents' answers for each dimension and for the overall level of participation. These scores were presented to the authors of the evaluation cases for reactions in the first part of the survey. Respondents' opinions were measured on an ordinal scale of agreement and an open-ended question asked respondents to justify their choice (i.e., "Why?"). The second part of the survey contained 11 four-point Likert-type questions from which the calculation of the Evaluation Involvement Scale (EIS) was derived (Toal, 2009).

Respondents generated qualitative data in their responses to the survey's open-ended questions that contained richer data than the evaluators had anticipated, and so they decided to conduct a thematic analysis of the qualitative comments. In addition, two of the authors of the original 40 published studies supplemented their survey responses with substantive comments made in e-mails; these were also included in the qualitative data analysis. Following the analysis from this round of data collection, the evaluators decided to revise the instrument to respond to the concerns raised by the authors of the articles that were part of the literature review. In the final stage, the evaluators used the revised instrument to again quantitatively rate the level of participation in the published articles from the first stage. They then surveyed the authors again, sharing with them the change in scores that resulted when the revised instrument was used to rate their work.

Data analysis: In the first stage, the authors' scores were compared with the raters' scores for agreement. The evaluators noted that the article authors only somewhat agreed that the PEMI score accurately represented the level of participation from their point of view. The evaluators decided to integrate this quantitative finding with a qualitative analysis of the comments respondents wrote for the open-ended questions and e-mails. The evaluators then decided that the qualitative data included rich data, so they conducted a thematic analysis of the survey and e-mail comments. They used these data to revise the instrument and then conducted a quantitative stage of data collection to obtain psychometric data about the quality of the instrument. Analysis consisted of comparison of the scores from the first use of the instrument to those obtained with the revised instrument. The Mann-Whitney U test was used to compare the responses of article authors whose scores stayed the same in the first and second administration of the scale with those whose scores increased.

Results: The initial quantitative stage indicated an acceptable level of reliability and weak to strong convergent validation. However, when the evaluators completed the qualitative thematic analysis, they found that people who felt the instrument underrepresented the extent of participation had expressed disagreement with the way the concept of participation was rated, the relevance of participation by different types of stakeholders, and inability of the scale to capture the multifaceted nature of the participation. The revised instrument resulted in 20% of the scores being unchanged and increased the scores for the other 80%, thus supporting increased validity of the instrument. The level of disagreement about the accuracy of the scores as measures of stakeholder participation yielded by the PEMI decreased, again supporting increased validity.

Benefits of using MM: The use of mixed methods led the evaluators to revise the PEMI: "The results generated in the mixed methods phase provide additional evidence of the necessity of revising the PEMI. Quantitative data indicated that the alignment between the scores derived from the PEMI and the respondents' opinions with respect to the level of participation was only partial. Qualitative data revealed that an overarching theme derived from the respondents' answers was the underrepresentation of stakeholder participation by the PEMI's scores, thus suggesting the need to find a less conservative concept structure for the revised version of the instrument" (p. 16). The evaluators used the integrated results of the first stage to revise and test the validity of the PEMI during a second quantitative stage.

Guidance for Designing an Instrument Development Study in the Use Branch

The instrument development and construct validation developed by Onwuegbuzie et al. (2010) contains 10 phases:

1. *Conceptualize the construct of interest.* Conduct a literature review and consult with a diverse set of experts on the construct to be measured. Conducting a pragmatic mixed methods systematic literature review is discussed further in Chapter 5 and can provide guidance for the evaluator at this stage. Input from experts can be obtained by a mixed methods strategy involving focus groups and surveys.

2. *Identify and describe behaviors that underlie the construct.* This phase involves the analysis of the data collected in Step 1. Data from the experts can be analyzed using qualitative strategies such as thematic analysis, grounded theory, or ethnographic analysis. The preliminary construct elements can be shared with experts through a quantitative strategy such as the Delphi technique. This process can be repeated as many times as necessary to reach a clear concept of the construct.

3. *Develop initial instrument.* A team can contribute to the item writing using a table of specifications to ensure coverage of the construct. The items should be formatted into a quantitative form, such as a Likert scale, with added room for qualitative comments about each item.

4. *Pilot test initial instrument.* The draft instrument should be administered to a pilot group to obtain input into the quality of the items by asking about such characteristics as clarity, relevance, and cultural responsiveness. It is possible to calculate reliability and validity coefficients at this stage, but these should be treated with caution because the pilot group is typically quite small. It is also possible that the evaluator could conduct focus groups or interviews following the pilot administration to collect additional qualitative data. The instrument should be revised based on this process.

5. *Design and field test revised instrument.* A larger sample is needed for field testing the instrument in order to permit the use of factor analysis of the responses. In a mixed methods design, the evaluator should include qualitative data collection through open-ended questions in addition to the quantitative responses to the items.

6. *Validate revised instrument.* Quantitative analysis phase: In this phase, the evaluator employs the traditional quantitative analytic strategies to establish the validity and reliability of the instrument (e.g., factor analysis, correlational analysis, discriminant and convergent validity).

7. *Validate revised instrument.* Qualitative analysis phase: The qualitative data from Stage 5 can be analyzed using any number of qualitative analytic strategies (e.g., narrative analysis, content analysis, and semiotics).

8. *Validate revised instrument.* Mixed analysis phase: **Qualitative-dominant crossover analyses**. This involves either qualitizing quantitative data or conducting a quantitative analysis of the qualitative data. This could take the form of disaggregation of groups based on high, medium, or low scores and comparing their qualitative data.

9. *Validate revised instrument.* Mixed analysis phase: Quantitative-dominant crossover analyses. This involves quantitizing qualitative data perhaps by noting themes that emerge and transforming them into factors that could be analyzed quantitatively.

10. *Evaluate the instrument/construct evaluation process and product.* The evaluator should review all the data and findings that emerged from the nine previous steps and engage in a debriefing with members of the team and experts. If concerns arise about the items or the process, then the instrument should be revised and the steps repeated until a satisfactory version of the instrument emerges (adapted from Onwuegbuzie et al. 2010).

Note: Additional examples of the development of quantitative instruments that used the Onweugbuzie et al. (2010) framework include (1) Koskey, Sondergeld, Stewart, and Pugh (2016) in their development of a quantitative instrument to measure the transformative experiences that students in school have in the form of extending their classroom learning into everyday experience and (2) David, Hitchcock, Ragan, Brooks, and Starkey (2016) in their development of a quantitative instrument to measure trust between college students and their athletic trainers.

Extending Your Thinking

Use Branch Instrument Development

1. The teacher accreditation organization requires that universities provide data on the change in teacher candidates' dispositions as they progress through their university program and in the first 5 years of their teaching careers. The measurement is to be used several times during the program and needs to align with the conceptual framework that guides the programmatic decisions. Design a mixed methods instrument development study using the Use branch characteristics for an instrument that could be used to address this need.

2. Examine the development of instruments used in evaluation studies in a domain of your interest. To what extent does the development process include the use of mixed methods and reflect the Use branch characteristics?

● SOCIAL JUSTICE BRANCH: INSTRUMENT DEVELOPMENT

Development of instruments in the Social Justice branch reflects the assumption of the transformative paradigm (Mertens, 2015b; Mertens & Wilson, 2012). Participation of stakeholders is a priority throughout the entire process of development in order to incorporate diverse values and meanings based on people's experiences and understandings. Specific efforts are made to ensure that inclusion of traditionally underrepresented groups is accomplished in culturally respectful ways. The transformative ontological assumption holds that different versions of reality emerge from different social positions and that different methods are needed to accurately understand the realities of those who are marginalized and oppressed. Mixed methods within the Social Justice branch can "capture the diversity of people's viewpoints with regard to their social locations" (Ungar & Liebenberg, 2011, p. 128). Cultural differences are of the utmost importance, and evaluators in this branch ask themselves questions such as "Does a measure in one culture relate to the measure of the same factor in another?. . . [And] how do we balance assumptions of homogeneity across Minority and Majority World contexts with the need for sensitivity to within group and between group heterogeneity?" (Ungar & Liebenberg, 2011, p. 129).

Ungar and Liebenberg (2011) worked with a team of instrument developers across the world to develop a measure of youth resilience (see Sample Study 3.5). They stated their goal as follows: "Our goal when constructing the CYRM-28 [Child Youth and Resilience Measure] was to build a more culturally sensitive measure with face and item validity (we wanted a measure that was perceived as relevant by all our global partners and showed the potential for discriminant validity in multiple contexts). Achieving this goal meant a more reciprocal research design congruent with mixed methods as used within a transformative paradigm" (p. 129).

Sample Study 3.5: Social Justice Branch

Instrument development: Measuring youth resilience (Ungar & Liebenberg, 2011).

Problem: Many studies of youth in low- and middle-income countries focus on what is wrong with young people. However, youth who survive in challenging contexts have strengths that, if recognized, can be seen as part of the solution to the problems they face. A good measure of youth resilience grounded in cultures across the world could assist in the identification of resilience.

Evaluand: Child and Youth Resilience Measure (CYRM-28)

Design: Transformative mixed methods multistage design (see Figure 3.1)

(Continued)

Figure 3.1 Transformative Mixed Methods Instrument Development Design

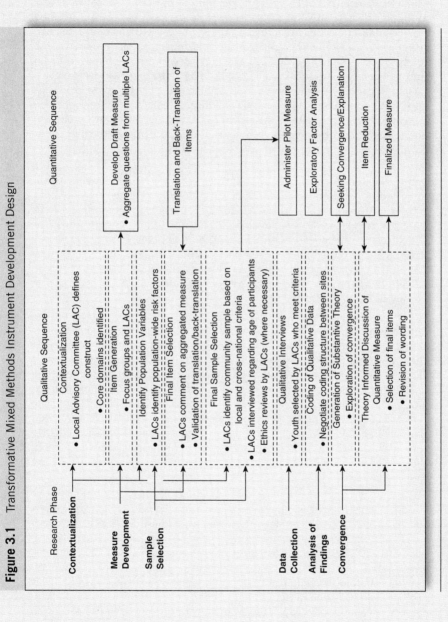

Source: Ungar & Liebenberg (2011), p. 130.

73

(Continued)

Sample: The instrument was pilot tested with 1,451 youth, and 89 youth participated in interviews in 11 different countries. Sites were purposefully chosen to maximize variation. The qualitative sample of youth was chosen to meet these criteria: "(a) cultural differences, (b) differences in the nature of the risks facing individual youth (all participants were sampled from one population of youth-at-risk identified locally, such as youth living in poverty, exposed to violence, or racially marginalized), and (c) the ability of the principal investigator to locate an academic partner with the capacity to supervise the research locally" (p. 131). For the quantitative testing of the instrument, 60 or more youth were purposefully chosen by the local advisory committee who knew youth who were placed at risk by virtue of living in a conflict zone, poverty, family breakdown, marginalization, or addiction in the family.

Data collection: A team of instrument developers from 14 communities in 11 countries collaborated on the creation of CYRM-28. Local advisory committees (LAC) were established at each site; these were composed of five individuals who were knowledgeable about youth in their communities. The evaluators conducted an audit of strengths that "were the most relevant to populations under stress by conducting focus groups (and later qualitative interviews) with youth and those responsible for their well-being from Minority and Majority World contexts where their youth are exposed to extreme adversity" (p. 128).

Data analysis: Initial listing of elements that reflected resilience were created by the members of the international team in a three-day conference. The group analyzed the elements using qualitative strategies that resulted in 32 domains (e.g., assertiveness, problem-solving ability) organized into four clusters (individual, relational, community, and cultural). Following the focus groups and comments by LAC members, the evaluators analyzed the items to identify common and unique elements and constructed the draft instrument. The data from the piloting of the instrument were analyzed using factor analysis. The factor analysis revealed commonality and redundancy across some items, allowing the evaluators to reduce the common core of questions on the measure to 28.

Results: "As such, by having begun with exploratory qualitative data, the questions contained in the quantitative measure are rooted in the experiences of individuals from multiple cultures and contexts. Findings from the analysis of additional qualitative data also informed the quantitative analysis and findings, affecting the structure of the CYRM-28. In this way, the CYRM-28 is designed to demonstrate good content validity within each research site in which it was piloted while still sharing enough homogeneity to make it useful for cross-national comparisons" (Ungar & Liebenberg, 2011, p. 128). The CYRM-28 consists of 28 items that are standard and also allows local areas to add questions that do not appear in the common list of elements in order to reflect specific local aspects of resilience. The questions are answered using a 5-point scale ranging from 1, Not at all, to 5, A lot.

Benefits of using MM: "Mixed methods were necessary to identify emic factors (including community values related to resilience) relevant to young people in cultures and contexts that are underrepresented in the Minority World literature. The use of mixed methods also allowed us to compare the results of our quantitative findings with young people's descriptions of their experiences of complex interactions to nurture and maintain well-being within their challenging social ecologies" (Ungar & Liebenberg, 2011, p. 128). Mixed methods also contributed to stronger internal validity and generalizability across contexts.

Guidance for Designing a Transformative Mixed Methods Instrument Development Study

Development of an instrument in the Social Justice branch follows a logic similar to that used in the development of any instrument. However, the influence of the transformative paradigm's assumptions leads to considerations of inclusion and representation that might not surface in other evaluation branches. The following guidance is offered:

1. *Defining the problem.* The meaning of the construct being measured needs to be negotiated across cultures and in a way that is inclusive of marginalized populations within the cultures. This means that local knowledge is needed to ascertain how individuals can be invited and supported in respectful ways. The use of literature review is also an appropriate part of this first step; however, it needs to be conducted with a critical eye toward whose voices are being represented in the literature.

2. *Identifying the study design.* Mixed methods designs allow for inclusion of qualitative methods that encourage discussions of variability and opportunities for tolerance and celebration of differences and commonalities. Quantitative methods of instrument construction can be used to establish psychometric properties and can be paired with qualitative data collection to ascertain the meanings and acceptability of the items as interpreted by the targeted population.

3. *Identifying participants.* The selection of participants for the various stages of the mixed methods study needs to be done with an awareness of the diversity within the communities. The use of local advisory committees can be helpful in this regard if the members are engaged with the communities and understand the power structures and bases of discrimination.

4. *Construction of the measure.* Evaluators can rely on the scope of the concept to be measured as it is represented in the literature

(Continued)

(Continued)

> with an important caveat. They need to ensure that the items for the instrument are grounded in the culture and complexity of the community. A good way to accomplish this is to have an intensive qualitative process that precedes and operates continuously throughout the development of the items. If comparisons are to be made across groups, then attention needs to be given to the language and translation issues.
>
> 5. *Analysis and interpretation.* The use of mixed methods encourages the co-construction of meaning of the constructs and helps to refine the selection of items. Face-to-face meetings within sites and between sites help ensure the measure demonstrates high face validity across cultures (adapted from Ungar & Liebenberg, 2011, p. 142).

Extending Your Thinking

Social Justice Branch Instrument Development

1. You have been hired by a firm to develop an instrument to determine if people in a community understand changes that need to be made in order to address environmental pollution and their willingness to engage in the recommended behaviors. How would you begin this process? Design a social justice mixed methods study to develop an instrument for this purpose.

2. Attitudes toward law enforcement officials is noted as a problem in trying to establish positive relationships between police officers and community members. What advice would you provide a community organization that wants to explore how to improve relationships with law enforcement in their community based on a measurement instrument that you develop? Design a social justice mixed methods study to develop an instrument for this context.

● DIALECTICAL PLURALISM: INSTRUMENT DEVELOPMENT

Dialectical pluralism applied to instrument development is similar to the description provided in Chapter 2 on evaluation of interventions in that two or more paradigms are used to frame the study (Shannon-Baker, 2015b). The processes used to develop the instrument stay true to the assumptions of the paradigms used in the framing of the study and then are brought into conversation with each other to identify new understandings that emerge from the different perspectives (Greene & Hall, 2010). Johnson and Stefurak (2013) recommend that the qualitative and quantitative parts of the study be conducted by cross-perspective research teams that represent expertise in each of the methods used. Through respectful dialogue among the team members, it is possible to incorporate understandings into the instrument development that would not be available if one method of data collection was used alone.

De-la-Cueva-Ariza et al. (2014) provide a description of a method for applying DP in the development of an instrument to study patient satisfaction with nursing care in intensive care contexts. Their publication consists of a description of their proposed methodology; therefore no results of the study can be presented.

Sample Study 3.6: Dialectical Pluralism Instrument Development

Patient satisfaction with nursing care in Spain (de-la-Cueva-Ariza et al., 2014).

Problem: Patient experience with nursing care is different in intensive care settings than in other health settings. No instrument exists that is specific to the intensive care context.

Evaluand: Survey for intensive care patients to measure their satisfaction with nursing care in Spain.

Design: Dialectical pluralism sequential MM design.

Sample: The qualitative sample size is estimated to be from 27 to 36 participants who will be purposefully chosen for maximum variation with individuals who meet the following criteria: be at least 18 years old, have spent at least 48 hours in the intensive care unit, and are able to describe their experience in the intensive care unit. The quantitative sample will be about 200 patients who were admitted to the intensive care unit using the same criteria used for the qualitative stage.

Data collection: The study will begin with a qualitative stage that will include in-depth interviews with patients who were admitted to intensive care and have spent at least 48 hours in that unit. Qualitative data collection will include an in-depth interview, field diaries, and a discussion group with experts. Documents will also be analyzed; the evaluators do not specify what the documents will be. The questionnaire itself will be the data collection

(Continued)

(Continued)

instrument for the quantitative part of the study. It will be developed based on the findings from the qualitative part of the study.

Data analysis: Grounded theory will be used to analyze the qualitative data. The evaluators described their data analytic process for the qualitative portion of the study as follows:

> First, an open encoding will allow for conceptualization (identification of concepts) and finding the properties and dimensions in the data. Therefore, we have the foundation and the initial structure to build a theory. Second, an axial codification consisting of matching categories to subcategories and linking them based on their properties and dimensions: accommodating the properties of a category and its dimensions (this task begins during the open codification); identifying the variety of conditions, actions/interactions and consequences associated with the phenomenon of satisfaction; matching category with its subcategories by sentences indicating the relationship among them; and searching for clues in the data denoting how they can be related to the main categories.
>
> Finally, the selective codification in the analysis will lead to the integration of concepts around a central category and completing the categories that need to be further perfected and developed, showing the depth and complexity of thought of the theory being developed. (p. 206)

Quantitative analysis will include descriptive and inferential statistics. The psychometric properties of the instrument will be determined using standard Methods branch strategies. "The scale's metric properties will be determined by: content validity with establishment of the Pearson correlation for quantitative variables and the sensitivity and specificity for the qualitative ones. The construct's validity will be defined through factorial analysis of the instrument's items. And reliability decided by the internal coherence established by Cronbach alpha and temporal stability through test-retest reliability calculated using the intra-class correlation coefficient will be cross-checked" (p. 207).

Results: The qualitative data will be used to categorize items that can be included in the questionnaire. The quantitative data will be used to establish the instrument's psychometric properties.

Benefits of using MM: The dialectical pluralism approach to instrument development allows the evaluators to adhere to the criteria for rigor that are defined for qualitative data collection in the Values branch, as well as those for quantitative data collection as defined in the Methods branch. The instrument will be developed based on the real experiences of patients in the intensive care unit and will have rigorous psychometric properties.

Guidance for Designing a Dialectical Pluralism Instrument Development Study

Instrument development using a DP approach borrows ideas from the paradigms used to frame the DP approach in each particular study.

1. If the plan for the study begins with a qualitative portion that reflects the assumptions of the constructivist paradigm and the Values branch, then the evaluators need to adhere to the methodological assumptions associated with that stance. This can include a comprehensive literature review. However, in the de-la-Cueva-Ariza et al. (2014) study, the evaluators propose using a grounded theory approach in the qualitative portion of the study that does not rely on preestablished categories that might emerge from the literature. The basic logic of **grounded theory** is that the inquiry begins without preestablished categories of concepts; rather, relevant ideas are allowed to emerge from interactions with participants in the field (Charmatz, 2014; Corbin & Strauss, 2008). Data are collected and analyzed simultaneously, and then data from each instance of interaction are compared with the analysis of others. This provides for a refinement of tentative categories that emerge from earlier data collection and analysis through a process of constant comparison. The intent is to develop an understanding of the concept to be measured that is grounded in the experiences of the target population. For example, de-la-Cueva-Ariza et al. (2014) plan to develop a grounded theory that explains the concept of patient satisfaction in relation to nursing care in intensive care contexts. The specifics of their grounded theory analysis are found in the summary of Sample Study 3.6.

2. The quantitative phase of the instrument development is informed by the results of the qualitative phase, thus bringing the qualitative and quantitative perspectives into dialogue with each other. Items for the questionnaire are developed that reflect the concepts that emerged from the qualitative data analysis. It is common practice to have these items reviewed by a group of experts in the field prior to administering them in a draft form to a sample from the target population. A revised draft is usually administered to a sample of the target population in a format that allows for determining the appropriateness, comprehension, and interpretation of the items. The draft instrument is then revised again based on the analysis of this administration.

3. At this stage, the instrument is generally tested quantitatively to determine its reliability and validity by administering it to another sample and conducting factor analysis and comparison to other known instruments for validity and calculating reliability coefficients such as Cronbach alpha and the test-retest approach.

Extending Your Thinking

Dialectical Pluralism Instrument Development

1. You have been hired by a community outreach group to help them measure the impact of their programs in terms of attitudes of community members toward members of a variety of religious groups. How would you use DP to frame an approach to the development of an instrument for this purpose?

2. If an organization says it has heard of this concept of DP but doesn't understand exactly what that would mean for its development of instruments, how would you explain the concept to that organization? Think of an example you can use as part of your explanation and integrate the example into the information you would share with the organization.

SUMMARY AND MOVING FORWARD

Part of the strategies for instrument development share common territory across the philosophical frames and evaluation branches in that a literature review is generally used as a starting point and engagement with stakeholders is necessary to collect quantitative and qualitative data about their experience with the instrument. However, mixed methods evaluation designs for instrument development manifest different emphases depending on the philosophical framing and evaluation branch used by the evaluators. For example, in the Methods branch, the emphasis is on quantitative data to establish the reliability and validity of an instrument, often in relation to a norm group. Qualitative data can be used to determine coverage and understanding of items. In the Values branch, the focus is much more on the collection of qualitative data to inform the development of the instrument. This can take the form of an ethnographic study to determine nuances of cultural understandings. The quantitative part of the study is also used to determine reliability and validity. In the Use branch, the goal is to develop an instrument that is psychometrically sound, and qualitative data are used to serve that goal. As in the sample study in this chapter, the qualitative data were "accidentally" collected by comments shared with the instrument developers. For the Social Justice branch, evaluators are more likely to spend more time upfront collecting qualitative and quantitative data to understand the context and complexity of the stakeholders more fully. They will also be consciously inclusive of members of marginalized populations in the sample that participates in the instrument development. In DP, separate strategies are used for qualitative data collection (which may include literature reviews and focus groups), and these are used to inform the development, implementation, and interpretation of quantitative data collection.

In the next chapter, we look at another important venue in which evaluators work: policy evaluation. This area is replete with complexity because of the explicitly political nature of the context and the power relations inherent in such contexts.

4

Mixed Methods Evaluation Designs for Policy Evaluation

The conception of RCTs as belonging to the highest tier of the hierarchy of evidence, whilst single-case studies, expert opinion and qualitative investigations are placed in the lowest ranks, is not only out of date but also potentially harmful and misleading; if we wish to address real-world issues such as how best to help depressed young people whose difficulties can potentially have long-term consequences, we need to see more mixed methods studies in which qualitative data are nested within RCT designs. (Midgley et al., 2013, p. 136)

Adopting a pragmatic worldview as the philosophical basis in which the research question is the decisive factor for selecting the research methodology—not the paradigm from which the method derives (Teddlie & Tashakkori, 2010)—researchers have chosen to utilize MM in their studies to answer questions that could not be answered monolithically (Johnson & Onwuegbuzie, 2004). (cited in Tsushima, 2015, p. 107)

In This Chapter

- Overview of mixed methods and policy evaluation
- Mixed methods designs for policy evaluation from the Methods branch
- Mixed methods designs for policy evaluation from the Values branch
- Mixed methods designs for policy evaluation from the Use branch
- Mixed methods designs for policy evaluation from the Social Justice branch
- Mixed methods designs for policy evaluation from dialectical pluralism

● POLICY EVALUATION AND MIXED METHODS

In some evaluation contexts, the evaluand is not a program or a practice but a policy that is of importance. Evaluators contribute to **policy evaluation** both to provide information as to what a policy should include as well as to determine the effects of policy. Policies are by definition developed within political contexts, and thus the decisions made about policies are influenced by multiple factors, evaluation evidence potentially being one of those influential factors. Evaluators sometimes express frustration in their attempts to bring evaluative thinking into policy development and evaluation (Kelly, 2015; Segone, 2015). This raises two important questions: What counts as evidence in policy evaluation, and how can this evidence be integrated effectively into the policy process?

If evidence is to have a greater impact on policy and practice, then four key requirements are necessary before such an agenda can be developed. The key requirements are these:

1. Agreement as to what counts as evidence in what circumstances

2. A strategic approach to the creation of evidence in priority areas, with concomitant systematic efforts to accumulate evidence in the form of robust bodies of knowledge

3. Effective dissemination of evidence to where it is most needed and the development of effective means of providing wide access to knowledge

4. Initiatives to ensure the integration of evidence into policy and encourage the use of evidence in practice (Nutley, Davies, & Walter, 2002)

Other characteristics of policy evaluation that have been found to influence policymakers are tailoring the message to the specific stakeholder group and providing access to an online registry of systematic reviews of policy evaluation studies (Dobbins et al., 2009). A systematic review of barriers to the use of evidence by policymakers revealed the most frequently cited barriers were poor accessibility to the findings and lack of timeliness in the provision of those findings (Oliver, Innvar, Lorenc, Woodman, & Thomas, 2014). Factors that facilitated policy use included collaboration between evaluators and policymakers and improved relationships and skills. Oliver and colleagues note that a weakness in many policy-related studies is lack of involvement with the policymakers themselves. They suggest a need to obtain information from policymakers as to what they consider to be clear, relevant, and reliable data and when and why they would use such data. As you read through the examples, examine how the evaluation design chosen reflects these important variables that influence use of evaluation findings for policymaking.

METHODS BRANCH: ●
MIXED METHODS POLICY EVALUATION

Several design options reflect the Methods branch in policy evaluation. I bring three designs that fit in this category to your attention: mixed methods with randomized controlled trials, mixed methods with time series design, and the use of surveys and interviews in a mixed methods design. A recent World Bank publication (Basu, 2013) supports the use of mixed methods designs that incorporate RCTs: "To get to policy conclusions requires combining the findings of randomized experiments with human intuition . . . even non-randomized empirical methods combined with reasoned intuition can help in crafting development policy" (p. i.). A concurrent time series mixed methods design is illustrated in the following section on a study of the effects of a policy change related to lead-based paint in houses in a major metropolitan area in the United States (Iregbu, 2008). A second example of a Methods branch mixed methods policy evaluation using a survey and interviews follows this study.

Sample Study 4.1: Methods Branch

Concurrent time series mixed methods study: Lead paint disclosure policy: Implications for eliminating childhood lead exposure in Baltimore (Iregbu, 2008).

Problem: Lead poisoning is a public health hazard that disproportionately affects children in low-income areas. Elevated levels of lead in the blood are associated with difficulties in learning and behavior. Children generally get high levels of lead in their blood by ingesting lead dust or chips when they live in houses built between 1946 and 1973 with walls covered with lead paint. Baltimore, MD, an area with significant older low-income housing, has a higher rate of elevated lead blood levels than its surrounding counties and cities.

Policy: In 1978, the United States banned the use of lead-based paint and the U.S. Congress passed a policy that called for landlords and homeowners to perform lead abatement or take other lead risk-reduction measures to eliminate or reduce exposure to lead (U.S. Code of Federal Regulations [CFR] 40:745, CFR-24 Subtitle A 5-1-01). The policy included a loophole provision for a disclosure policy that "provided a waiver for property owners of rental housing units and home sellers from performing lead abatement or other risk-reduction measures before signing rental or sales agreements" (p. 6). In 1996, the Environmental Protection Agency established the Lead Residential Lead-Based Disclosure Program (Section 1018 of Title X) that stated that landlords/owners were supposed to disclose the information about the lead hazards in a residence prior to selling or renting houses built prior to 1978. The EPA rule does not require any testing or removal of lead-based paint by the sellers or landlords. In Baltimore, the policy effective date was the end of 1996. In Iregbu's study, the prepolicy dates included 1994–1996. The postpolicy phase was 1997–2006.

Design: The evaluator used a concurrent mixed methods design, using a time series design for the quantitative portion and interviews for the qualitative portion. The time series design included the collection of quantitative data over several years prior to the implementation of the policy (1994–1996) and several years after the policy was implemented (1997–2004).

Sample: The sample for the quantitative portion consisted of the entire city of Baltimore. The qualitative sample consisted of 14 lead-based paint program managers from selected government and community-based organizations.

Data collection: Databases maintained by Baltimore and the Maryland Department of Environment Lead-based Paint Prevention Program were used to obtain quantitative data such as the number of lead-based paint abatements, number of children with elevated lead in their blood, and the number of children suffering from lead poisoning. U.S. Census data were used to obtain information about educational levels, value of real estate properties, race, and income levels. Qualitative data were collected by means of interviews with the lead-based paint program managers that focused on their perceptions of the need to revise the disclosure policy. The evaluator specifically mentions the need to avoid biasing the results of the interviews by avoiding any personal preknowledge of the interviewees prior to data collection. He states, "The interview questions were constructed free of political tones, personal confrontation, and interest group biases" (p. 89).

Data analysis: The evaluator used an inductive strategy to perform open coding for the qualitative data. The inductive coding involved allowing generalized conclusions to emerge from the codes based on probabilistic occurrence and interpretation. The evaluator then used descriptive statistics to summarize the frequency of qualitative comments made by participants. Quantitative data were analyzed by calculating descriptive statistics (e.g., the number of lead abatements each year) for each year. He also used analysis of variance and covariance to compare pre- and postpolicy dependent variables. The analysis of covariance allowed him to control confounding variables such as economic status.

Results: There is an increase in the number of lead abatements by landlords and owners since the implementation of the policy. However, many homes are still not free of lead. The level of elevated blood lead levels is highest in the African Americans who live in the low-income part of Baltimore. The qualitative data revealed that not everyone agrees that lead abatement is the solution to the problem because it is expensive for the property owner. It also revealed that tenants may choose not to press for lead abatement because they are afraid they might get evicted, they cannot afford to live anywhere else, or their reading skills are too low to understand what the property owner shares with them.

Benefits of using MM: The quantitative data revealed progress in the reduction of lead in housing and elevated levels of lead in children's blood. However, it also revealed an ongoing problem more prevalent for people who live in low-income housing and are from racial and ethnic minority groups. The qualitative data revealed that the disclosure policy is not effective in preventing people from living in lead-painted houses and that there is lack of enforcement of the lead abatement policy.

Guidance for Designing a Methods Branch Concurrent Mixed Methods Study With Time Series and Interviews

1. In a time series study, data need to be available over a reasonable period of time, or the study needs to continue over a reasonable period of time so the data can be collected at several points before and after the intervention. The term *reasonable* here is defined in relation to the evaluand. For example, an evaluation of an educational program might collect data several times in the beginning of the

(Continued)

(Continued)

school year to establish a baseline, an intervention could be implemented, and then data would be collected several more times. In Iregbu's (2008) study, annual data were available through databases maintained by the state of Maryland on the variables of interest.

2. In a concurrent MM design, the quantitative and qualitative data are collected simultaneously. In Iregbu's (2008) study, the quantitative data were available from existing databases. He identified a number of variables that had relevance to his research questions related to the frequency of lead abatements and the level of lead in children's blood, as well as demographic data. For the interviews, he selected people who had experience with housing in the lower-income neighborhoods and used open-ended questions to interview them.

3. The sample sizes were much different for the quantitative (very large, in the 1,000s) part of the study as compared to the qualitative part (14 people were interviewed).

4. The data were integrated at the point of interpretation; the evaluator used the qualitative data to provide insights into the continued presence of lead in houses and the continued elevated levels of lead in the children's blood.

• METHODS BRANCH: MIXED METHODS SURVEY/INTERVIEW EMBEDDED POLICY ANALYSIS

Policy analysis can also be conducted using a large-scale quantitative strategy with a smaller-scale qualitative strategy embedded in the study. This is the approach used by Beletsky et al. (2015) when they evaluated a reform in Mexico's drug policy to ascertain changes needed to improve treatment for people who use drugs.

Sample Study 4.2: Methods Branch

Embedded quantitative qualitative design for policy analysis: Treatment for people who use drugs (Beletsky et al., 2015).

Problem: Many countries are decriminalizing small-scale drug possession because an excessive number of people incarcerated for possession results in overcrowding in prisons and some would say injustice. Problems were identified in Mexico related to this issue, and the Mexican government decided to take a progressive stance and pass legislation with the goal of decreasing arrests for small amounts of illegal drugs and to increase participation in treatment programs for drug users.

Policy: In 2009, Mexico passed a drug reform policy aimed at increasing the use of drug treatment diversion programs instead of incarceration for people who inject drugs. Diversion programs are designed to provide support for individuals arrested for drug use so they can change the conditions of their lives toward a goal of more healthy living. The purpose of the evaluation was to determine the impact of the reform policy on people who inject drugs. The focus was on the drug users' knowledge of the policy and their encounters with police (arrest, detention, or treatment diversion).

Design: The evaluators used an embedded quantitative qualitative design that included a dominant quantitative portion with a smaller qualitative part of the study. The quantitative study was used to identify a subsample that could be used in the qualitative study.

Sample: Trained staff visited areas in Tijuana where drug users were known to gather; they recruited 737 participants, 95% of whom reported injecting drugs at least once a day and 76% of whom reported being stopped or arrested by police in the past 6 months. The qualitative subsample included 32 participants who were purposefully selected to be representative of gender and deportation experiences. All of the interviewees reported being stopped and/ or arrested by police in the previous month.

Data collection: "The quantitative study survey instrument assessed sociodemographics, injection and risky behaviors, migration history, knowledge of Mexican drug laws, and police encounter history, among other domains. Items designed to assess the implementation of the drug law reform included questions assessing knowledge, firsthand experience, and attitudes toward the Mexican drug law and its enforcement" (p. 5). Interviewers were also trained to collect the qualitative data; the interviews lasted between 40 and 90 minutes. "Interview guide domains included knowledge and attitudes about drug possession and paraphernalia laws; perceived recent changes in those laws and the sources of information about any change; perceived consistency of law enforcement and the adherence of police practices to the formal law; in-depth description of the last police encounter and its comparison with a 'typical' encounter; and perceived behavioral and mental health effect of police encounters on drug use and daily activities" (p. 5).

Data analysis: Quantitative data analysis included calculation of descriptive statistics, nonparametric statistical tests, and univariate logistical regression to compare responses of drug users who had encounters with police and those who did not. The qualitative data were transcribed from audio tapes and then were translated from Spanish to English. The evaluators used bilingual interviewers to check the translations. The analysis included writing memos about initial impressions of the data, development of criteria for assigning codes to text, and independent coding by at least two staff. They described the integration of the quantitative and qualitative data in the following way:

(Continued)

(Continued)

> We present quantitative findings to characterize the prevalence of phenomena within the entire study population. We then invite the reader to reflect on respondent narratives to contextualize, enrich, and personalize our quantitative findings. We also use our qualitative findings to draw out conceptual and theoretical insights from our quantitative data, as well as to inform our discussion of next steps. (p. 6)

Results: The quantitative findings indicated that 98% of respondents reported that police behavior was not in keeping with the new law. The evaluators used the qualitative data to explain the ways that the drug users experienced this—they were locked up for having syringes or if they had one dose of heroin. Only 2% of the respondents reported that they were diverted to a drug treatment program. The qualitative data revealed that drug users had been beaten by police, asked for bribes, and had drugs planted on them so they would have a longer jail sentence.

Benefits of using MM: The quantitative findings were expanded and contextualized by the use of the qualitative interview data. The use of mixed methods enabled the evaluators to document the prevalence of the problems with the drug reform policy and to gain insight into the reasons for the failure of the policy. The evaluators wrote: "Our qualitative analysis demonstrated that it was not merely a lack of knowledge about the drug law that influenced participants' behavior, but also a deeply rooted sense of mistrust that existing laws will be applied as written" (p. 13). The desired impact of the new policy will require changes in police officers' knowledge about the law, attitudes toward drug users, and incentives to implement the reform.

Guidance for Designing a Methods Branch Embedded Quantitative Qualitative Study

1. In the context of policy analysis, it is important to identify the stakeholders impacted by the policy. In the Beletsky et al. (2015) study, they focused on drug users. If they had asked different evaluation questions, they could have sampled from policymakers, health or social service providers, or families of drug users.

2. Typically, the sampling plan will include a larger sample for the quantitative part of the study and a smaller sample for the qualitative part. This disparity in sample sizes is related to the labor-intensive nature of collecting qualitative data as compared to quantitative data (in many circumstances). The qualitative sample can be independent of the quantitative sample or it can be a subset of the quantitative sample. In the Beletsky et al. (2015) embedded MM study, the quantitative sample was used to identify the appropriate sample for the qualitative study.

3. Integration of quantitative and qualitative strategies can occur at many stages in the evaluation. For example, the sampling can depend on integration of quantitative and qualitative aspects. The data collection in the qualitative portion can be influenced by the results of the quantitative survey. The interview questions can be designed to explore the issues that were salient in the quantitative portion.

4. In an embedded design, either the quantitative or the qualitative portion of the study can dominate. However, in the Methods branch, the quantitative portion of the study is usually dominant. Either the quantitative or the qualitative portion of the study can occur first in the implementation of the evaluation.

5. Integration of findings is very important and needs to be included to fully maximize the benefit of using mixed methods. In MM policy evaluations, the results need to be brought into conversation with the policy itself and shared with policymakers.

Extending Your Thinking

Methods Branch Mixed Methods Policy Evaluation

1. In the United States, the primary legislation governing education from 2002 to 2015 was the No Child Left Behind (NCLB) Act. In 2015, the U.S. Congress passed a new education law, Every Student Succeeds Act (ESSA). NCLB was heralded because the concept was that no child, no matter what his or her race/ethnicity, disability, gender, or economic class, should be deprived of educational achievement. The mechanism for the NCLB law was a source of criticism and angst in many schools because it focused on standardized tests in math and reading; carried sanctions for nonachievement; offered very little in resources or support to achieve goals; and left out other subjects such as history, art, music, and science. ESSA greatly reduces the use of testing, mandating testing in the third and eighth grades and once in secondary school, and supports a more inclusive curriculum. Design a policy study using either a concurrent time series mixed methods design or an embedded quantitative qualitative mixed methods design to explore the effects of the change in policy.

2. Select a policy issue of your choice. Design a mixed methods study using either concurrent time series mixed methods design or an embedded quantitative qualitative mixed methods design to explore the effects of the change in policy.

● VALUES BRANCH: MIXED METHODS POLICY EVALUATION

Evaluators often think that quantitative evaluations involve large samples and qualitative evaluations involve small samples. This perception is supported by many of the studies included in this book. However, qualitatively dominant studies can be large scale, thus requiring more resources because of the labor-intensive nature of qualitative data collection. Nevertheless, evaluations can begin with fieldwork that has many benefits, as is clear in this statement by Hunt et al. (2013): "The benefits of fieldwork include the ability to note contextual features that may not be readily apparent in interviews, to gain a lived, tactile sense of the social worlds of the participants, and to witness and experience the interactions that comprise this social world" (p. 437). Being present in the context in which the evaluation is taking place can have the additional benefit of facilitating the development of a sampling frame, identifying diversity within the population, and forming relationships that support recruitment of participants.

Hunt et al. (2013) conducted a Values branch evaluation to inform policy related to preventing youth drug use. The qualitative component of the study was dominant, based on the rationale that drug policy needs to be informed by both epidemiological data and by an understanding of the perceptions and meanings of illegal drug use by young people.

Sample Study 4.3: Values Branch

Large-scale qualitative policy evaluation: Drug use by youth (Hunt et al., 2011).

Problem: Drug use by youth puts them at risk for health, economic, psychological, and social problems. Despite programs to decrease youth use of illicit drugs, the practice continues to flourish, especially in the dance club scene. The drug Ecstasy is increasingly used at electronic dance parties (raves) and is associated with risky behaviors and danger to health and life.

Policy: Policies about drug use in the cultural context in which drug use is prevalent in San Francisco, Hong Kong, and Rotterdam.

Design: Concurrent mixed methods on a large scale involving participant observation to map the field, in-depth interviews, and quantitative data through a survey.

Sample: Youth who attend raves and go to dance clubs might be considered a hidden population in that the use of illicit drugs makes access to them more difficult. Over 300 youth who went to clubs and raves in San Francisco, Hong

Kong, and Rotterdam were recruited through ethnographic observations of the nightlife venues and engagement with youth in that subculture. However, sampling strategies had to be adjusted to include different cultural groups, such as Asian American gay and bisexual men. With this group, the evaluators had to develop contacts, maintain a presence in the scene, engage with community-based organizations, use advertising that was culturally acceptable, and use online recruitment and networking. In Rotterdam, the sample was recruited by first obtaining information from over 100 clubs and then using this set of data to recruit directly from the clubs and by means of flyers taken to these clubs. In Hong Kong, snowball sampling was used as well as contacts at drug treatment centers. Key informants were also part of the sample, including nightclub owners, promoters, DJs, local government officials, and police.

Data collection: The data collection began with ethnographic fieldwork, including observations at raves, clubs, and bars. Observers used an observational protocol to record interactions among the youth and staff in the venues, such as alcohol and drug procurement and consumption, prevalence of violence, and gender roles. In-depth interviews were a dominant part of the data collection. The interviews were conducted by trained staff using a semistructured open-ended guide to gather data about the youth's social world and the narrative they used to describe their lives. The interviews lasted from 2 to 4 hours. Quantitative data were also gathered at the same time that included demographic information and drug and alcohol use data.

Data analysis: Data analysis involved all members of the evaluation team from senior members to fieldworkers. In this way, the perceptions of the line by line coders, the personal experiences of the interviewers, and the experience of the senior members could all be brought into the discussion of the data analysis. In addition, evaluators from the three countries all participated in the data analysis of the other three countries.

Results: The evaluators began the results reporting with quantitative data describing the demographics; frequency and type of drug use; and different patterns by ethnicity, age, socioeconomic status, etc. The results of the data analysis were then combined for the quantitative and qualitative data. In this way they could report on the differences in the narrative surrounding drug use within specific subgroups, with a focus on motivations for use, meanings, and contextual influences. They revealed that youth described their engagement in this culture as a way of developing self-identity and having a structured social group. Globalization of the drug and dance culture was apparent in the similarities found in the youth groups in the three cities.

Benefits of using MM: The use of mixed methods allowed the evaluators to both describe what was happening in terms of drug use and to provide an interpretation of that use from the youth's perspective. Evaluators were able to provide theories about youth drug use that can be used to understand both the process and the outcomes. Such information is invaluable in designing interventions to decrease use of illicit drugs by youth. By combining the qualitative

(Continued)

(Continued)

data from literature review and ethnographic data collection with the quantitative data, the evaluators were able to identify the influence of acculturation and acculturation stress on the drug use practices of Asian Americans. Some described their drug use as part of their American acculturation; others described it as a response to stress associated with American acculturation. The results reveal the perceptions by youth of the normalization of drug use across cultures, which is quite a different picture from that held by policymakers that focuses on the risks of using illegal drugs. Knowledge of this disconnect between the perceptions of youth and policymakers can provide a basis for development of policy that might more effectively address the problem.

Guidance for Designing a Values Branch Policy Evaluation Study

1. A large-scale qualitatively dominant mixed methods study has several challenges associated with it that are magnified because of the number of people involved and the massive amount of data. Hunt et al. (2011) described their data set: "With 300 or more interviews, each generating 60–70 pages of transcripts, a single project can generate over 20,000 pages of transcribed interviews, in addition to the quantitative survey results, field notes, and the memos and coding" (p. 441).

2. Data collection in such large studies takes a lot of time for the evaluators and stakeholders. Consideration needs to be given to stakeholders (especially youth) asked to give up 4 hours of time without the use of their smartphones or to respondents who have jobs or family responsibilities. This might include paying an honorarium, provision of food and drinks, providing child care, or persuading the participants that a social good will come from their participation.

3. Strategies for data management need to be given consideration so that important findings do not get lost in the mountains of data being processed. Hunt et al. (2011) recommended constructing a **focus sheet** shortly after each interview that captured the major themes and observations of the interviewer. Thus, the focus sheet served as a prememo for the data analysis by highlighting key characteristics associated with the respondents.

4. With massive amounts of data, the use of computer-assisted qualitative data analysis packages is essential. This allows the evaluators to organize the information contained in the transcripts and field notes and to facilitate the coding of the data. Codebooks are essential with large qualitative data sets so that the coders can share understandings

of the various codes. A process of independent coding can be used with a sample of the transcripts to ensure shared understandings.

5. Be aware of options for recruiting participants into large-scale qualitative studies, especially those that might involve recruitment of hidden or hard-to-access populations. Fieldwork can provide opportunities for understanding the population in its diversity and to build relationships necessary for respectful recruitment of participants. Recruitment at venues where targeted stakeholders congregate is one strategy; others include use of flyers, advertisements, online networking, and snowball sampling.

6. Strategies for bringing Values branch evaluation findings to policymakers are very important. Evaluators need to emphasize the rigor of the qualitative methods and the richness of the findings and demonstrate how the findings can improve policies about important problems.

Extending Your Thinking

Values Branch Mixed Methods Policy Evaluation

1. Poverty reduction is a critical goal for international development specialists. Design a large-scale qualitatively dominant mixed methods study to evaluate a poverty reduction program in a selected country, critically examining the policies relevant to the program. What are the benefits of such an approach? How would you include representatives from the selected country?

2. In your evaluation work, in what circumstances would you recommend the use of a large-scale qualitatively dominant mixed methods design for a policy evaluation? How would you persuade funders to support the additional resources needed for such a study?

USE BRANCH: MIXED METHODS POLICY EVALUATION ●

Because some policymakers seek an evidence base that supports the continuation or modification of implemented policies, Use branch evaluators have an opening to provide useful evaluative findings for the policy decisions that need to be made. Veitch et al. (2012) state, "Policy concerns are identified as access, complexity, cost, distribution of benefits, timeliness, effectiveness, equity, policy consistency, and community and political acceptability" (p. 1).

Veitch et al. (2012) proposed a Use branch MM multistage design to provide policymakers with evidence on the effectiveness and need for modification to policies related to the delivery of services for people with disabilities in New South Wales, Australia. The article used for this sample study is a proposed methodology, hence, results of the study are not reported.

Sample Study 4.4: Use Branch

Multistage MM policy evaluation in the Use branch: Disability service delivery in rural Australia (Veitch et al., 2012).

Problem: Rural and remote communities have fewer allied health workers to serve people with disabilities over large geographic areas. Staff retention and dispersion of clients continue to be barriers to provision of services.

Policy: New South Wales Government Family and Community Services Ageing, Disability and Home Care–Western Region (ADHS-WR) Intake Policy (ADHC-WR, 2001) and Priortisation and Allocation Policy (ADHC-WR, 2001) and proposed policies regarding transportation of people with disabilities to services.

Design: Use branch multistage MM policy evaluation: Four interrelated stages over 5 years that align with a full policy cycle (see Figure 4.1).

Stage 1 adopts a policy analysis approach in which existing relevant policies and related documentation will be collected and reviewed. Policymakers and senior managers within the region and in central offices will be interviewed about issues that influence policy development and implementation.

Stage 2 uses a mixed methods approach to collecting information from allied health professionals, clients, and carers. Focus groups and interviews will explore issues related to providing and receiving allied health services. Discrete choice experiments will elicit staff and client/carer preferences (using a fractional factorial experimental design with a fixed number of attributes and levels for each attribute).

Stage 3 synthesizes Stage 1 and 2 findings with reference to the key policy issues to develop and implement policies and procedures to establish several innovative regional workforce and service provision projects.

Stage 4 uses mixed methods to monitor and evaluate the implementation and impact of new or adapted policies that arise from the preceding stages.

Sample: Existing policies and related documents in the form of agency policies, guidelines, and national legislation, adding to the pool by purposeful

Figure 4.1 Multistage Use Branch Mixed Methods Policy Evaluation Design

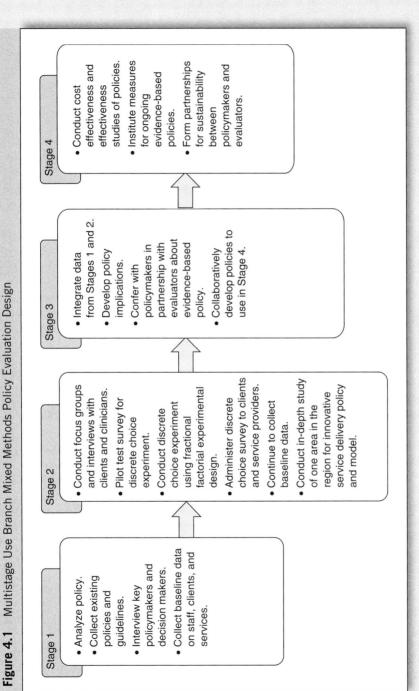

Stage 1
- Analyze policy.
- Collect existing policies and guidelines.
- Interview key policymakers and decision makers.
- Collect baseline data on staff, clients, and services.

Stage 2
- Conduct focus groups and interviews with clients and clinicians.
- Pilot test survey for discrete choice experiment.
- Conduct discrete choice experiment using fractional factorial experimental design.
- Administer discrete choice survey to clients and service providers.
- Continue to collect baseline data.
- Conduct in-depth study of one area in the region for innovative service delivery policy and model.

Stage 3
- Integrate data from Stages 1 and 2.
- Develop policy implications.
- Confer with policymakers in partnership with evaluators about evidence-based policy.
- Collaboratively develop policies to use in Stage 4.

Stage 4
- Conduct cost effectiveness and effectiveness studies of policies.
- Institute measures for ongoing evidence-based policies.
- Form partnerships for sustainability between policymakers and evaluators.

Source: Adapted from Veitch et al. (2012).

(Continued)

and snowball sampling strategies. Purposeful sampling will be used to identify 50 senior staff and 100 service users who work at ADHC or provide supportive services. For the discrete choice experiment, all service providers
(total = 100) will be used; 180 service users will be randomly selected to
represent different travel distances from services. In Stages 3 and 4 similar
sampling strategies will be used to select professional staff, service providers,
and service users.

Data Collection

Stage 1: Collect relevant policies and related documents based on policies
and guidelines currently being used in ADHS-WR. Interview key policymakers
and decision makers. Collect baseline data on staff, clients, and services and
identify measures that inform policy development and monitoring.

Stage 2: Focus groups and interviews with clinicians, clients, and carers.
A survey will be used to conduct a discrete choice experiment with staff to
determine their preferences in terms of work characteristics. Service users will
also complete a discrete choice experiment to determine their preferences
for service design and access. Both surveys will be pilot tested. Baseline data
will be collected on staff and clients and carers using available data sources
where feasible at 6-month intervals during the study (e.g., Australian Bureau of
Statistics). An in-depth study will be conducted of one region's service delivery
model focusing on formulation, implementation, and cost-effectiveness.

Stage 3: Synthesize data from first two stages with specific focus on policy
issues and guiding policy questions from policymakers. Confer with policymakers about evidence-based policy. Collaboratively develop strategies based
on trial study in Stage 2.

Stage 4: Conduct cost-effectiveness study of policies formulated in previous stages. Institute measures for ongoing policy evaluation. Form partnership between evaluators and stakeholders to sustain evidence-based policy
strategies.

Data analysis: Policy documents and guidelines will be analyzed to identify
themes that will guide individual interviews. Summary notes will be prepared
for each interview in Stage 1; these data will be analyzed using thematic analysis that will reveal key policy issues. Data from the focus groups and interviews
in Stage 2 will be analyzed using grounded theory and constant comparison.
Results from the discrete choice experiments will include descriptive and com-
parative statistics using both parametric and nonparametric tests. A random
parameter of a multinomial mixed logit model will be used to analyze the survey data in order to reveal staff and client preferences and their relations to
demographic characteristics. Stage 3 data analysis will involve a partnership
between policymakers and the evaluators to develop strategies for implementation of evidence-based policy. The final stage will include an assessment of the reliability and utility of outcome measures included in the policy.

In addition, focus groups will be held with health professionals, ADHC staff, and clients to ascertain their experiences with the changes in policy and service delivery.

Results: The results are intended to provide policymakers with evidence to support complex policy decisions related to equitable allocation of resources, prioritization of policies and eligibility criteria, constraints and strengths of workforce, and evidence-based clinical practice.

Benefits of using MM: The results of each stage of data collection and analysis will be used to inform the next stage. For example, qualitative data from policy analysis and first-stage interviews and demographic variables on resources, clients, and staff will be used in Stage 2 to inform the design of the in-depth interviews and discrete choice experiment surveys. The results of the discrete experiment studies will be used to identify choices that can influence future workforce and service delivery policies. Data from the discrete choice experiments will be used to design an alternative service delivery model that will be tested for cost-effectiveness and outcomes in one region. The ultimate goal is to improve health care delivery for persons with disabilities through bringing workplace preferences and experiences of service users together to provide evidence for improved policy.

Guidance for Designing a Use Branch Policy Evaluation Study

1. Evaluation of policies under the Use branch begin with an assumption that by working with policymakers in a cyclical way, it is possible to generate and interpret evidence that is applicable in the development and/or improvement of evidence-based policies. The partnership and the provision of timely evidence will result in improved policies and service delivery.

2. Evaluators may begin with a policy analysis of existing policies based on documents and related guidelines in a specific sector. Evaluation questions guide the policy analysis and are generated by the evaluators with a knowledge of the context of policy within that sector. Criteria of importance in policy analysis are used, including "access, complexity, cost, distribution of benefits, timeliness, effectiveness, equity, policy consistency, and community and political acceptability" (Veitch et al., 2012. p. 1). The policy analysis may include interviews with managers and staff members of the relevant agencies.

3. Baseline quantitative data can be collected from extant sources if feasible, or additional data collection can be implemented as necessary.

(Continued)

(Continued)

4. Additional data may be collected through a variety of methods that engage service providers and clients, such as focus groups and interviews. An experimental design can also be used to test assumptions about choices stakeholders would make based on different policy options.

5. Findings from the policy analysis, focus groups, interviews, and experiments can be used to work with policymakers to develop new policies.

6. A test of the new policies can be conducted using strategies similar to those used in earlier stages such as interviews and focus groups.

Extending Your Thinking

Use Branch Mixed Methods Policy Evaluation

1. Find a MM policy evaluation study that is located in the Use branch. Analyze the study. What characteristics support your assertion that this study illustrates the Use branch? What is the design used in the study? How would you recommend improving the design to increase the possible use of the findings?

2. You were hired to design a Use branch MM policy evaluation study of practices related to refugees entering the country (you pick the country). How would you begin the study? Design a MM multistage policy evaluation study that reflects the Use branch for this assignment.

● SOCIAL JUSTICE BRANCH: MIXED METHODS POLICY EVALUATION

Social Justice branch MM policy evaluations are conducted through a lens of human rights. Under international human rights treaties, everyone's rights should be respected. When conditions suggest that a group of people's rights are not being protected based on race/ethnicity, gender, sexual identity, religion, disability, deafness, prisoner status, refugee or immigrant status, or other characteristics, then the policy analysis will start at that point to examine how policies are either supporting an oppressive status quo or how they can be changed to support human rights. Marra (2015) argues that Social Justice branch policy evaluations must take into account the complexity of the systems in terms of **power relationships** and how dominant groups may "benefit from denying others access to material and social resources, such as adequate child care, paid work opportunities, or political representation" (p. 32). Thus, evaluation of policies needs to include a critical look at measures that can shift the balance of power such as provision of a living wage, affordable child care, and universal health care.

As noted by Todrys et al. (2011), policy evaluation is only part of the problem; the policy evaluation has to be conducted in ways that create the political will for change that will increase responsiveness to human rights. International treaties and conventions do not automatically mean that rights will be respected; it is necessary to analyze the policies in-country and to determine the extent to which the country's policies align with the international treaties and conventions and how those policies are implemented in practice. A key aspect of the social justice MM policy evaluation is the importance placed on the voices of those who are most vulnerable and the safety of individuals who witness or experience human rights abuses.

Sample Study 4.5: Social Justice Branch

Transformative concurrent MM design: HIV and TB prevention and treatment in Zambian prisons (Todrys et al., 2011).

Problem: Zambian legislation and policies in prisons and the criminal justice system have not been effective in protection of the human rights and health of prisoners.

Policy: Zambian legislation and policies governing prisons and the criminal justice system. The Zambian government has a policy that all antiretroviral drugs are to be disseminated for free. Yet the infection rate for HIV is 2 to 50 times higher and TB is 6 to 30 times higher in the prison population.

Design: Social justice concurrent MM design. Quantitative and qualitative data were collected at the same time.

Sample: Legislation and policies on prisons and criminal justice. Sample consisted of 246 prisoners and 30 prison officers at 6 Zambian prisons. Key informant interviews were conducted with government and nongovernment organizations and representatives of international agencies and donors

(Continued)

(Continued)

(18 government officials; 28 representatives of international NGOs and donor governments and agencies). Purposeful sampling was used to obtain representation from different prisons, locations, and reasons for being in prison (e.g., convicted of a crime, immigrant detainee), as well as for inclusion of women and juveniles.

Data collection: Facility assessments were conducted based on interviews with inmates and prison officials and observational data about the condition, proximity, and accessibility of prison medical care, prisoner cells, and punishment and medical isolation cells. In-depth interviews and surveys with prisoners and semistructured interviews with prison officers were given in French or English or in a tribal language such as Bemba or Tonga. The evaluators also conducted a review of Zambian legislation and policies for prisons and criminal justice, and key informant interviews with Zambian government and NGO officials.

> This methodology was chosen in order to develop a comprehensive understanding of the conditions faced by prisoners, primarily through prisoners' self-reporting, but also through information provided by prison officials and key informants, and through information on prison and justice system laws and policies. Prisoners were asked to complete both a survey and an in-depth interview to provide a way of systematically presenting key indicators, as well as of allowing more thorough documentation of conditions and nuanced understanding of the interrelation of key variables. (p. 2)

Private areas were provided for the interviews to ensure confidentiality and safety of the respondents who had witnessed or been victims of human rights violations.

Data analysis: Quantitative data from the surveys and interviews were analyzed for frequency counts and compared by prison and prisoner characteristics. Chi square tests were done to test for differences in categorical data. Evaluators conducted content analysis of the qualitative data from the interviews to develop a code set and then develop themes across interviews. The data from all sources were integrated by organizing them by theme and used as a basis for developing recommendations.

Results: Facilities assessments revealed that serious barriers existed for prisoners to get services for prevention and treatment of TB and HIV. Only 15 of the 76 prisons in Zambia have a medical clinic, many of which only distribute pain medications. Access to care is controlled by nonmedical untrained prison officials. These findings were corroborated and extended by the results of the in-depth and key informant interviews. Also, lengthy pretrial detention and overcrowding exacerbate conditions and contribute to a lack of appropriate preventive services (prisoners reported that because of overcrowding they have to sleep sitting up or with five other people on one mattress). Observational data revealed the inadequacy of isolation cells for people with TB; in one case, the isolation cell was 10 by 8 meters and contained 57 prisoners, of whom 34 were not receiving TB treatment.

Yet health conditions in Zambian prisons indisputably violate international prohibitions on cruel, inhuman or degrading treatment; and the medical care available, and support provided by international donors, is far from that available in the general population. Zambian law establishes minimum standards for medical care, and requires that the officer in charge of each prison maintain a properly secured hospital, clinic or sick bay within the prison. A serious gap, however, exists between these legal requirements and practice, with little or no medical care available at most of Zambia's 86 prisons. Criminal justice system failures lead to extended pretrial detention in violation of international law, and abuses of inmates' rights exacerbate overcrowding, poor conditions and inadequate medical care. In addition to calling upon, and supporting, Zambia to respect its human rights obligations to prisoners, international donors should examine their own portfolios of health grant-making. International human rights law indicates that donors should honor the principles of non-discrimination and equality in their funding of such services as health. (p. 9)

Benefits of using MM: Policies need to change in the way international donors fund health services for prisoners. The focus needs to include respect for human rights; nondiscrimination; and prevention of cruel, inhumane, and degrading treatment. Such policies are needed to stop the spread of HIV and TB in prisons, especially if Zambia is to reach the sustainable development goals established by the UN. The prison policy acknowledges that vulnerability to HIV is higher in prisons and that prevention methods should be available. However, evidence from prisoners and prison officials indicates that prevention and treatment are rarely provided in prisons. Despite Zambia's policy that a comprehensive prevention package should be provided, the facility assessment indicated that condoms are not available in all the prisons the evaluators visited.

Guidance for Designing a Social Justice Branch Policy Evaluation Study

1. Marra (2015) notes that in order to have effective policies that address solutions to problems "deeply embedded in structural inequalities that characterize the 21st century, we need to understand the ways in which race, class, gender, sexuality, nationality and other systems of inequality intersect" (p. 32). Hence the review and synthesis of relevant publications as a starting point for evaluation of policy from a Social Justice branch perspective takes on a bit of a different character. To the extent possible, this review should include these aspects: (1) the cultural specificity and relevance displayed in the studies, (2) complications introduced by having multicomponent interventions

(Continued)

(Continued)

in diverse contexts, and (3) evidence of which study findings have been used to inform policy. This will help identify gaps in knowledge and conduits from the evaluation world to the policy world.

2. Build on existing relationships to identify organizations that have a stake in the policy and populations affected by the policy. Use existing data if available to analyze the severity of the problem to be addressed by the policy and to identify subgroups within the population that might be in a position to benefit more from a policy change. Use qualitative approaches such as focus groups, town meetings, online forums, and interviews to obtain rich information about the experiential side of the problem as viewed by multiple stakeholder groups, with appropriate attention to issues of power and safety.

3. Look for opportunities to increase the strength of the findings of the study by supporting linkages among organizations, agencies, and potential beneficiaries. This can be part of the process of data collection, interpretation of findings, and sharing of results in the form of preparing an action plan based on the available evidence. This can have the effect of creating coalitions that share the desire to see conditions improved by changes in policies.

4. Include **capacity building** in the use of evaluation findings in the design of the study. Kelly (2015) notes that "the likelihood of policy influence increases where there is an understanding of the political environment, policy-making processes, as well as the possession of robust evidence. Further, . . . engagement with the media, networking and advocacy efforts increase the efficacy of efforts to shape policy" (p. 206).

Extending Your Thinking

Social Justice Branch Mixed Methods Policy Evaluation

1. Choose a policy issue in a domain of interest to you—for example, child care, criminal justice, environmental issues, or health care. Identify policies that currently exist within that domain. Critically analyze the policies using a social justice lens, examining the extent to which the policies incorporate responsiveness to issues of power and culture. Design a MM social justice policy evaluation that could provide information for the revision of the policy in order to be more responsive to structural inequalities.

2. Identify a social justice policy evaluation study and critically review it to determine elements of a social justice lens evident in the way the study was conducted, its findings, and how it was used in the policy arena. Make suggestions for improvement of the study based on the use of a social justice lens for evaluation of policy.

DIALECTICAL PLURALISM: MIXED METHODS POLICY EVALUATION

As noted in previous chapters, DP adheres to the practice of following the principles of two or more branches/paradigms, maintaining the integrity of each and then putting the results of the different strategies into conversation with each other. An example of this process is provided by Hoddinott et al. (2010) in their evaluation of a policy in Scotland designed to increase breastfeeding by new mothers.

Sample Study 4.6: Dialectical Pluralism

Breastfeeding in Scotland (Hoddinott et al., 2010).

Problem: Scotland has one of the lowest rates of breastfeeding in the developed world. A new policy was implemented in Scotland to provide breastfeeding groups for pregnant and breastfeeding women; there was a need to evaluate its effectiveness.

Policy: A policy in Scotland to provide breastfeeding groups for pregnant women and breastfeeding mothers was evaluated for clinical effectiveness and cost-effectiveness.

Design: RCT with embedded qualitative case studies. A cluster randomized design was used to match pairs of similar localities and then randomly assign women to either the experimental group or the control group. The randomized trial portion of the study was used to compare women who participated in the breastfeeding group (experimental = 27 groups) with women who received routine care and did not participate in the group activity (control = 10 groups). They used qualitative and quantitative methods to conduct case studies to "investigate the amount of intervention delivered and the group characteristics and to compare group activity between intervention and control localities" (p. 2).

Sample: In the qualitative phase, 105 participants were interviewed; 13 professionals took part in focus groups; and 41 face-to-face and 27 telephone

(Continued)

(Continued)

interviews were conducted with professionals. The experimental groups included 1,310 women and the control groups 1,042 women. Of the 3,777 babies born during the time period to mothers in the intervention group, 845 (22%) completed the satisfaction questionnaire; in the control group, 3,525 mothers were eligible and 534 (15%) completed the questionnaire.

Data collection: Two years of pretrial data on the number of babies who were breastfed were collected from extant data sources prior to the trial. The quantitative data included the number of babies who were breastfed at 6–8 weeks and the number of babies getting breastmilk at 5–7 days and 8–9 months and a quantitative measure of mothers' satisfaction and social support. Health visitors and midwives routinely collected this data in the specified time periods. The questionnaire was completed by mothers who had breastfed their baby at least once and was returned by them through the post. Qualitative data were collected via ethnographic interviews with participants and focus groups with health professionals and peer support personnel. Face-to-face and telephone interviews were conducted with group facilitators, nurses, women participants, and women who did not participate.

Data analysis: Quantitative data were analyzed using analysis of covariance, comparing the amount of breastfeeding between the experimental and control groups while controlling for the preintervention rate of breastfeeding. There was no significant difference in mothers' satisfaction and social support between the two groups. Attendance diaries were kept to document attendance at the group meetings; these indicated that attendance was quite low (28%). The qualitative and quantitative data were combined to create seven embedded case studies.

Results: No significant difference was found in the number of women breastfeeding their infants between the experimental and control groups. The cost of running the breastfeeding groups was about the same as the cost of home visits. The breastfeeding rates declined in three of the seven intervention sites. The qualitative data revealed that in the sites where breastfeeding rates declined, "negative aspects of place including deprivation, unsuitable premises, and geographical barriers to inter-professional communication; personnel resources including staff shortages, high workload and low morale; and organizational change predominated" (p. 769). Thus, program managers were occupied with addressing these issues rather than implementing the policy.

Benefits of using MM: The quantitative data indicated that the breastfeeding group policy did not result in improved rates of breastfeeding in the first 6 to 8 weeks after birth. In addition the quantitative data revealed low attendance at the groups and that those who did attend were primarily white, higher income, and older, characteristics typically associated with higher rates of breastfeeding. Qualitative data suggested that interventions to encourage breastfeeding needed to be done earlier at antenatal groups or possibly through midwives before the mothers leave the hospital with support at home for the first few weeks.

Guidance for Designing a Dialectical Pluralism Study

1. The evaluator should examine the policy to determine what is prescribed within it in terms of requirements or recommendations. These elements then become the basis for the study of an intervention that is supported by a policy. In the Hoddinott et al. (2010) study, the elements of importance were those prescribed for breastfeeding groups as specified in the policy, such as weekly meetings, women only, and the presence of at least one health professional.

2. Policy evaluations conducted with a dialectical pluralism approach can be inclusive of randomized controlled trials and qualitative approaches such as ethnography or case studies. Both quantitative and qualitative data can be collected as part of the experimental design, as well as part of the case studies. The integrity of the randomized trial is important to maintain based on the principles of the postpositivist paradigm and the Methods branch. For example, Hoddinott et al. (2010) developed a model of how the policy should be implemented prior to conducting data about its implementation to minimize bias by observations in the field. The researchers who analyzed the quantitative data were blind to the condition from which the data came.

3. For the qualitative portion of the study, the evaluator should follow the principles appropriate to the philosophical framing of the study. For example, in the Hoddinott et al. (2010) study, they used ethnographic interviewing and grounded theory strategies. They noted that their process reflected the recommendations of Corbin and Strauss (2008) in this regard:

> The chief investigator and trial coordinator adopted an ethnographic approach to trial design and conduct, kept reflective diaries and were explicit about their respective backgrounds as a general practitioner and a former breastfeeding volunteer and their research roles. Qualitative data collection and analysis proceeded concurrently and iteratively from recruitment (2004) until the trial end (2007). This informed changes in interview topic guides, sampling and data collection method (focus groups, individual/pair interviews, breastfeeding group observations). We reflected regularly on the research questions, emerging analysis and how to identify disconfirming cases and differing perspectives in accordance with grounded theory. . . . Informal locality meetings, telephone conversations and e-mails contributed to reflective diaries and theory development. (p. 771)

(Continued)

(Continued)

4. The integration of qualitative and quantitative data from the separate data collection methods is an important element of MM evaluations of policies using DP. Hoddinott et al. (2010) used a case study as defined by Stake (1995) to integrate the results of their study. The case was a primary care organization with indistinct geographical boundaries. The case itself consisted of "mothers of the babies included in the outcome data, midwives, health visitors (community nurses with a remit to promote health for families with children aged 0–5), ancillary staff, managers and volunteers and the relationships between them, their organisations and places where they interact" (Hoddinott et al., 2010, p. 771).

5. Presentation of results from a DP policy evaluation study can be made in a variety of formats, with the caveat that they should put the quantitative and qualitative data into conversation with each other. Hoddinott et al. (2010) accomplished this by the use of a matrix to display the results that included the "four most challenging components of the policy (rows) and six emergent explanatory themes, each combining several categories (columns). The cells summarized data using respondent's text and referring to the source" (p. 771). The evaluators produced seven such matrices, one for each of the localities. This revealed patterns of similarities and differences and highlighted attributes of health service delivery necessary for the implementation of the policy.

Extending Your Thinking

Dialectical Pluralism Policy Evaluation

1. You are in negotiations with an agency for a possible policy evaluation to examine the effectiveness of a policy designed to improve public transportation access in rural communities. Imagine that this is the first meeting you are having with the client where you explain your ideas about planning the evaluation. Prepare an argument for the use of DP as the framing for the evaluation. What would you say to support the use of this approach? What options would you present to the client for the quantitative and qualitative parts of the study? How would you propose staffing for such a project? How would you propose integrating data for this project?

2. Identify a policy evaluation that did not use a DP approach in an area of interest to you. How would you redesign the study to use a DP approach? What would be the advantages and disadvantages of using such an approach for that particular policy evaluation?

SUMMARY AND MOVING FORWARD

Evaluators can play a potentially powerful role by providing credible information for policy development and evaluation. The different philosophical frameworks and evaluation branches yield insights into how evaluators can engage in this process in different ways, depending on their assumptions. In the Methods branch, we saw the use of time series and surveys as the dominant data collection methods combined with qualitative data collection to bring in different perspectives about the policies. In the Values branch, the emphasis is on having a deeper cultural understanding of the phenomenon relevant to the policies, and collection of quantitative data is more limited. The Use branch evaluators are concerned with what kind of information will be found useful to the policymakers, and therefore, their mixed methods designs are crafted to be responsive to the policymakers' needs. The Social Justice branch examines policies through the lens of how they address structural inequalities and how they are responsive to diverse marginalized communities. The DP approach illustrated in this chapter used an RCT to determine intervention effectiveness with qualitative data providing insights to reasons why the policy was not implemented as planned. Thus, evaluators need to be aware that policies are not always implemented as planned, and a valuable service they can offer to policymakers is insight into the reasons those challenges occur and possible solutions to the challenges.

In the next chapter, I provide examples of mixed methods designs used in systematic reviews of literature in evaluation. This approach to evaluation is favored by those who argue that a single evaluation study cannot provide the same degree of useful insights as can be obtained from looking across a larger number of studies.

5

Mixed Methods Evaluation Designs for Systematic Reviews

Systematic reviews aim to identify, evaluate and summarise the findings of all relevant individual studies, thereby making the available evidence more accessible to decision makers. When appropriate, combining the results of several studies gives a more reliable and precise estimate of an intervention's effectiveness than one study alone. (Centre for Reviews and Dissemination, 2009, p. v)

Being more explicit about the personal and political in research and increasing the potential for the increased involvement of different sections of society nationally and internationally is an important goal for systematic reviews. (Gough, Oliver, & Thomas, 2012, p. 13)

In This Chapter

- Overview of mixed methods and systematic reviews
- Mixed methods designs for systematic reviews from the Methods branch

- Mixed methods designs for systematic reviews from the Values branch
- Mixed methods designs for systematic reviews from the Use branch
- Mixed methods designs for systematic reviews from the Social Justice branch
- Mixed methods designs for systematic reviews from dialectical pluralism

● MIXED METHODS AND SYSTEMATIC LITERATURE REVIEW

Systematic literature reviews are powerful ways to bring together the learnings from a large number of studies of a particular type of intervention or policy. Gough, Oliver, and Thomas (2012) provide the following definition of a **systematic review**: "a review of research literature using systematic and explicit, accountable methods" (p. 2). Systematic reviews can be used by evaluators to answer questions such as What does the available evidence say about the effects of a particular intervention? Or, What is the impact of a particular policy? The results of systematic reviews do not provide uncomplicated answers to these questions because of the limitations of studies included in the review in terms of methodological approaches, reporting of results, and populations included or excluded from the studies. The general process for systematic reviews includes these elements: identify a research question, develop a protocol that specifies the search strategy and establishes criteria for inclusion and exclusion of studies, identify and describe the relevant research, critically appraise research reports in a systematic manner, and synthesize findings into a coherent statement.

Systematic reviews can take many forms; the decision about how to proceed with a systematic review is influenced at least in part by the philosophical stance of the reviewers. Some systematic literature reviews focus on RCTs or quasi-experimental studies that yield quantitative statistics for purposes of compiling the results, such as the Cochrane Collaboration (www.cochrane.org), which focuses on health care; the Campbell Collaboration (www.campbellcollaboration.org), which focuses on education, social welfare, and crime and justice; and the U.S. Department of Education's What Works Clearinghouse (http://ies.ed.gov/ncee/wwc). However, systematic reviews that only use quantitative measures result in a loss of information if the studies on the topic used mixed methods or qualitative only designs. Mixing results of research that come from different traditions raises many complex issues. Caracelli and Cooksy (2013) described a systematic review process that incorporates quantitative, qualitative, and mixed methods studies that emphasize the importance of both the intellectual quality of the original studies and the context, culture, and values relevant in evaluation studies.

Before jumping into the sample studies, I want to clarify two terms often associated with systematic reviews: scoping reviews and meta-analysis. **Scoping reviews** are generally conducted when a topic "has not yet been extensively reviewed or is of a complex or heterogeneous nature. . . . They are commonly undertaken to examine the extent, range, and nature of research activity in a topic area; determine the value and potential scope and cost of undertaking a full systematic review; summarize and disseminate research findings; and identify research gaps in the existing literature" (Pham et al., 2014, p. 371). They can be done as a stand-alone study or as a preliminary step in a systematic review. The intent is to map the knowledge domain of available literature, rather than to provide a summary of the best available research on that topic. **Meta-analysis** is a statistical approach to synthesizing findings based on the effect sizes to standardize outcomes and facilitate comparisons across studies (Mertens, 2015b). Meta-analysis is used with studies that attempt to establish causal claims between interventions and outcomes. It is commonly used with studies that use randomized controlled trials (RCTs) or quasi-experimental designs. It can be part of a systematic review if the types of studies included in the review meet the criteria for inclusion and have the appropriate statistical data available in the article.

METHODS BRANCH: MIXED METHODS SYSTEMATIC REVIEWS

The Cochrane Collaboration has a 25-year history of quantitative systematic reviews of studies that use randomized or quasi-experimental designs. More recently, it has also begun to explore ways to include qualitative data in systematic reviews. Noyes (2010) explains how this collaboration has included qualitative studies in systematic reviews in the *Cochrane Handbook for Systematic Reviews of Interventions*.

Qualitative research can contribute to Cochrane intervention reviews in four ways:

1. Informing reviews by using evidence from qualitative research to help define and refine the question, and to ensure the review includes appropriate studies and addresses important outcomes;

2. Enhancing reviews by synthesising evidence from qualitative research identified whilst looking for evidence of effectiveness;

3. Extending reviews by undertaking a search to specifically seek out evidence from qualitative studies to address questions directly related to the effectiveness review; and

4. Supplementing reviews by synthesising qualitative evidence within a stand-alone, but complementary, qualitative review to address questions on aspects other than effectiveness. (Noyes, Popay, Pearson, Hannes, & Booth, 2008, cited in Noyes, 2010, p. 532)

The Cochrane Collaboration has made progress on using qualitative research for Items 1, 2, and 3 but not so much progress on the final item. It has produced a guide for mixed methods systematic reviews (Pluye & Hong, 2014) and one for the conduct of reviews of qualitative data (Noyes & Lewin, 2011).

Thomas et al. (2004) conducted a systematic review related to healthy eating in children in the United Kingdom that used the Cochrane systematic review process as well as a systematic review of qualitative studies on the topic.

Sample Study 5.1: Methods Branch

Mixed methods systematic review: Effectiveness of healthy eating programs for children (Thomas et al., 2004).

Problem: Many programs have been developed to improve healthy eating in children, but findings have been conflicting and little is known about the barriers and facilitators for healthy eating among children. Their overall question was "What is known about the barriers to, and facilitators of, healthy eating among children aged 4–10 years?" (p. 1010).

Evaluand: Studies that evaluated the effectiveness of programs that focused on increased consumption of fruits and vegetables.

Design: MM systematic review was achieved by combining a quantitative review using the Cochrane system with a qualitative review of the studies that focused on children's perceptions of and experience with eating fruits and vegetables, as well as on healthy eating in general.

Sample: Twenty-one quantitative studies were found that met the criteria needed for conducting a meta-analysis. Eight qualitative studies were found that met the criteria of quality of reporting, sufficiency of strategies for establishing reliability and validity, and rooted in children's perspectives. The quantitative studies were chosen if they provided data on outcomes before and after the intervention and data on all outcomes measured and if they used an equivalent control or comparison group.

Data collection: Data were collected using a two-stage process. The evaluators started with a mapping (scoping) exercise to determine the range of studies available and to develop inclusion and exclusion criteria. They searched multiple databases (e.g., Medline) using the terms *children*, *barriers and facilitators of health promotion*, and *healthy eating*. They then hand searched journals by searching through their reference lists; they also contacted authors of the included studies and other key organizations in the United Kingdom that promote healthy eating. They identified studies that fell into the specified scope and analyzed those studies to determine if they met the criteria for inclusion. The evaluators searched for two types of studies: "controlled trials (randomized or non-randomized) that examined interventions to promote healthy eating and studies that examined children's perspectives and understandings (views studies), often by using qualitative research methods—for example, in-depth interviews and focus groups" (p. 1010).

Data analysis: An in-depth analysis was conducted for each study that included data extraction and assessment of study quality. The quantitative analysis used meta-analysis for studies with sufficient data. Qualitative analysis techniques were used to synthesize the findings of the studies of children's views; they entered the data into a computer-assisted data analysis program and looked for similarities and differences for barriers, facilitators, and implied recommendations. The evaluators then integrated the findings from the quantitative and qualitative results through a cross-study synthesis. The evaluators combined the findings using a matrix that "juxtaposed the barriers, facilitators, and implied recommendations against the actual interventions that had been implemented and evaluated. . . . We had to go back to the original interventions evaluated in the trials to identify those that built on the barriers and facilitators suggested by the children" (p. 1011).

Results: The results of the meta-analysis indicated that intervention programs have a small but significant effect. The effect size from the pooled studies suggest that, on average, children will increase their fruit and vegetable intake by a half a portion a day. The qualitative analysis revealed that children do not have a high opinion of healthy foods, hence it might be advisable to encourage children to eat tasty fruits and vegetables, rather than "healthy" ones. The cross-over analysis revealed that studies that did not emphasize health messages were more likely to yield an increase in consumption of fruits and vegetables.

Benefits of using MM: The main benefit of using mixed methods "is that the conclusions of reviews may be substantially altered by the inclusion of

(Continued)

(Continued)

qualitative data, which are more likely to reflect the experiences of the target groups for intervention" (p. 1012). Greater insights from the target population may lead to more appropriate recommendations for modified interventions. "The method allows the integration of quantitative estimates of benefit and harm with qualitative understanding from people's lives. The insights gained from the synthesis of qualitative studies allow exploration of statistical heterogeneity in ways that it would be difficult to imagine in advance" (p. 1012).

Guidance for Designing a Mixed Methods Systematic Review Study in the Methods Branch

1. Systematic reviews can begin with scoping reviews to get an understanding of the range of published and unpublished literature on the specified topic.

2. Systematic reviews must be carried out according to predetermined standards, including the search process, the criteria for inclusion and exclusion, and processes for data analysis.

3. Evaluators can start by identifying evaluation questions to frame the study. What is the problem, and what kind of reviews have already been conducted on this problem? The understanding of the problem can evolve as the reviewers move through the process of reading articles.

4. Protocols need to be developed for identifying studies. This usually includes deciding on the types of study designs (e.g., RCTs, quasi-experimental, case studies), the search terms, and the databases to be searched. It can also include searching gray literature, following up on reference lists, and asking experts in the field.

5. Establish or find criteria that exist to assess the quality of the identified studies. Rate the studies according to quality.

6. Extract data from the studies, including both quantitative and qualitative data, and record it in a systematic manner.

7. Synthesize the findings using a statistical procedure where possible, such as meta-analysis, or using narrative or matrix analysis to look at effects across the studies (adapted from Caracelli & Cooksy, 2013).

Extending Your Thinking

Mixed Methods Systematic Review in the Methods Branch

1. What are your thoughts about combining quantitative and qualitative and mixed methods studies in a systematic review? Should these be kept separate? How can the data from quantitative, qualitative, and mixed methods studies best be integrated in a review?

2. Choose a topic of interest to you. Search scholarly databases and web-based resources to see if there is a systematic review on that topic already. If there is, compare the methods used to those recommended in this chapter. What are the strengths and weaknesses of their methods?

3. Design a study for a systematic review on a topic of interest to you, following the guidelines found in this chapter.

VALUES BRANCH: QUALITATIVELY DOMINANT SYSTEMATIC REVIEWS

The process of conducting a systematic review of literature at a surface level looks similar in the Methods and Values branches, that is, research questions are developed, criteria are set for inclusion and exclusion, searches of literature are conducted, and data from the selected articles are coded. However, in the Values branch, systematic literature reviews begin with an acknowledgment of the evaluator/researcher as instrument, that is, what are the characteristics of the evaluators framing and conducting the study, and how do these characteristics come into play in the review process? Inclusion of quantitative, qualitative, and mixed methods studies in the literature sample means that strategies need to be formulated for coding both quantitative and qualitative processes and findings. Archibald et al. (2015) conducted a qualitatively dominant systematic review of literature on the use of mixed methods in qualitative research journals (see Sample Study 5.2).

Sample Study 5.2: Values Branch

Qualitatively dominant mixed methods systematic review: Mixed methods in qualitative journals (Archibald et al., 2015).

Problem: Mixed methods use is increasing in the research and evaluation communities, yet there remains a great deal that is unknown about the concept of how mixing actually occurs, especially in qualitatively dominant studies.

Evaluand: Articles published in six leading qualitative research journals from 2003 through 2014 that were mixed methods in nature.

Design: Systematic review with coding of quantitative and qualitative data on each article simultaneously. Integration of the quantitative and qualitative data at the analysis stage.

Sample: Forty-four theoretically oriented articles and 50 empirical articles made up the sample. The articles were chosen through team discussion to identify the six qualitative research journals based on their awareness of their importance and influence in the field. Selection of the articles for inclusion was based on their including both quantitative and qualitative components or by self-identifying as mixed methods studies. If articles used several qualitative methods but no quantitative methods or strategies, then they were excluded.

Data collection: The evaluators first discussed the reviewer as the instrument, giving information about themselves that was relevant to the choice of journals, criteria for inclusion and exclusion, and coding and interpretation. The evaluators hand searched the six journals for the prescribed date range using keywords such as *mixed* and *quantitative and qualitative*. Each article was read by two reviewers independently to ensure it met the inclusion criteria.

Data analysis: Two reviewers independently coded each article; for empirical articles, they coded the "research topic/problem, purpose/rationale/ philosophy, research questions, design, method fidelity, and implementation, as well as overall mixing, interpretive rigor, and rhetoric/terminology" (p. 10). Theoretical articles were coded for "focus, conceptual position taken, and conclusions drawn/practice recommendations" (p. 10). Quantitative data were analyzed using descriptive statistics and nonparametric statistics.

Results: Quantitative data revealed that less than 2% of the articles published in the qualitative journals included mixed methods, with an increasing trend in the number of articles from 2003 through 2012 and a decrease in the subsequent years of the study; 52 percent of the articles specifically identified as mixed methods. Qualitative data revealed that the definition of mixed methods tended to be rather simplistic, mentioning the combination of quantitative and qualitative techniques. Almost half the studies reported that the article was based on a larger study, which typically meant that the quantitative portion was published in another journal. Hence, it increased the challenge of the reviewers to identify the point of integration for the qualitative and quantitative portions of the study.

Benefits of using MM: The combination of qualitative and quantitative methods of coding and analysis allowed the evaluators to address the breadth and quality of mixed methods research published in the preeminent qualitative research journals. They were able to describe the extent of integration as well as gain insight into the rationales and methods used for integration of the two types of data. Integration was most commonly explained in articles that involved the development of instruments. The second most common type of integration was for purposes of triangulation. The predominant use of sequential designs probably contributed to the separate reporting of quantitative and qualitative portions of studies and may be a legacy of paradigmatic silos in professional journals. Nevertheless, this study's findings highlight the impact of such publishing practices as not providing sufficient examples of truly mixed designs.

Guidance for Designing a Mixed Methods Systematic Review Study in the Values Branch

1. Practice critical reflexivity to identify characteristics and values relevant to your evaluation work on the chosen topic.

2. If possible, work with a team to identify the pool of possible literature sources for the study. Conduct a literature review using standard procedures for database searching, make use of hand searches of reference lists, and make contact with authors and key organizations.

3. Develop research questions to guide decisions about what to review and what criteria to use for inclusion and exclusion. Allow these decisions to be flexible in the early stages of the review process so that modifications can be made to accommodate what is learned about the topic.

4. Develop coding processes that allow for both quantitative and qualitative entry of data so that the combination of data can be used to prepare results and to inform interpretations. Engage in discussions with team members to reach consensus about the coding and the ratings of quality in the articles.

5. Develop and implement strategies to integrate the data from the quantitative and qualitative codes into the results and conclusions.

Extending Your Thinking

Mixed Methods Systematic Review
in the Values Branch

1. Identify another study that used a qualitatively dominant systematic review design. How did that design differ from the one used by Archibald et al. (2015)? What do you identify as the strengths and weaknesses of each approach?

2. Using your own work in evaluation, select a topic for which you can design a qualitatively dominant systematic review. Design the review process. What kind of criteria will you use for inclusion and exclusion? How will you include diverse perspectives in the study design and implementation?

● **USE BRANCH: MIXED METHODS SYSTEMATIC REVIEWS**

Systematic reviews under the Use branch can use the same strategies used in the Methods branch (i.e., meta-analysis of experimental studies), but they can also use other strategies to be more inclusive of studies that are quantitative but not experimental in design, as well as include mixed methods and qualitative studies. The Evidence for Policy and Practice Information and Co-ordinating Centre (EPPI-Centre) (Boaz, Ashby, & Young, 2002) developed a method for systematic review based on the pragmatic position that what works is not all that matters. Rather, systematic reviews can be used to examine other questions such as what the problem is, what causes it, and what is being done about it.

Sample Study 5.3: Use Branch

Use branch systematic review: Children and young people with diabetes in educational settings (Edwards, Noyes, Lowes, Spencer, and Gregory, 2014).

Problem: Type 1 diabetes frequently occurs in children and youth in schools, colleges, and universities. Whereas students in college and university can generally self-manage the disease, evidence is needed on how to optimally support children's diet, exercise, blood glucose monitoring, and insulin regime when they are in school.

Evaluand: Studies of the effectiveness of intervention-based studies and children, parent, and professional views of barriers and facilitators to optimal support.

Design: Mixed methods systematic review from the Use branch. Edwards et al. adapted the mixed methods synthesis guidelines developed by the EPPI-Centre.

Sample: Eleven intervention studies and 55 views studies (i.e., studies that reported the views of children, parents, or professionals). MM triangulation was used as a guiding framework for building the sample of studies included in the review. They identified very few randomized controlled studies and so they continued to search for quantitative studies that provided evidence on attitudes and experiences of participants, as well as nonintervention survey and qualitative studies.

Data collection: The search strategy included databases such as Medline, Scopus, Cochrane Library, and PsychINFO. Reference lists and published reviews were also searched. The primary criteria for inclusion was that the studies focused on young people with type 1 diabetes in an educational setting or on parents, peers, educational setting personnel, and health professionals who worked with this age group. Quantitative studies were excluded if they did not include a before-and-after measure, and surveys and qualitative studies were excluded if they did not report the views of the children, parents, or professionals. Independent reviewers rated the quality of the studies based on criteria appropriate for quantitative, survey, and qualitative methods.

Data analysis: Meta-analysis was not possible because of the heterogeneity of the populations, interventions, and outcomes. Quantitative outcome data were entered into a narrative summary table. Qualitative analysis was performed using Atlas.ti with a coding framework derived from the study's conceptual framework and other codes that emerged. Evidence from quantitative studies on attitudes and experiences was mapped onto evidence from surveys and qualitative studies. They then conducted an overall narrative synthesis that integrated the findings from both types of studies.

> A final overarching synthesis of intervention and non-intervention studies was conducted. For this final synthesis a matrix was constructed that mapped best practice guidance against the age-related barriers and facilitators identified by children and young people, parents, school personnel and school health professionals and age-related interventions and outcomes in [quantitative studies]. . . . We were particularly interested to see the extent to which interventions were effective and addressed the barriers identified by children, parents and teachers/health professionals, and built upon the facilitators to providing optimal care and management of children and young people with T1D [type 1 diabetes] in educational settings. (p. 6)

(Continued)

(Continued)

Results: Interventions that were effective included health plans and school nurse support. Short-term effectiveness was noted for telemedicine in school for individual cases, but there was no evidence that this was linked to longer-term follow-up. The views studies revealed that children, parents, and professionals experienced many barriers, including school structure, organizational policies, educational practices, and nonsupportive attitudes. Even though schools had intervention plans, the plans were not implemented in a comprehensive way. When staff were supportive, children and parents were very appreciative.

Benefits of using MM: "This novel mixed-method systematic review is the first to integrate intervention effectiveness with views of children/parents/professionals mapped against school diabetes guidelines. Diabetes management could be generally improved by fully implementing and auditing guideline impact. Evidence is limited by quality and there are gaps in knowledge of what works" (p. 3).

Guidance for Designing a Mixed Methods Systematic Review Study in the Use Branch

The steps for conducting a Use branch systematic review are adapted from EPPI's recommendations (Boaz et al., 2002):

1. Identify a specific question on which to focus the review. The questions can emerge from knowledge of extant literature and be combined with perspectives from professionals and participants in the programs.

2. Identify as much research as possible, including published studies that use multiple methods, extant reviews, Internet searches, and personal and professional networks. Examples can be found in most published reviews, including those on the EPPI-Centre website (http://eppi.ioe.ac.uk).

3. Develop exclusion and inclusion criteria for the studies based on the focus questions.

4. Evaluate the quality of the evidence in each study using a protocol that addresses methodological rigor. Use criteria that are appropriate to the methodology in the reviewed study, that is, different criteria apply to quantitative, qualitative, and mixed methods studies. Examples of protocols can be found at the Centre for Reviews and Dissemination (2009) website, which also provides detailed guidance on how to put together a protocol (see www.york.ac.uk/inst/crd/report4.htm).

5. Synthesize the studies in different ways, using both meta-analysis and narrative synthesis. Recognize that meta-analysis might not be possible because of the different methodologies and outcomes included in your pool of studies. Use narrative synthesis to compare studies on similarities and differences in terms of methods and outcomes to support claims made about the effectiveness of interventions.

6. Integrate quantitative and qualitative data from systematic reviews by creating tables that display the narrative data from the studies. The use of narrative analysis allows for discussion with stakeholders of complex interventions that have multiple outcomes.

Extending Your Thinking

Mixed Methods Systematic Review in the Use Branch

1. You have been hired by a firm to conduct a systematic review using Use branch framing on the topic of reducing recidivism for youthful offenders. How would you begin the study? What question would you draft as a beginning point for discussions with stakeholders for the review? How would you design the study using the guidelines provided in the preceding section?

2. What is already known about settling refugees who come from conflict zones? What literature is already available? How would you design a systematic review using Use branch framing to evaluate the current state of knowledge about resettling refugees?

SOCIAL JUSTICE BRANCH: ●
MIXED METHODS SYSTEMATIC REVIEWS

Systematic reviews in the Social Justice branch follow a similar pathway as systematic reviews in other branches in that they use systematic processes for identifying studies and coding the findings of the studies. However, these reviews are different in that there is a focus on a marginalized population (which can also be the case under other branches but is essential in the Social Justice branch) and because there is a focus on the systemic barriers and facilitators that impact the effect of the intervention under study. This means there is greater interest in identifying qualitative and mixed methods studies that are inclusive of the systemic barriers and facilitators. The intended use of the systematic review is to inform practice or policy in ways that overcome barriers of specific relevance in marginalized communities.

Everson-Hock et al. (2013) conducted a Social Justice branch systematic review of the effect of interventions designed to impact changes in diet and exercise to prevent type 2 diabetes in poor communities in the United Kingdom. Their study provides an example of how the inclusion of systemic barriers and facilitators can be achieved for the purpose of informing policy.

Sample Study 5.4: Social Justice Branch

Transformative mixed methods systematic review (Everson-Hock et al., 2013).

Problem: Type 2 diabetes is increasing in the United Kingdom, and the increase is especially large in low-income populations. People in low-income populations are less likely to live in conditions that support having a healthy diet or that permit regular exercise regimes.

Evaluand: Thirty-five studies on diet and exercise to prevent diabetes in the United Kingdom: 9 quantitative, 23 qualitative, and 3 mixed methods. The focus was on studies that used public health campaigns like mass media and mailings to change behavior.

Design: MM social justice systematic review.

Sample: The evaluators searched multiple databases (e.g., Medline, PsychINFO, and the Cochrane Library) using search terms such as low socioeconomic status, diabetes, exercise, community physical activities, and diet. They also searched the gray literature through the Internet and hand searched relevant literature. They established criteria for the inclusion of studies. Quantitative studies had to include community-based physical activity and dietary interventions for a low-SES group, with a comparison to usual care or a placebo, or no comparison group. The qualitative evaluations and mixed methods studies were included if they assessed beliefs and perceptions of physical activity and diet for low-SES adults or health care providers. The studies all had to be from the United Kingdom because the purpose was to influence national policy. Thirty-five studies were included in the final sample.

Data collection: Two reviewers read each study and extracted the following data: sampling, aims, intervention, measured outcomes, themes, barriers, and facilitators.

Data analysis: The quality of the studies was ascertained using the National Institute for Health and Clinical Excellence (NICE) quality assessment checklists (NICE, 2009). The interventions and populations in the quantitative studies were very heterogeneous; therefore the authors decided not to do a meta-analysis, opting instead to do narrative synthesis of these studies. For the qualitative data, they conducted thematic analysis, deriving the themes from the data. To integrate the quantitative and qualitative studies, the authors developed a matrix that allowed them to assess the extent to which "the interventions incorporated the barriers and facilitators identified in the qualitative synthesis" (p. 266).

Results: The results of the analysis of the quantitative studies revealed mixed effectiveness in terms of changes in diet and exercise: "While no single intervention demonstrated a clear positive effect on all outcome measures considered, some studies showed positive impacts on some outcomes and no intervention had a negative impact on any outcome" (p. 270). The qualitative analysis yielded 48 barriers and 32 facilitators of healthy eating and physical activity. The juxtaposition of quantitative and qualitative findings in the matrix showed that about half the barriers and facilitators were included in the intervention studies and about half were not. None of the interventions addressed barriers mentioned by participants such as fear of crime, unsafe neighborhoods, cost of healthy eating, and family attitudes about health and weight. Thus, interventions could be improved by increased responsiveness to the needs of the low-SES population.

Benefits of using MM: A purely quantitative systematic review of the impact of programs designed to decrease type 2 diabetes in poor communities would have resulted in an inability to draw a definitive conclusion about their effectiveness because of the limited number of studies, their heterogeneity, and the exclusion of contextual factors that explain the results. By using a social justice mixed methods approach to the systematic review, the evaluators were able to include studies that did examine the barriers and facilitators within each context. In addition, the qualitative analysis part of the study provided insights into variables that could be introduced into national policies that would potentially increase the effectiveness of interventions. They concluded:

> A strength of this review was the inclusion of many types of evidence, which allowed us to explore effectiveness findings in contextual detail and create explicit links between quantitative and qualitative evidence, using methods appropriate for the data. . . . This enabled us to identify gaps in the intervention evidence base and thus directions for future research. (p. 270)

Guidance for Designing a Mixed Methods Systematic Review Study in the Social Justice Branch

1. Define the questions to be investigated in a way that includes a focus on marginalized populations and takes barriers and facilitators into account.

2. Design the search protocol to reflect issues of relevance to the marginalized populations. For example, Everson-Hock et al. (2013) included topics such as crime and safety in their search for barriers and facilitators, concepts that may or may not have surfaced in a systematic review of interventions to address type 2 diabetes under other branches of evaluation. Also make note of the barriers and facilitators not addressed in the studies reviewed. For example, Everson-Hock et al. noted that none of the reviewed studies had included the use of qualitative data to inform the content or implementation of the interventions themselves, thus revealing a gap in the responsiveness of culture and context that could have implications for program effectiveness.

3. Expand the search to include consultation with community members to determine if there is information of relevance that has not been published in scholarly journals but would provide insights into the variables that influence program effectiveness, particularly of a cultural or contextual nature.

4. Expand the analysis of the extant data using strategies other than or in addition to quantitative meta-analysis. After critically evaluating each study (often by more than one reviewer), determine what analytic strategies make the most sense given the nature and quality of the quantitative and qualitative data. Be aware of the heterogeneity of the interventions and the conditions under which the interventions are implemented; code for these characteristics. For example, Everson-Hock et al. (2013) noted that the goal of the interventions in deprived communities focused on different outcomes, such as increasing fruit and vegetable intake or choosing and cooking healthy food. They also found that the interventions were quite heterogeneous, ranging from introducing a new retail outlet for selling food in a deprived community to an environment-focused community awareness campaign designed to increase exercise. The differences in the chosen interventions and variables resulted in differences in outcomes. For this reason, the evaluators felt it was not appropriate to synthesize across the studies using meta-analysis. Quantitative data may be better analyzed using a narrative synthesis than a meta-analysis if the heterogeneity among the studies is high. Thematic analysis can be conducted of the qualitative data that are presented in quantitative, qualitative, and mixed methods studies.

5. The use of a matrix is one method for integrating quantitative and qualitative data. This strategy is useful, particularly when the quantitative studies have been analyzed using a narrative synthesis. This allows for the juxtaposition of concepts and can provide greater insights into barriers and facilitators that influence impact.

6. Develop a mechanism for disseminating the results of the study to practitioners, policymakers, and members of the evaluation community so that the results can be used for transformative purposes. Unfortunately, this is a weak link in the chain of many evaluations and needs to be consciously addressed if it is to be a reality. Everson-Hock et al. (2013) made recommendations for practitioners, policymakers, and evaluators regarding how to improve programs, evaluation designs, and policies by taking cultural and contextual factors into account, especially the role of family, attitudes and perceptions relating to behavior and weight, and fear of crime that are not typically addressed in the current work on improving health.

Extending Your Thinking

Mixed Methods Systematic Review in the Social Justice Branch

1. Pick up the newspaper or consult a website. Look for a story about a social problem that is difficult to solve (e.g., climate change and environmental justice, police-community interactions, health issues). Design a Social Justice branch systematic review study using the guidelines presented in this chapter.

2. Find a systematic review that does not use a social justice lens as its framing. Critically analyze the study to identify aspects of the topic that may be overlooked because social justice was not a focal point in designing or carrying out the study. How would you redesign the study to bring a social justice lens to the topic?

DIALECTICAL PLURALISM: MIXED METHODS SYSTEMATIC REVIEWS

DP systematic reviews include adherence to the principles used in the separate evaluation branches that are brought together under the DP approach. Therefore, if the intent is to conduct a DP study that adheres to the Methods and Use branches, the evaluator would use a strategy similar to that available from the Campbell Collaboration or the Cochrane Institute and explained earlier in this chapter under the Methods branch section, and the qualitative design would reflect the Use branch strategies explained earlier in this chapter. The key to a DP approach is to bring the results of the two approaches together to identify issues that arise from that juxtaposition.

Petrosino and colleagues (2013) used only experimental or quasi-experimental studies in the quantitative portion of their study, following the recommendations of the Campbell Collaboration in that regard. They also conducted a narrative analysis of the same studies for the qualitative portion of the review and compared the results of the two approaches.

Sample Study 5.5: Dialectical Pluralism

Dialectical pluralism and MM systematic review: Scared Straight (Petrosino et al., 2013).

Problem: Strategies used to deter juveniles from becoming delinquent may do more harm than good. Scared Straight is one strategy that attempts to scare youth by giving them firsthand observation of prison life and interaction with incarcerated adults. It might have negative effects.

Evaluand: Studies published up until December 2011 that used either an experimental or quasi-experimental design and involved programs that brought youth to penal institutions in order to scare them into avoiding criminal behavior.

Design: Systematic review using quantitative methods and narrative review.

Sample: Literature covered the years 1945 to 2011. Of over 500 citations found through the search process, only 9 studies met the criteria for design and outcomes; the sample of these studies all together was in excess of 1,000 students. These spanned the time frame of 1967 to 1992. No more current studies met the criteria for inclusion. They used the same nine studies for both the quantitative and qualitative portions of the study.

Data collection: Studies were collected by means of hand searches of 29 leading criminology and social science journals; review of prior systematic reviews' bibliographies; electronic search of relevant databases such as PsycINFO, ERIC, the Campbell Collaboration Register, the Cochrane Central database, and the Criminal Justice Abstracts; outreach to researchers and research centers; and in association newsletters. Quantitative data were extracted from the reports in the form of rates of new offenses or violation of a probation order. Qualitative data were extracted in the form of the description of the interventions and the methods used in the studies.

Data analysis: Meta-analysis of postintervention offending rates using official data and narrative analysis of qualitative data in nine studies. Data were extracted from each study using a data collection instrument developed by Petrosino. Quantitative and qualitative results of each individual study are included in Petrosino et al. (2013). The quantitative data were analyzed as the proportion of each group that reoffended. The qualitative data were analyzed using a narrative approach.

Results: The meta-analysis and narrative analysis indicated that the programs actually do more harm than doing nothing. Scared Straight actually increases delinquency. The narrative analysis revealed that the descriptions of treatment were quite varied, sometimes not providing much detail, and that the description of methods used to randomize individuals to groups was not well reported. In one study, 43% of the experimental group and 17% of the control group reoffended; this quantitative finding was remarkable in that the study's authors did not discuss it as a troubling negative outcome in their narrative. Narratives of other studies also reported negative or nonsignificant outcomes concerning contact with the police, yet they also reported positive attitudes of parents, teachers, and inmates about the program.

Benefits of using MM: The quantitative analysis based on a meta-analysis of quantitative experimental and quasi-experimental studies clearly shows a negative effect of the Scared Straight program in terms of increased juvenile delinquent behaviors. The narrative data provides insights into problems with prior studies in terms of the amount of detail about the intervention and methods used but also in terms of ignoring no differences and negative outcomes for students and inclusion of positive outcomes in the form of parents, teachers, and inmates' perceptions. The conundrum that continues about Scared Straight is why policymakers continue to fund the program when the evidence supports that it is at best ineffective and at worst harmful. It is ironic that no randomized trials have been conducted on the program since 1992.

Guidance for Designing a Mixed Methods Systematic Review Study for Dialectical Pluralism

1. If DP is planned to include Methods and Values branch approaches to systematic review, then evaluators can choose the approaches to quantitative and qualitative design from those two approaches. For example, Petrosino and colleagues (2013) used the specific procedures for a Methods branch systematic review as prescribed by the Campbell Collaboration. Their approach to the qualitative parts of the studies might be characterized more as a pragmatic, Use branch design because they did not seek out additional qualitative studies as would have been done under the Values branch.

(Continued)

(Continued)

2. If the qualitative portion of the study reflects the Use branch, then the narrative analysis follows procedures as outlined for this approach with a specific focus on finding information that would be useful to policymakers and practitioners. This is what Petrosino and colleagues did; they wanted to impact federal policy in the United States by demonstrating the lack of positive outcomes on young people of the Scared Straight program.

3. Combine the quantitative and qualitative results so that implications can be drawn from both aspects of the study. Petrosino et al. (2013) did this by noting that the meta-analysis indicated either no or a negative effect of the Scared Straight program on youth. The qualitative portion of their study revealed that the authors of the studies had downplayed the negative outcomes for youth and emphasized the positive perceptions of teachers, parents, and inmates about the program. They noted that this way of presenting the findings may have led to the justification to continue funding for a program that is not having the intended effect on youth and might actually be harmful.

Extending Your Thinking

Mixed Methods Systematic Review for Dialectical Pluralism

1. Identify a Campbell Collaboration or a Cochrane Institute meta-analysis on a topic of interest to you. Use that as a basis for a DP systematic review by conducting a qualitative review on the same topic. Bring the results of the two studies together. What insights do you gain by adding the qualitative review? What challenges did you encounter in this exercise?

2. Design a DP systematic review on a topic of interest to you. Be explicit about the two branches of evaluation you are using for the quantitative and qualitative parts of the study. Also be explicit about how you would bring the results of the two parts of the study into conversation with each other.

SUMMARY AND MOVING FORWARD

Systematic reviews provide a potentially powerful tool for informing policymakers and other stakeholders about the effectiveness of a program by bringing together the results of many studies conducted on a particular topic. The outcomes of systematic reviews clearly depend on what type of and how many studies are used in the reviews, determined by the evaluator's search strategies and inclusion and exclusion criteria. In the Methods branch, the emphasis has been on experimental and quasi-experimental design studies and the calculation of effect sizes. Qualitative strategies have only recently been making inroads into Methods branch systematic reviews and take the form of noting contextual information available in the experimental studies. In the Values branch, more emphasis is placed on the qualitative analysis of articles and development of themes to understand outcomes expressed in quantitative form. In the Use branch, the quantitative portion of the study can use the criteria for systematic reviews found in the Methods branch. This can be combined with qualitative data that can provide insights into different stakeholders' perspectives. In the Social Justice branch, literature is consciously chosen to include the experiences of members of marginalized communities, and the qualitative data are analyzed to reveal power inequities and systemic discrimination at the root of intransigent social problems. The focus is also on resilience in communities and identification of strategies that work. Less emphasis is placed on aggregating quantitative data across studies, and more attention is given to the contextual factors that support or impede effectiveness. In the DP approach, evaluators may use the quantitative strategy of meta-analysis combined with qualitative analysis of information about the interventions in the studies.

In the next chapter, we look at mixed methods designs in evaluation that are used for particular purposes, such as needs assessment, gender analysis, Indigenous settings, evaluations with people with disabilities, arts-based evaluations, evaluations in conflict zones, evaluations that use visual spatial analysis, and evaluations that focus on ongoing development in an organization rather than a specific program. I chose these specific variations in mixed methods design because the issues that arise are unique and require different mixed methods approaches.

6

Variations in Mixed Methods Evaluation Designs

Gender-responsive evaluation methodology and techniques are those that allow for both the substantive assessment of gender equality issues and those that seek to ensure that evaluation practice itself is gender-responsive in its processes. Some key aspects that can be included to improve the gender-responsiveness . . . include: Requiring the use of mixed-methods approach and gender disaggregation of evaluative evidence. (UN Women, 2015)

In This Chapter

- Mixed methods designs and gender-responsive evaluation
- Mixed methods designs and Indigenous evaluation
- Mixed methods designs using universal design with persons with disabilities and Deaf persons
- Mixed methods designs and developmental evaluation
- Mixed methods designs and needs assessment

- Mixed methods designs and visual data: spatial data and arts-based evaluation

- Mixed methods designs in conflict zones

The focus of Chapters 2 through 5 is on specific types of evaluations commonly undertaken in the field of evaluation. In this chapter, I provide illustrations and guidance on other types of evaluations that are important for evaluators because they have a specific focus, such as gender-responsive evaluations, Indigenous evaluations, developmental evaluations, and needs assessment. I also provide illustrations and guidance for evaluations that make use of visual data in the form of visual spatial data or data from the arts. Finally, I provide illustration and guidance for evaluators who work in conflict zones. These studies can also be characterized by their paradigmatic framing, but they are chosen here to illustrate advances in mixed methods within particular contexts and/or emergent innovations in mixed methods designs.

● MIXED METHODS DESIGNS AND GENDER-RESPONSIVE EVALUATION

Gender-responsive evaluation is "a systematic and impartial assessment that provides credible and reliable evidence-based information about the extent to which an intervention has resulted in progress (or lack thereof) towards intended and/or unintended results regarding gender equality and the empowerment of women" (UN Women, 2015, p. 4). Given this definition, gender-responsive evaluation is most aligned with the transformative paradigm because of its focus on human rights and its focus on social transformation in the form of gender equity. Gender-responsive evaluation applies mixed methods (quantitative and qualitative data collection methods and analytical approaches) to account for complexity of gender relations and to ensure participatory and inclusive processes that are culturally appropriate. UN Women (2015), along with other international evaluation organizations, supports the combination of mixed methods with a gender analysis framework because "the emerging consensus in literature on impact evaluation appears to be that most questions can best be answered by 'mixed methods.' This might involve a mix of both quantitative and qualitative methods, or a mix of specific approaches within either of the two categories. Furthermore, approaches which 'blend' methods, such as quantifying some aspects of qualitative data, are also increasingly seen as valuable" (pp. 53–54).

UN Women developed a handbook to provide guidance in the planning and management of gender-responsive evaluation because it views this as a strategy for combining the rigor of evaluation with the goal of achieving gender equality and women's empowerment. A guiding principle of gender-responsive evaluation is that "evaluations should be conducted with an understanding of contextual power and gender relations. Evaluations can foster empowerment through the participation of stakeholders in the creation of knowledge about the intervention and other aspects of the evaluation process, and in the communication of its results" (UN Women, 2015, p. 3). The goals of gender-responsive evaluation are to improve accountability, provide evidence for decision making, and promote social change; mixed methods can contribute to these goals by providing a critical understanding of this complex phenomenon that would not be possible with a mono-method study.

Ackerly's (2012) evaluation of a funding project provides an excellent example of how gender-responsive evaluations incorporate mixed methods into their designs. She clearly ties her work to the use of a gender-responsive framework and feminist theory. **Feminist theory** "is a broad term that describes the application of feminist thought and ideas to a range of disciplines and discourses" (Brisolara, 2014, p. 3). There is no one definition of feminist theory; however, there is general consensus that it focuses on gender inequities and offers a way to examine and understand "social issues and dynamics that elucidate gender inequities as well as women's interests, concerns, and perspectives. . . . Most feminist theories are applied with the intent of contributing to the promotion of greater equity, the establishment of equal rights and opportunities, and the ending of oppression" (Brisolara, 2014, p. 3). The project that Ackerly (2012) evaluated focused on the improvement of women's equality through grants designed to address issues of importance to women: decreasing poverty, reduction of violence, and increased participation in governance. The focus of the evaluation is on systemic changes needed to increase women's equality (see Sample Study 6.1).

Sample Study 6.1: Mixed Methods in Gender-Responsive Evaluations

An external rights-based evaluation of grant making for gender equality (Ackerly, 2012).

Problem: Women in Asia and the Pacific experience violence, insufficient participation in governance, and poverty partially as a result of denial of inheritance rights and poor employment opportunities.

Intervention/evaluand/policy: The evaluand is the Global Fund for Women's (GFW) grant-making effectiveness in terms of its ability to meet the goals of the Global Fund for Women Breakthrough Project: Catalyzing Activism to Achieve MDG3 in Asia and the Pacific. The Breakthrough Project is designed to increase the availability and accessibility of resources for women in Asia and the Pacific through supporting women-led civil society organizations. The project works with the assumption that violence, governance, and poverty can be addressed by supporting conditions that enhance transformative and sustainable gender equality through rights-based grant making and movement building for social activism. The Breakthrough Project (the evaluand) provided three years of funding to the GFW for grant making in Asia and the Pacific.

Design: "The evaluation uses a rights-based approach to evaluation that is informed by the most recent advances in feminist and social science research methods as well as a feminist research ethic" (Ackerly, 2012, p. 10). It was a mixed methods design inclusive of a gender analysis framework originally developed by Aruna Rao and David Kelleher that they called Gender at Work (Rao, Sandler, Kelleher, & Miller, 2016) (see www.genderatwork.org). This fits within the Social Justice branch of evaluation.

Sample: The portfolio of grants gathered from all funded individual applications and final reports (147 grants); applications of all declined and funded from India in 2010 (87 applications); observation at one board meeting and selected other meetings; site visits in Bangladesh and Hong Kong; participants at a convening held in the Philippines; staff at the GFW; and GFW's annual plans for 4 years.

Data collection: Portfolios were available from the GFW for the grant recipients that included individual applications and final reports. Data were also collected through participant observation at the Global Fund's offices; interviews; and reviews of internal, external, and convening reports. To conduct gender analysis, data were collected on the improvement of accessible funding for members of marginalized groups; transformation of the legal and political environments; and transformation of social values, practices, and norms because feminist theory suggests these are the changes needed for feminist movement organizations to effect sustainable transformative social change. Data from the portfolios were collected to match the gender analysis framework. These included qualitative and quantitative data on changes in individual awareness; access to resources; changes in cultural norms; and changes in institutions, laws, and policies.

Data analysis: Descriptive statistics were used to analyze quantitative data available in the individual applications and final reports to provide evidence regarding the accountability for the grant-making activities. Using these same portfolios, quantitative data analysis was conducted by coding and converting to statistical data to determine if the GFW used a rights-based approach and whether the results contributed to gender equality. Qualitative analysis was also conducted based on the portfolios, site visits to two locations, interview data, and report reviews. For the gender equality analysis portion of the evaluation, the final reports were analyzed to identify factors that contribute to the effectiveness of social movements, including the capacity to think strategically "measured by ideological and strategic autonomy from internal (government or social) or external (donor, women's movement) pressures; continuity, sustainability, and credibility of the organization; linkages with other movement actors and connected activism with partners and stakeholders; impact; and financial responsibility" (p. 77). The quantitative data from this analysis were then combined with the qualitative data from fieldwork and descriptions found in the reports of strategic actions that gender equality grantees identified in their work.

Results: The GFW "met its output and impact goals. It issued $2,215,400 (in Euros) through 147 grants to 125 women-led civil society organizations working on economic justice, women's political participation, and gender-based violence in 26 countries" (p. 12). It also held three convenings for collaboration and connection that supported the organization of social and political movements in the countries that participated. The portfolio analysis indicates that grantees are using "a rights-based approach to social movement work that is consistent with the important advances in gender politics and feminist theory globally" (p. 13). The portfolios also revealed that women used their skills to advocate for changes in the judicial system, legislation, and popular opinion to improve workers' rights; reduce gender-based violence; and increase women's land rights.

Benefits of using MM: Complex forces contribute to gender inequality and influence efforts to improve gender equality. Mixed methods with a gender analysis framework allowed for the collection of data that could inform accountability and learning about building social movements and what contributes to their success (or lack thereof). Mixed methods allowed the evaluator to document how the GFW addressed systemic changes needed in the form of enabling marginalized groups to improve access to resources; transform the legal and political environments; and transform social values, practices, and norms. For example, quantitative data could be collected on the passing of a law. However, sometimes passing a law is insufficient because the law is not enforced. Quantitative and qualitative data about the process of change and observational data about the enforcement of the law give a more complete understanding of transformations. Inclusion of qualitative data that illustrate the types of strategic actions engaged in by grantees provides insights for others interested in effective strategies for systemic change for women's equality.

Guidance for Designing a Gender-Responsive Mixed Methods Study

Guidance for conducting gender-responsive mixed methods designs in evaluation can be found in documents developed by UN Women (2015), such as the handbook it developed on managing a gender-responsive evaluation. I integrate the design guidance from the mixed methods community with the guidance provided by UN Women in designing a gender-responsive evaluation.

1. Frame the study using feminist theory and methodologies inclusive of both quantitative and qualitative data collection strategies.

2. Include a gender analysis framework that provides both quantitative and qualitative data such as the Harvard analytical framework, Moser gender planning framework, social relations framework, or the women's empowerment framework (see Table 6.1 for a brief description and references).

3. Ensure the appropriateness of the design and data collection plan for both men and women by engaging with members of the community.

4. Develop the design using participatory methods and continue the use of participatory methods throughout the evaluation.

5. Be aware of and responsive to constraints and challenges of informants and participants, including gender roles and power relations, in order to be context and culturally responsive.

6. Include plans for disaggregation of data by gender and other appropriate characteristics that could be used as a basis for discrimination in the particular context of the evaluation.

7. Emphasize the usefulness of mixed methods in the development of the design.

Table 6.1   Gender-Responsive Frameworks: Descriptions and References

Framework	Description	Reference
Harvard analytic framework	Developed by the Harvard Institute for International Development and USAID: identifies activities and resources by gender	Overholt, Anderson, Cloud, & Austin (1984) International Labour Organization: http://www.ilo.org/public/english/region/asro/mdtmanila/training/unit1/harvrdfw.htm

Framework	Description	Reference
Moser gender analysis framework	Developed by Moser in conjunction with DFID; includes six tools to capture activities, needs, access and control, and intervention effects by gender	Moser (2005) Chronic Poverty Research Centre: http://www .chronicpoverty.org/ uploads/publication_ files/WP32_Bolt_Bird.pdf Chronic Poverty Advisory Network: http://www .chronicpovertynetwork.org
Social relations framework	Focuses on household, community, market, and state to ascertain the structural causes of problems by gender	March, Smyth, & Mukhopadhyay (1999)
Empowerment framework	Developed by Longwe (1995) to determine the process of empowerment by documenting a sequence of measurable actions by gender; highlights impact and political dimensions	Longwe (1995) Association for Women in International Development: http:// awidme.pbworks .com/w/page/36322701/ Women%27s%20 Empowerment%20 Framework#_ftn1

Extending Your Thinking

Mixed Methods Gender Analysis Design

1. You are considering responding to a request for proposals to evaluate a program in Africa designed to support women farmers. The funding organization indicated that it wants a plan for the evaluation that uses a variety of methods to collect and analyze data and bring out a clear gender analysis throughout the evaluation. It wants suggestions for methodological approaches that address the objectives

(Continued)

(Continued)

and evaluation questions that include strong gender-responsive or feminist evaluation principles. What resources would you consult to begin your response to this request for proposals? Sketch out a mixed methods gender-responsive design that you could propose for this client.

2. Find a mixed methods evaluation study designed to evaluate issues of importance to women, such as poverty, reduction of violence, economic development, health care, child care, or participation in governance. Does the study include a gender analysis component? If so, what framework is used, and does it address systemic issues? If not, redesign the study to use a gender analysis framework. How does that add to the possibility of the usefulness of the findings?

3. *Gender* is a contested term, and the binary of male/female "perpetuates a lack of clarity about sex, sexual orientation, gender, and gender identity" (Mertens, Fraser, & Heimlich, 2008, p. 96). Mertens and colleagues suggest that evaluators could benefit from engaging in discussions with members of the LGBTQ community to come to a better understanding of power dynamics that surround the use of the term *gender* and to explore alternative ways to make meaning of the different identities. This challenge of representation of gender as being multifaceted offers mixed methods evaluators an opportunity to advance understanding of how to conduct evaluations that are responsive to diverse sexual identities. Design a mixed methods study that allows for the exploration of diverse sexual identities in respectful ways and that examines the effects of a program designed to decrease discrimination on the basis of sexual identity.

MIXED METHODS DESIGNS AND INDIGENOUS EVALUATION

Indigenous evaluators have increased their presence in the mixed methods community and have contributed to understanding the importance of their involvement and leadership in such evaluations (Chilisa, 2012; Cram & Mertens, 2015). As mentioned in the first chapter, Indigenous scholars have described their approach as a paradigm, framework, methodology, theoretical lens, or perspective. Mertens (2015b; Mertens & Wilson, 2012) included the Indigenous approach as a theoretical position under the transformative paradigm. However, in light of Chilisa's (2012) and Cram's (2016) delineation of an Indigenous paradigm, I chose to treat it as such in this text, rather than as a theoretical position under the transformative paradigm. The distinctiveness of an **Indigenous paradigm** is reflected in the axiological, ontological, epistemological, and methodological characteristics explained by Indigenous scholars. Distinctive earmarks of an Indigenous paradigm for evaluation rest in the history of colonization, loss of land, questions of sovereignty, beliefs nested in spirituality, and tribal/family relations that set Indigenous people apart from other marginalized groups. Whereas important differences exist across various Indigenous communities, there is sufficient overlap in their historical experiences to warrant discussion of an Indigenous paradigm.

Based on the work of Chilisa (2012), Cram (in press), and Smith (2012), I provide a very brief summary of the Indigenous philosophical assumptions. The Indigenous axiological assumption calls for attention to cultural norms and protocols that are relevant for the community. Ontologically, Indigenous people acknowledge their connectedness with each other, the environment, their ancestors, generations to come, and all living and nonliving things. Thus, concepts of reality include what is present and tangible, as well as what is spiritual and relational. In epistemological terms, knowledge is viewed as a sacred trust handed down through tribal elders. Knowledge has a cognitive and spiritual dimension and should be used to improve the quality of relationships and health in the community. Methodologically, the Indigenous paradigm raises questions about control of the study; who has power in the definition of the problem, questions, approaches, and use of results? Methods can go beyond quantitative and qualitative methods to include culturally responsive methods through engagement with tribal leaders and members in traditional rituals. Non-Indigenous evaluators can work with Indigenous evaluators; however, this must be done with respect for the Indigenous philosophical assumptions.

Cram et al. (2015) conducted an Indigenous mixed methods study of the effects of a program designed to improve the secondary achievement of **Maori** (Indigenous people from Aotearoa New Zealand) and **Pasifika** (Indigenous people from the Pacific Islands and Polynesia). The program began in 2011 because a youth pastor and community worker from Chicago noticed that the young men he worked with had limited access to quality secondary education. Geographically, they lived in areas, some rural, where this limitation would reduce their life opportunities. He established a program that would invite the young men to live in the zone that was served by the Auckland Grammar School (AGS). The program was called InZone and was conducted in collaboration with the AGS, a prestigious school with a history of high academic achievement. Socioeconomic circumstances presented a barrier to the young men living in this zone in the absence of the program because their families lack the wealth to purchase or rent a home in that zone.

Sample Study 6.2: Mixed Methods Design in Indigenous Evaluation (Cram et al., 2015)[1]

Problem: Maori and Pasifika in Aotearoa New Zealand live with a legacy of colonization and oppression, resulting in underachievement in secondary education that is exacerbated by poverty and the presence of violent gangs in some communities. These communities also live with the legacy of having their parents and grandparents having been sent to boarding schools intended to destroy their linkage with their culture, language, and families. They have limited access to high-quality education because of economic segregation; they do not live in high-income communities where many high-quality schools operate.

Intervention/evaluand: A youth pastor and community worker from Chicago began the InZone Project in 2011 with a program to improve young male Maori and Pasifika access to quality secondary education. The pastor worked with members of the Maori community and the executive staff at the Auckland Grammar School (AGS) to design a program that reflected Maori culture and needs. The InZone Project works in collaboration with the AGS to prepare young men for better experiences in secondary school. As the youth lived with their families in their home districts with restricted quality secondary education, they were provided with hostel live-in accommodations in which to live away from home so they could attend a prestigious school. The young men receive tutoring to support their academic studies; pastoral care with daily devotions; a home environment in the Owens Road hostel; and training in leadership, employment skills, and financial literacy.

Design: The evaluators used an Indigenous mixed methods design rooted in the Kaupapa Maori methodology (by Maori, for Maori) (Cram, 2009; Smith, 2012) and made space for a "by Pasifika, for Pasifika" approach as well. The mixed methods design was developed with important Indigenous values and beliefs in mind, such as the need to include a structural analysis of the problem, respect for the importance of *whanau* (family), and ensuring that the community viewed the evaluation agenda as representing their priorities before making decisions about specific methods. This fits within the Social Justice branch of evaluation.

Sample: The evaluators reviewed literature on the history of boarding hostels, national policies, and Maori and Pasifika educational research. Interviews were held with the InZone founder and director, 12 key informants, and some of the staff and students. Seven whanau members of five whanau were also interviewed. Observations (including videos and pictures) were conducted in the Owens Road hostel between September 2014 and March 2015. The AGS provided student achievement data on all students from 2011 to 2014, and 46 AGS staff responded to an online survey.

---

[1] My appreciation to Fiona Cram and the staff from the AGS school for commenting on this summary of their study and offering important revisions in the spirit of an accurate representation of their work and their community.

Data collection: "This mixed method evaluation included a literature review and analysis, interviews with the InZone founder and director, observation and interviews at the InZone Owens Road hostel, *whanau* interviews, key informant interviews, AGS staff survey, and analysis of AGS student achievement data . . . , and a review of media representations of IZP" (Cram et al., 2015, p. 1).

Data analysis: Qualitative data were digitally recorded and transcribed and then analyzed for common themes. Quantitative data were analyzed using descriptive statistics and graphic representation. The evaluators included quantitative comparisons between InZone students, students who stayed in their communities for school, and other AGS students. The integration of the quantitative and qualitative data occurred at the data reporting stage.

Results: The qualitative data revealed that the young men and their families were pleased with the opportunities provided through the InZone project and with the positive environment in which the students lived. The families were not happy with the connotation that there was something "wrong" with their sons coming from their whanau. Quantitative data from the survey indicated that the majority of the teaching staff believed in InZone students; achievement was on par with students who lived in the zone. Quantitative analysis of achievement data indicated mixed results in that about half the InZone students at Year 11 achieved at a lower rate on the National Certificate in Education Achievement (NCEA) assessment than the nation as a whole or for other Maori and Pasifika who attended AGS not as InZone students. At Year 12, 90% of the InZone students achieved Level 1 in the NCEA and 83% achieved Level 2. All the students who completed Year 13 graduated with either NCEA Level 2 or 3. Six graduates enrolled in higher education and four were employed. Differences in achievement were explained by the variation in the number of years that the young men participated in the project. The longer the students are there, the more improvement that is seen. A number of the boys were also selected to positions of leadership in AGS in sports teams and classrooms. The Maori community sees value in the project and wants to have greater involvement in supporting its continuation.

Benefits of using MM: The evaluation began with a welcoming ceremony that used both the Maori language (*te reo Māori*) and the Pasifika language (Samoa). This is appropriate for the building of trusting relationships that is the foundation for evaluations conducted in the Indigenous paradigm. The study was explained to the stakeholders and their opinions were sought regarding culturally appropriate methods for data collection. The stakeholders suggested inclusion of observations that included pictures and videos and interviews that were conducted like conversations to reflect their oral culture and traditions of art and storytelling. The qualitative data permitted the community's voice to be heard about structural problems rooted in economic segregation as well as to express concerns about being depicted as having something wrong with them. Quantitative data produced the documentation of specific educational achievement patterns as well as the collection of data from a relatively large number of InZone staff members.

Guidance for Designing an Indigenous Mixed Methods Study

1. The first point of importance is to be cognizant of who is on the evaluation team. Members of the Indigenous group should be on the team, and the team should be structured so that their cultural knowledge is given the proper value. In some contexts, Indigenous scholars have all the credentials and experience necessary to be the team leaders. If this is not the case, then the team should be structured in ways that both value their contribution and build their capacity to enhance their evaluation skills. Explicitly address issues of power to ensure that relationships can be identified, developed, and maintained (Bowman & Francis, 2015).

2. A key point about any evaluation done with Indigenous communities is to recognize the sovereign status of the community. This necessitates a historical understanding of the territory in which the Indigenous peoples are residing, whether it is on their own lands or as minorities in other places. Where possible, remember to use words or statements in the Indigenous language because in some situations this language describes things more accurately than in English.

3. Be aware of cultural protocols and respect the rituals of first encounters. Develop strategies for local involvement that are respectful of cultural protocols. Evaluators are visitors to a community; they need to do their homework to know what is appropriate and inappropriate from a cultural lens. To the extent possible, begin the evaluation process with visits to the communities, meeting with tribal elders as a matter of respect and to build advocacy for the evaluation through honest and open discussions. Quantitative data about incidence and demographics can also be collected at this stage.

4. Critically analyze theories of change and proposed interventions to ensure that they are viewed as valid and appropriate by community members. This might mean the evaluator needs to use data from the community to challenge theories of the problem and appropriate interventions held by the funder. The understanding of the nature of the problem and the appropriateness of the solution should come from the community. Keep in mind that codesign of evaluations is a fundamental strategy of partnerships.

5. Use multiple and mixed methods to collect data reflective of the multidimensional concept of knowledge held by Indigenous communities.

6. Be aware that everything about the evaluation belongs to the community, including instruments developed and knowledge gained. The Indigenous belief holds that evaluations should be conducted to bring benefits to the community. Thus multiple and mixed methods need to be used to be sure that interpretations are culturally appropriate and results are accessible to community members for action purposes (Jacklin & Kinoshameg, 2008).

Extending Your Thinking

Mixed Methods Indigenous Design

1. Find another mixed methods evaluation study done with Indigenous peoples. What characteristics do you find in the study that align with the guidance for conducting such evaluations based on the assumptions of the Indigenous paradigm?

2. Design a mixed methods study that could be conducted with an Indigenous population, paying particular attention to the assumptions of the Indigenous paradigm. If you are not Indigenous yourself, how would you begin your discussions with members of the Indigenous community? If you are Indigenous, how would you represent yourself to the Indigenous community in which you are proposing to work?

UNIVERSAL DESIGN: MIXED METHODS DESIGNS WITH PERSONS WITH DISABILITIES AND DEAF PERSONS

People with disabilities are ubiquitous. Many of us are either temporarily abled or temporarily disabled. Many disabilities are invisible. Lack of awareness of or responsiveness to the needs of people with disabilities can jeopardize the quality of findings in evaluations. Gothberg (2015) argues that evaluators need to understand the complexities and challenges inherent in the design, implementation, and management of evaluations that involve people with disabilities as a matter of ethics and validity. **Universal design** is a concept that emerged from the architectural community; it means that products and environments are designed to be usable by all people to the greatest extent possible. In evaluation design, universal design has relevance in terms of making evaluations accessible, inclusive, and usable by all people, including those with disabilities, chronic illnesses, or who use a language other than English (including Deaf American Sign Language users).

Suleweski and Gothberg (2013) developed the Universal Design for Evaluation Checklist (4th ed.) that provides guidance for evaluators in the design of their evaluations, as well as in instrument design, data collection and analysis, and dissemination of findings. The checklist is based on seven principles of universal design to provide guidance for evaluators (for the complete checklist, see http://comm.eval.org/communities/community-home/librarydocuments/viewdocument?DocumentKey=62107753-a359-40d1-96d7-2fc113ae9ba8).

The elements of the Universal Design for Evaluation Checklist are used in part in the section that follows on guidance for designing a mixed methods study following Sample Study 6.3. The Improve Group (2013) in Minnesota undertook a mixed methods evaluation study of the accessibility, quantity, and quality of services for people in Minnesota with a disability, mental illness, or chronic illness. The evaluators worked with the following principle: "In order to treat all people with respect we must be sensitive to individual needs and respect differences, without judgment. This study was also guided by the understanding that relationships are important to helping people feel comfortable and share stories about sensitive topics" (Improve Group, 2013, p. 11). To this end, their mixed methods study was designed to align with the principles of universal design as described in Sample Study 6.3.

Sample Study 6.3: Mixed Methods Design Using the Universal Design Framework for Inclusion of Persons With Disabilities (Improve Group, 2013)

Problem: In Minnesota, there is an increasing number of people who have a disability, mental illness, or chronic health condition that requires long-term services and support. Systems to provide such services are complex and expensive; the Minnesota Department of Human Services spends $3.5 billion annually in state and federal funds for services and supports to serve this population. Information was not available about the perceptions of the people who need the services and their families and caregivers, how the services were or were not meeting their needs, and how services and the system could be improved.

Intervention/evaluand: The Minnesota Department of Human Services Continuing Care Administration and the Chemical and Mental Health Services Administration share the responsibility for providing long-term support and services to people who have a disability, mental illness, or chronic health condition. The evaluand included the system and services overseen by these two offices. Stakeholders included those who receive services and those who are eligible but do not receive services, as well as families and caregivers.

Design: A mixed methods design informed by the principles of universal design was used in this study. It is a concurrent mixed methods design based on the principles of universal design. This fits within the Social Justice branch of evaluation.

Sample: Literature was selected based on its relevance to providing knowledge about previous studies conducted in the state, as well as to determine appropriate data collection methods for people with disabilities and/or mental illness, and people with chronic illness. Databases of previously conducted surveys were available for analysis. Focus group participants were selected to represent the three groups: people with disabilities, people with mental illness, and people with chronic illnesses and their caregivers. The selection of communities was made based on DHS recommendations with the criteria that the groups should represent diversity in terms of geographic location across the state and density of services. A total of 260 individuals were recruited for the focus groups in those communities by means of local contacts and newspaper ads. Seven providers and three tribal leaders from the Ojibwe community were selected based on recommendations of the tribal leaders. Twenty-four key stakeholders participated in phone interviews; they were identified through contacts provided by DHS, the Improve staff, and Internet searches of leaders in the field. A quantitative survey on availability of surveys was answered by 110 people who identified as having a disability, were parents or caregivers, or were older with a chronic illness. Twenty-three health plan coordinators were recommended by DHS to participate in an online focus group.

Data collection: Qualitative data were collected by a variety of means, including review of existing research, including two studies conducted by the Minnesota Department of Human Services on trends in service availability for specific populations and needs assessments that surveyed county staff. They also reviewed policies and court documents related to a suit brought against the state for inappropriate provision of services for people with mental illness. Data collection instruments and procedures were planned with the use of a universal design framework in order to be responsive to the needs of the various constituencies. Qualitative and quantitative data were collected from people receiving and needing support, people with disabilities, people with mental illness, older people and their families and caregivers, tribal leaders, and advocates. Quantitative data were used from a survey of human services waiver reviews that determined compliance with program requirements. Twelve group interviews were held with county government staff members. A quantitative online survey was also used to collect data across the state about the availability of services. In keeping with the principles of universal design, this survey was also made available at a conference for people with developmental disabilities where Improve staff administered the survey by reading the items to participants and recording their responses. Leaders of the Ojibwe tribal community were contacted to determine the best methods for gathering data from their members. Qualitative data were collected from them in two sessions that included a meal, interviews, and focus groups. Sixteen focus groups were conducted with the primary audiences of persons with disabilities and/or mental illness, older persons, and caregivers. Following the principles of universal design in evaluation, support services such as provision of transportation were provided to enable people to participate in the focus groups. Focus group locations were chosen to be convenient and accessible. A strategy used in the focus group was designed to give everyone an opportunity to contribute, to lessen anxiety about participation in the groups, to bridge cultural and language barriers, and to be accessible to people with disabilities.

(Continued)

(Continued)

> The focus groups used an interactive image-based exercise—
> Image Grouping—in which participants were instructed to rate dif-
> ferent areas of their life, or the life of the person they care for, by
> placing the life domain stickers on a scale from "good" to "bad."
> Participants were given a choice of three stickers with different
> images for each domain area: community membership; health and
> wellness; independence; relationships; and employment, volun-
> teerism, and school. Participants were instructed to choose one
> or more stickers per domain area to place on their scale. (Improve
> Group, 2013, p. 9)

Focus group invitations were translated into Hmong, Somali, and Spanish
and were also available in large print. The evaluators arranged for interpreters in American Sign Language and in other languages through a language
line service. Materials at the focus group were also available in large print and
Braille.

Data analysis: Qualitative data were analyzed using the constant comparison
method and were organized by theme in Excel spreadsheets. The quantitative data were then "analyzed and assigned to themes where it supported or
supplemented qualitative data. . . . The data were used to support and verify
findings from the qualitative analysis" (p. 12).

Results: Quantitative and qualitative data supported the desire on the part of
persons with disabilities, those with mental illness, and people with chronic
illnesses to be part of a community; however, they also revealed feelings of
stigma attached to people like them and a lack of comfort about getting out
into the community. Participants also expressed a desire to eat healthy and
exercise, and they noted barriers (particularly financial, security, transportation,
and accessibility) to being able to follow through on these desires. Results
were disaggregated by the type of community (urban, rural, suburban, and
tribal) and by type of disability. For example, transportation was more available in urban areas, but the waiting stations were not always accessible during
inclement weather.

Benefits of using MM: The use of mixed methods had many benefits in this
study. The use of existing literature and extant databases allowed for a broader
understanding of issues and eliminated the cost of collecting new data that
would be redundant. The use of the universal design principles allows for the
inclusion of diverse people in culturally appropriate ways. People with disabilities, mental illness, or chronic illnesses are often represented in research by
the voices of their service providers. By using mixed methods designed using
universal design principles, the evaluators were able to provide evidence of
the quality and quantity of services available from many perspectives. These
data are of value for service providers and policymakers.

Guidance for Designing a Universal Design Mixed Methods Study

As mentioned earlier, the Universal Design for Evaluation Checklist (Suleweski & Gothberg, 2013) is organized by seven principles of universal design; each principle is accompanied by recommendations for its implementation in evaluation design. The guidance for the design of a mixed methods evaluation using universal design principles is based on the work of Suleweski and Gothberg (2013); Jenson (2015); and Kohler, Gothberg, and Coyle (2012).

1. Ensure equitable use by involvement of stakeholders in supportive and accessible means throughout the course of the evaluation.

2. Flexibility in evaluation design means that multiple formats and methods should be used in order to be responsive to the needs of diverse stakeholders, including people with disabilities and those whose first language is not English. This might entail providing interpreters, extra time, and variations in the data collection tools.

3. Keep the design for the evaluation simple and intuitive in order to incorporate different communication needs, reading levels, language, low vision, and color blindness.

4. Be sure the design is responsive to the sensory capabilities of the stakeholders, using interpreters, large print, Braille, and multiple media options for the presentation and collection of information. If using web-based data collection or sharing, ensure that the web materials follow recommended standards for accessibility (https://www.w3.org/WAI). Jenson (2015) notes that people with disabilities are more likely to have experienced trauma than persons without disabilities and that this should be kept in mind in the design and implementation of the evaluation to minimize renewed trauma and allow them to meaningfully participate. Mixed and multiple methods can be a means to increasing comfort levels for participation by people who have experienced trauma.

5. Data collection instruments should be pilot tested with diverse stakeholders and modified to ensure that they are clear and that the respondents are able to respond to them. Kohler, Gothberg, and Coyle (2012) recommend considering adaptations of focus groups procedures such as those seen in the Improve Group (2013) evaluation or giving the questions to participants in

(Continued)

(Continued)

advance so they can write down their thoughts and bring them into the focus group. This can help people with cognitive challenges to remember what they want to say and to reduce anxiety levels.

6. Be aware of the amount of physical effort required to participate in terms of accessible and available transportation, comfort in seating, and allowance for extra time and breaks as necessary. Physical surroundings for persons who have experienced trauma also need to provide easy access to the exits, good visual access, and respect for personal space (Jenson, 2015).

7. Be sure that areas chosen for interviews, focus groups, meetings, presentations, or other gatherings are accessible and that restrooms are also accessible. Provide supportive accommodations (e.g., reader, interpreter, or computer) as necessary.

Extending Your Thinking

Mixed Methods With Universal Design

1. Find an evaluation study done with persons with disabilities. Analyze the study's design and methods to see how it aligns with the recommendations found in the Universal Design for Evaluation Checklist.

2. Design a mixed methods study that explicitly addresses the universal design principles (Suleweski & Gothberg, 2013). How did the universal design principles support the use of mixed methods?

3. Universal design was developed specifically for use with persons with disabilities. However, as exemplified in the Improve Group (2013) study, it is possible to use this tool in a mixed methods design with other sensitive populations because of its sensitivity to language differences and abilities. One sensitive population consists of undocumented workers who take great risk by participating in evaluation studies because of the possibility of deportation and discrimination. Find a MM study that focused on undocumented workers or a similar group that are at risk when participating in evaluation studies (e.g., sex workers) and determine what additional components of the design are needed to safely include members of these populations. See, for example, Kuehne, Huschke, and Bullinger's (2015) evaluation of access to health care for undocumented workers in Germany.

MIXED METHODS DESIGNS AND DEVELOPMENTAL EVALUATION

So far, the examples [...] interventions, policies, ins[...] that occur within time boun[...] ds evaluations have focused on many situations in which evalu[...] pment, and systematic reviews circumstances, particularly in organ[...] (2011) noticed that there are continuously, rather than having time[...] f use that do not fit these evaluated. Therefore, he developed an ap[...] want to learn and grow **evaluation** that can be used to evaluate proj[...] jects that need to be organizational changes, policy reforms, and syst[...] ed **developmental** occur in dynamic and complex contexts. Develop[...] rams, products, is most appropriate in contexts in which innovation is[...] ventions that with adaptive management. The evaluation processes st[...] evaluation asking evaluative questions and applying evaluative logic, but [...] ed along [...] clude of the evaluator becomes one of serving as a team member to provide data and opportunity for reflection for "new approaches in a long-term, ongoing process of continuous development, adaptation, and experimentation" (Patton, 2011, p. 1). Developmental evaluation shares some characteristics with the mixed methods cyclical designs we have seen in earlier chapters; however, one difference is that the goal is not necessarily to have a "summative evaluation." Rather, the goal is to have ongoing learning and reflection and to be responsive to issues that arise as an organization's role evolves and contexts change.

Patton (2011) noted that social innovators resist having specific outcomes determined prior to development and implementation of a program or policy: "Principles for operating in complex adaptive systems inform the practice of developmental evaluation" (p. 9). Thus, complexity theory is an integral part of developmental evaluation and allows evaluators to reject the notion that a single prespecified solution should be tested. Rather, the evaluator works with stakeholders to question what the nature of the problem is and what system dynamics underlie the perceptions of the problem. The purpose of developmental evaluation is to provide data to inform decisions and facilitate ongoing innovation.

Examples of developmental evaluation do not always include the use of mixed methods, nor do they reflect the conditions of ongoing changes in an organization or program (Patton, McKegg, & Wehipeihana, 2016). Hargreaves and colleagues (2013) provide an example of a mixed methods developmental evaluation that focused

and treat obesity in
opmental evaluation are
he project was intended to
rvention, rather than support

on the development of a prog
children and families. Some ele
well illustrated in this exam
support the development o
ongoing change.

Sample Stud ixed Methods Developmental
Eva (Hargreaves et al., 2013)

Problem: Child esity is very high in the United States and is linked to
obesity in ad heart problems, diabetes, and psychological and social
problems. F decisions about food and physical activity influence weight
in childh

Eval a: The Healthy Weight Collaborative (HWC) is a program funded
ough the U.S. Department of Health and Human Services to "create
partnerships between primary care, public health, and community-based
organizations to discover sustainable ways to promote healthy weight and
eliminate health disparities in communities across the United States" (p. 104).
The evaluand includes the partnerships and an integrated change package
of six evidence-based clinical and community-based strategies to prevent
and treat obesity. "The change package included writing a community action
plan, creating a community-wide obesity prevention message, assessing the
weight status of the target population, developing and implementing the
healthy weight plans, and initiating organizational and environmental policy
changes supporting healthy eating and active living" (p. 105).

Design: A developmental mixed methods design was used to track the evolution of the HWC over time. The evaluation design was responsive to the
need to change and adapt the model for implementation in multiple communities. The evaluation also focused on the nature of the team activities to
track changes in their collaborative capacity, using a collaboration scale and
social network analysis. A third component of the evaluation design focused on
the multilevel, multisectoral governance structure, using complexity theory to
examine the development of community-wide partnerships and organizational
linkages. This fits within the Use branch of evaluation.

Sample: The HWC teams consisted of between 10 and 27 members and
included representatives from primary care, public health, and community-
based organizations. The sample of teams used in this study were selected
from 10 geographic regions across the United States—six from urban locations
and four from rural areas.

Data collection: Quantitative and qualitative measures were used, including
observations of learning sessions during which evaluators rated the sessions

on their logistics, content, and facilitation. They conducted qualitative interviews with individuals and groups with leaders, project managers, faculty, and staff. Project documents were reviewed and analyzed that included team performance measures, progress reports, and learning session materials. The evaluators surveyed team members to obtain data about the learning sessions, collaborations, and levels of interaction. Evaluators also conducted a literature review of models for obesity reduction interventions.

Data analysis: The specifics of data analysis were not discussed in the published article. The integration of the quantitative and qualitative data were evident in the results section that reported on the extent to which the teams interacted and the quality of those interactions.

Results: Teams reported that they had a greater sense of shared vision and felt that their goals were more concrete and attainable. The level of interaction was high (4 or 5 on a 5-point scale). All teams developed a community action plan and had a consistent healthy weight message. Some teams created a healthy weight plan, but they all varied in the extent to which they were able to assess the weight status of the targeted population. Because the period for evaluation was only 1 year, no team was able to implement an environmental policy change. Opportunities for interaction among team members yielded a chance to improve the program and to identify gaps that required additional attention.

Benefits of using MM: The mixed methods provided information for the funders and other stakeholders that could be used to improve the partnerships in terms of the processes used to develop them and to implement the HWC. The combination of developmental evaluation with mixed methods was appropriate because the HWC was conceptualized as a program that needed to be adapted to specific communities. Hence, collection and analysis of qualitative and quantitative data enabled the identification of needed changes in each of the communities.

Guidance for Designing a Mixed Methods Developmental Evaluation Study

1. Be aware of initial conditions and changes that might be unpredictable or unexpected. Use mixed methods to capture changes both quantitatively and qualitatively. Small changes can have big impacts; document the effects of small and large changes.

(Continued)

(Continued)

2. Be aware of the human dynamics operating in the context. Use mixed methods to document formation of subgroups and explore the differential experiences and perceptions of members of emerging subgroups. Use an emergent evaluation design that includes such data collection strategies as mapping networks, system relationships, and subgroups, and tracking information flows, communication, and emergent issues. Make note of what occurs and what does not occur; what appears and what disappears. The evaluation design needs to be emergent and responsive based on changes occurring in the system.

3. Keep the evaluation adaptive in order to be responsive to changing conditions and perceptions. Use mixed methods to collect data on perceptions from diverse stakeholders and put these perspectives into dialogue with each other. Share information about adaptations needed in the evaluation as well as observations about adaptations that are or are not occurring in the organization.

4. Uncertainty about the nature of the problem and solutions is a key characteristic of complex systems. The evaluator has a role to play in identifying sources of uncertainty and in providing methods of data collection to help reduce uncertainty. In some circumstances, there may be a need for rapid feedback and adjustments; the evaluator needs to be responsive to this need. Hence, use of different methods of data collection that can provide a quick turnaround should be in the developmental evaluator's repertoire.

5. Collect data about changes that occur (quantitative) and how and why the changes occur (qualitative). "Create a flexible and responsive data collection system that can mirror adaptive, emergent, and dynamic/dynamical developments, so that fieldwork can speed up and slow down in sync with the intervention's rhythms of change. Engage in ongoing monitoring of shifts in levels and activity to capture dynamic/dynamical transitions. Analyze and distinguish contextual factors and participation patterns that are static, dynamic, and dynamical, and implications of these different patterns" (Patton, 2011, p. 151).

6. Developmental evaluation designs need to evolve with the evolution of the evaluand. Quantitative and qualitative data need to be collected on process as well as outcomes and impacts.

Extending Your Thinking

Mixed Methods Developmental Evaluation

1. You have been hired by an organization because it senses that its normal way of doing business is not being responsive to changes in the surrounding community. Choose a situation in the community in which you live where you suspect this to be true (e.g., health services where many people now live in the community who speak languages other than English). Propose a developmental mixed methods evaluation design to the organization that will allow it to have ongoing learning as it adapts to the new circumstances.

2. Find a developmental evaluation study. Critically analyze the study, identifying those aspects of developmental evaluation and mixed methods that are present and absent in the study. How would you recommend improving the design of the study?

MIXED METHODS DESIGNS AND NEEDS ASSESSMENT

Needs assessment has already been addressed in some of the evaluation studies that used mixed methods cyclical designs in which evaluators engaged in data collection to determine what was needed for whom and in what manner it should be implemented and evaluated. However, needs assessment can be a stand-alone evaluation purpose and is very important in the repertoire of evaluators. The use of mixed methods has enhanced evaluators' abilities to provide useful information prior to the development and implementation of an intervention. Therefore, in this section, we take a look at the use of mixed methods in needs assessment studies.

Jacklin and Kinoshameg (2008) undertook a needs assessment in Canada to determine the health needs in an Aboriginal community. The community was hesitant to participate with the evaluators because they had not seen benefits from previous studies conducted on them. The community members agreed to participate "only if it's going to mean something" (Jacklin & Kinoshameg, 2008, p. 53). The needs assessment was designed to incorporate critical theory, Indigenous theory, and participatory action strategies. This is in keeping with the Social Justice branch.

Sample Study 6.5: Mixed Methods Needs Assessment for an Aboriginal Health Research Project in Ontario, Canada (Jacklin & Kinoshameg, 2008)

Problem: The Wikwemikong Health Centre (WHC) needed to conduct a community needs assessment as part of its community health plan, a requirement for its participation in a nationally funded health transfer project that allows the transfer of funding for health services from the government to local communities. The first author of the study is a member of an Aboriginal community but not of the bands that live in the study area. The Indigenous community members were suspicious of researchers and evaluators who entered their community from the "outside" because they have experienced exploitation and misrepresentation at the hands of past investigators.

Intervention/evaluand/policy: No intervention was being evaluated; rather, the goal was to identify the health needs of members of this community.

Design: A mixed methods needs assessment design was developed that reflected a critical theoretical framework to consciously address social inequities, Indigenous teachings, and participatory action research strategies. Before the design of the study could be developed, the evaluator needed to go through a lengthy process to obtain permission to enter the community that included meetings with the health director, following health board protocols, obtaining a recommendation to the chief and council, and ensuring that the knowledge gained from the study would be for the use of the community to meet the requirements for their health transfer funding. Jacklin then conducted informal interviews with the staff and community members to get their input into the design of the study. The second author of the study was the lead for the health center management team and a member of the reserve band. Qualitative data were collected by the first author over a 2-year period; a community-based needs assessment survey was developed and implemented during that period. Another aspect of the design that emerged as part of the community consultation process was the need to advertise the survey widely in the community prior to its implementation by posting flyers, running advertisements on local television, and putting advertisements in the local newspaper. This was done in order to respond to questions local residents might have about the study. This fits within the Social Justice branch of evaluation.

Sample: The participants in this study came from the Wikwemikong Unceded Indian Reserve, located in Ontario, Canada. The band members are Ojibwa, Odawa, and Potawatomi; they use three dialects of the Algonquian language family and English. The sampling strategy for the community-based needs assessment survey was a random sample in order to be sure that the health plan represented all age groups, genders, and villages. The sampling frame consisted of all households on a 911 emergency phone list selected using random numbers. Three hundred fifty band members (20% of households) were interviewed. "Key informant interviews were conducted with specialized informants such as health center staff and managers working in various program areas, directors of community organizations, and community informants" (p. 58).

Data collection: "Methods included literature reviews, two years of participant observation, key informant interviewing and a community needs assessment" (p. 55). The survey used for the community needs assessment contained both quantitative and qualitative questions and was developed based on a literature review. It was then reviewed by health center and band office staff members; this was followed by review by community organization representatives and four local research assistants. The survey was pilot tested and a final draft was given to the WHC and the university ethical review board. The survey data were collected by four local postsecondary students who had been trained as research assistants and who spoke the Indigenous languages and English. During their training, the assistants raised questions about the comfort level of revealing personal information during interviews. Based on their experience with the community, they worked with the evaluator to revise the process in the interview to allow community members to write their answer to sensitive questions privately. The identifying information was kept in one envelope and the completed surveys were sealed in an unmarked envelope in front of the participant.

Data analysis: Data analysis was conducted jointly with the first author and the four local research assistants who met frequently to examine emerging themes. Quantitative data were analyzed using descriptive statistics. The integration of data came in interim reports in newsletters distributed to all 350 participants.

Results: The results were viewed as valid by the community members who asked that the findings be disseminated in several formats such as newsletters to participants and research briefs for the health center in a form that allowed them to use the information in a proposal for future funding. They also used community bulletin boards with posters of the results on different topics—for example, tobacco use and health promotion on stopping smoking. The community ownership and control resulted in findings that the community could use for their own purposes to improve their ability to provide culturally responsive health services.

Benefits of using MM: A quantitative survey provided information about the extent of health concerns; however, this alone would not have met the demands of the Indigenous community for a respectful relationship and credible data. The process of obtaining permission to enter the community and the qualitative data collected through participant observation and other methods served to convince the community that this evaluator was there to do something that mattered to them and would serve their information needs.

Guidance for Designing a Mixed Methods Needs Assessment Study

1. Be aware of existing information available about needs in the community; this information may be available in published articles but also in internal reports and in the lived experience of members of the targeted community. If evaluators do not search for and acknowledge what is already known about needs, the community members may feel resentful and see the evaluator as another person who has come to take information from them to advance his or her own career.

2. Establish relationships with community members and service providers and other stakeholders to be sure that there is an opportunity to modify the design of the study to really meet the needs of the stakeholders. Needs assessments framed using participatory action research strategies and culturally responsive approaches may be more acceptable to community leaders and members.

3. As much as possible, collect qualitative data through informal interviews, participant observation, and being of service to the community. This gives a richness to understandings and strengthens the sense of credibility and ownership of the findings.

4. Consider combining multiple methods such as concept mapping (Trochim & Kane, 2005), photovoice (Han & Oliffe, 2016), key informant interviews, focus groups, and use of secondary data.

5. For quantitative data collection, work cooperatively with community members to ensure that the questions asked are comprehensible to the intended participants. Be aware of cultural norms that make some topics more sensitive and look for ways to obtain data that do not cause discomfort or reveal personal information. Include quantitative data as part of the process evaluation where it is appropriate— for example, to obtain information about usage and participation.

6. Look for ways to share findings that integrate the quantitative and qualitative results and are appropriate to the audience. This might mean through community bulletin boards, websites, research briefings, or newsletters.

Extending Your Thinking

Mixed Methods Needs Assessment

1. You have been contacted by a local school that is concerned with obesity in its students. Design a needs assessment mixed methods study that would help the school identify the nature of the problem

and what is contributing to it. How would you engage with the community in ways that would engender their willingness to collaborate with you? How would mixed methods enhance understandings of the existing needs?

2. Identify a needs assessment study. Does it use mixed methods? If so, what design is used? If not, how could mixed methods have added to the quality of the findings?

MIXED METHODS DESIGNS AND VISUAL SPATIAL DATA

The constructivist paradigm assumptions emphasize the importance of context in understanding the emergence of different versions of reality. One tool used widely in geographic and urban planning studies, but less so in education, health, and the social sciences, is **spatial analysis** (Rucks-Ahidiana & Bierbaum, 2015). The use of spatial analysis and qualitative approaches can be traced back as far as W. E. B. Du Bois's (1899) study of African Americans in Philadelphia. Spatial analysis on the surface might appear to be a quantitative approach because it is based on collection of statistical data that are then displayed as a map of the selected variables. However, maps are social constructions and thus inherently include a qualitative dimension as the data are used to understand patterns and trends and changes over time that can be linked to observational and interview data.

Fielding and Cisneros-Puebla (2009) describe several strategies for incorporating spatial analysis and qualitative approaches, such as having participants draw maps of their neighborhoods to indicate places where they feel safe and not so safe. The use of **geographic information systems (GIS)** illustrates the use of more sophisticated technology that produces maps that can be combined with graphs, figures, photos, stories, performances, and networks. Technological advances have added enormously to the potential to use spatial analysis in mixed methods studies—for example, interactive legends for maps, "data-exploration tools, user-controlled animation, virtual environments, real-time 3-D modeling, [and] wearable computing devices" (Knigge & Cope, 2006, p. 2027). Fielding and Cisneros-Puebla (2009) suggest that the integration of spatial analysis might represent a purely mixed methods study because the quantitative and qualitative aspects of the study intertwine so much.

Knigge and Cope (2006) applied a spatial analysis with ethnography in a study of community gardens in Buffalo, New York. Their study demonstrates many different qualitative strategies that fall under ethnographic grounded theory combined with spatial analysis. Their study reflects the Values branch of evaluation.

Sample Study 6.6: Mixed Methods Design Using Spatial Analysis

Spatial analysis and ethnography: Community gardens (Knigge & Cope, 2006).

Problem: The Lower West Side (LWS) of Buffalo, New York, has a high rate of crime, many empty dilapidating houses, and many different immigrant groups who live there. It also has a planning group and residents who want to see improvements.

Evaluand: A local planning organization wanted to design a plan to improve the safety and economic and environmental quality of the LWS.

Design: Knigge and Cope (2006) describe their design as grounded visualization that combined ethnography and GIS. They collected their data using a concurrent MM design with an emphasis on recursive analysis and integration of quantitative and qualitative data at the analysis stage of the study.

Sample: Residents from the LWS.

Data collection: The study began with a quantitative study of the demographics in the neighborhood through the use of existing data and having evaluation interns walk the streets of the neighborhood and rate the condition of the houses and other buildings. These data were mapped using GIS and presented at a public meeting to the residents, many of whom protested that their houses were not included in the mapped area. The evaluators expanded the target area to include those residents' houses. Knigge followed this meeting up with participant observation, walking and riding her bike through the neighborhood and observing the residents' attachment, agency, and marginalization. She asked questions about the heterogeneity in the neighborhood and how space was used. The evaluators did more data collection to produce maps that reflected vacant lots, housing values, and types of structures. Knigge attended public and neighborhood meetings, including those of the Coalition of the Buffalo Community Gardeners and Vacant Lot Task Force. She continued collecting data through attending meetings, inspecting and documenting community gardens, and engaging in participant observation.

Data analysis: Knigge used grounded theory coding processes to combine the quantitative and qualitative data, performing several rounds of recursive analysis using visualization and grounded theory (see Figure 6.1).

Figure 6.1   Map of Community Gardens

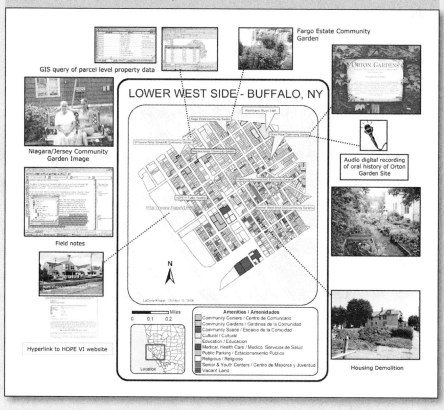

Source: Knigge & Cope (2006).

Results: The mapping revealed 265 vacant lots that were disproportionately located in areas where demolition was the policy being implemented by the city. The city records revealed that 31,000 houses were demolished between 1990 and 2010. Themes emerged related to "diversity, poverty, survival strategies and (potentially) community identity" (p. 2031). One significant trend emerged about how space was used. The themes encapsulated the vacant lots and abandoned dilapidated houses but also included gardens on the porches, front lawns, and community plots. Knigge identified seven community gardens in the LWS. See Figure 6.1 to view the mapping and additional data sources used in this study.

Benefits of using MM: Knigge's integration of qualitative and quantitative data led to revelations that would not have been possible with one type of data alone. For example, the initial quantitative part of the study did not reveal anything about the gardens residents kept; this came to her attention through her participant observation. At the same time, if she had relied

(Continued)

(Continued)

solely on qualitative data, she would not have been cognizant of the clusters revealed in the maps around wealth and vacant lots. The qualitative part of the study was necessary to learn the meaning of the community and individual gardens to residents in the LWS. The gardens provided residents with economic and political empowerment through the production of food and engagement in an informal economic sector. The results of the study can be used to inform policymakers in the areas of use of public space, housing, food security, and community gardens.

Guidance for Designing a Mixed Methods Visual Spatial Data Study

1. Formulate an evaluation question that will be answerable by spatial data and qualitative approaches.

2. If creating maps from existing data, identify data sources and extract the data relevant to the question. If maps are to be constructed by participants, provide a training session for the participants so they are able to display their knowledge through the mapping process.

3. If geographical information is to be captured as part of the data collection process, provide the technology and training as needed to produce the needed data. This can include handheld computers or smartphones. Jaskiewicz, Block, and Chavez (2016) provide a comparison of various spatial mapping tools that can be useful for evaluators in deciding which tool to use in such a study.

4. Plan for qualitative approaches that can be used in conjunction with the spatial analysis. This could include full ethnographic studies that include participant interpretation of the maps, town meetings, participant observation, interviews, or analysis of documents. If using grounded theory, plan for the recursive, iterative analysis of data that will allow the theory to emerge from the analytic procedure, recognizing that spatial representation is a social construction.

5. Be aware of software available to support the integration of spatial analysis and qualitative data. Fielding and Cisneros-Puebla (2009) review the computer-based qualitative data analysis packages (http://www.surrey.ac.uk/sociology/research/researchcentres/caqdas) and GIS computer systems such as ArcGIS and ArcInfo (http://www.esri.com/what-is-gis) that evaluators can use to support the integration of spatial data and qualitative data. Evaluators interested in using this approach will find many valuable resources at these two websites.

Extending Your Thinking

Mixed Methods and Visual Spatial Data

1. Imagine you are hired as an evaluator by a school system that wants to improve the safety of the neighborhood surrounding its schools. Create an evaluation design that integrates spatial analysis and qualitative methods. How could you include technology and students in the design?

2. Think about your own work in evaluation. How could your design of an evaluation be enhanced by the use of spatial analysis and qualitative approaches?

MIXED METHODS DESIGNS AND ●
ARTS-BASED EVALUATIONS

Arts-based evaluation means that the creative arts are integrated into the design of an evaluation when artistic expression is part of the intervention, intended outcomes, or methods of communicating findings of evaluations. Simons and McCormack (2007) argue that the inclusion of creative arts in evaluation design allows for accessing different ways of knowing, seeing, and understanding:

> Starting with an image instead of a category allows the imagination to work at an unconscious level and brings to the surface a different form of understanding. It frees the evaluator from the constraints of categories and reductionist analysis. Images can also act as a useful metaphor (i.e., way of resembling imaginatively) for what we are aspiring to understand in evaluation. Working with metaphor we can see how themes and patterns form an integrated whole and carry a message beyond formal explanation, reshaping the text from a unidimensional form to one that has multiple layers. (p. 295)

Arts-based evaluation as part of a mixed methods design presents different kinds of challenges as compared to other designs because it may include writing (e.g., poems), visual art (e.g., painting, photography), drama, music, and dance—a different mix of data that goes beyond typical quantitative and qualitative data. The creation of the data may even be considered the intervention itself in studies that investigate the effect of participating in creative expression on particular outcomes. Such methods of expression can reveal values that would not come to the surface with only words or numbers; they can also be personally engaging and revealing. Issues that arise in the integration of creative arts with mixed methods evaluation include the collection of the data, analytic criteria used, credibility of findings, external validity, and presentation of results.

Shannon-Baker (2015a) provides an example of a mixed methods arts-based evaluation of a study abroad program, focusing on the experience of culture shock for the students who traveled from the United States to South America. The use of arts-based methods was deemed to be appropriate because immersion in a different culture is an experience that cannot always be adequately captured with words or numbers. This study fits with the dialectical pluralism approach.

Sample Study 6.7: Mixed Methods in Arts-Based Evaluations

Arts-based mixed methods in a study abroad program (Shannon-Baker, 2015a).

Problem: Persons who travel to different countries sometimes experience culture shock because of unexpected experiences that are disconcerting and can lead to misunderstandings. Research on culture shock suggests that it can be linked with risk-related conditions such as excessive alcohol consumption or depression. In addition, higher levels of culture shock can impede the development of positive interpersonal relationships and limit involvement with the host culture. Culture shock can also be manifest when students return home and have difficulty adjusting to life back there.

Evaluand: A short-term study abroad program in which U.S. undergraduate students traveled to a South American country.

Design: Shannon-Baker (2015a) used a concurrent parallel mixed methods research design that used arts-informed, qualitative, and quantitative approaches. The evaluator placed her work within the dialectical pluralism framework for evaluation:

> In particular, dialectics informed this study at the integration stage by the careful consideration of how the results of the data sets informed one another, and in how to integrate the text and visual data. Also, given that dialectics emphasizes the multiple perspectives of a phenomenon have something to offer the inquiry . . . , I used both my own analysis of the data and the students' interpretations. Finally a dialectical approach, considering issues of validity, encouraged me to discuss any potential divergences, and why they might be there. (p. 37)

Sample: The students attended a midwestern university and were taking a course about the educational system and culture of a country in South America. As part of the course, they participated in a 10-day study abroad experience. Ten students from the course agreed to participate in the study and completed all the course requirements.

Data collection: Students completed reflective journals before, during, and after their time abroad. In their journals, the students answered open-ended questions and drew a self-portrait. The instructions for drawing the self-portrait directed them to depict their emotions shortly after the trip began. The students were also asked to write a statement about their self-portrait, explaining their use of symbols, color, etc. They also completed a quantitative survey, the Revised Sociocultural Adaptation Scale (Wilson, 2013). This 41-item scale assesses student adaptation to culturally based activities and skills and provides a quantitative self-report of their level of culture shock.

Data analysis: Data from each method were analyzed separately in the first phase of analysis. The evaluator used the criteria developed by Guillemin and Westall (2008) (see following Guidance section for the specific criteria) to analyze the self-portraits as images. She derived themes from the image analysis and then integrated this analysis with data from the artistic statements accompanying the images. She used an interpretive-based approach to analyze the data in the student journals. She analyzed the quantitative data using descriptive statistics. She integrated the arts-based, qualitative, and quantitative data using a matrix of the major themes and their presence in the three data sources. She identified similarities, differences, and conflicting representations in the data sets.

Results: The analysis of the self-portraits revealed that the students expressed mixed emotions such as showing a happy face with tears coming down the cheeks. Their artistic statements explained that they wanted to appear happy because they were grateful for the opportunity, but they still wanted to show that they were feeling nervous, confused, angry, and frustrated. The quantitative data revealed that the students felt mild to moderate culture shock while abroad. The dialectical process resulted in the evaluator being able to identify sources of tension for the students such as entering the situation thinking their language skills were adequate (quantitative data) but finding out that they experienced challenges in communication (illustrated in their self-portraits and written about in their journals).

Benefits of using MM: The use of a mixed methods arts-based design uncovered aspects of the experience that would not have been accessible through words or numbers. Students had difficulties in their study abroad placements, and the use of arts-based methods helped them process these experiences psychologically and emotionally. The use of mixed methods allowed for a better understanding of the complexities of the experience and contributed to expanding frameworks for addressing culture shock.

Guidance for Designing a Mixed Methods Arts-Based Evaluation Study

1. Evaluators interested in integrating arts-based approaches in their mixed methods studies need to decide (perhaps in consultation with the stakeholders) the type of creative expression appropriate in a specific context. Simons and McCormack (2007) advocate for involvement with the stakeholders in decision making about the form of creative expression in a study because this strengthens the connection between the evaluation plan and the experience of the participants.

2. Be prepared to assure stakeholders that the quality of the creative expression is not of concern in the study, rather, the focus is on the person's willingness to express his or her feelings through an artistic medium.

3. Criteria are available for analyzing artistic expressions within the context of evaluation that are different from judging an art show. For example, the following are questions from Guillemin and Westall (2008, p. 125):

   • What is being shown? What are the components of the image? How are they arranged?

   • What relationships are established between the components of the image?

   • What use is made of color? What colors are used? What is the significance to the drawer of the colors used?

   • What do the different components of the image signify? What is being represented?

   • What knowledges are being deployed?

   • Whose knowledges are excluded from this representation?

4. When establishing the quality of the data and findings from artistic-based evaluations, consider using criteria that include the extent to which participant engagement deepens, the quality of evaluator-stakeholder interactions, contextual and political aspects of people's lives, and the ability to have civil discourse about difficult topics.

5. Consider creative ways of sharing findings that integrate the arts into the presentations, through community art shows, web-based postings, dramatic presentations, and concerts.

Extending Your Thinking

Mixed Methods Arts-Based Evaluation

1. You have been hired to evaluate a program to determine the effect of dance on survivors of cancer. Develop a mixed methods, arts-based evaluation for this context. Explain how you will integrate the artistic expression into the evaluation.

2. Find an arts-based therapy evaluation. Critically examine it to determine if the evaluation includes arts, quantitative, and qualitative dimensions. Propose improvements to the design to allow for the inclusion of the three dimensions.

MIXED METHODS DESIGNS IN CONFLICT ZONES AND VIOLENTLY DIVIDED SOCIETIES

The methodological implication for evaluations in conflict zones is clear: the need to ensure that the scope and tools of evaluation are able—indeed required—to probe, explore, and measure peace and conflict impacts beyond short-term, measurable outputs of an intervention. (Bush & Duggan, 2013, p. 13)

Evaluators who work in conflict zones and violently divided societies know that the challenges that come with conducting their work are compounded by the volatility, unpredictability, and risk inherent in such places. Yet they have a commitment to working toward peacebuilding and development and have given considerable thought to how to design evaluation studies that contribute to these goals. Mixed methods has a role to play in addressing the challenges because it can incorporate information about the context not just of an intervention but of the conflict itself; local, national, international, and geopolitical political policies and activities; and strategies to catalyze positive political and social change (Bush, Duggan, McCandless, & Abu-Nimer, 2013). Mixed methods can contribute to better evaluation in violent contexts because there is a need to consider how the violence or conflict influences the environment:

physical, historical, social, cultural, political, organizational—within which evaluation practice occurs, and the ways in which the very existence of violence (its presence, legacy, or potentiality) may influence how stakeholders engage (or not) with projects programmes, research or evaluations. This includes the consideration of how conflict affects prospects for communication, uptake and actual use of evaluations for social change. Our contention is that in settings affected by significant levels of militarised or non-militarised violence, context is much more than a landscape or backdrop. It is a fact that permeates and affects all aspects of an intervention. (p. 2)

Bush and Duggan (2013) recognize specific aspects of evaluation in conflict zones that would be aided by the inclusion of mixed methods in study design. These include the concern that reliance on one method might exclude key stakeholders who are already marginalized, thus leading to a misrepresentation of a program's impact. Lack of representation of stakeholders can also be exacerbated by limited time, insecurity, and inaccessible geography. Evaluators may be restricted by vested interests of governments, program staff, or funders to view only successful sites. Insistence by a client on a specific design—for example, randomized control trials—may delegitimize more contextual methods needed to understand the complexity of the situation. Problems such as these can occur in any evaluation context; however, evaluators in a conflict zone need to be aware of the acute risk of harm to themselves and their stakeholders, shifts in control of geographic territory, and potential increases in suspicion or distrust that require a quick change in design, evaluation approach, and data collection.

Maphosa (2013) conducted an evaluation in Burundi, a country that has a long history of conflict. The design of the study is reflective of the transformative and Indigenous paradigms because it engaged with the Indigenous community using traditionally acceptable practices and was aimed toward transformation into a more peaceful country.

Sample Study 6.8: Mixed Methods
Designs in Conflict Zone Evaluations

Mixed methods in conflict zones: Peacebuilding in Burundi (Maphosa, 2013).

Problem: Burundi has experienced more than a decade of violence that began in 1993. The society is struggling to recover from structural violence, mistrust and fear, oppression, trauma, and lack of resources. The Centre

Ubuntu (CU) in Burundi undertook an intervention to engage with community elders and local groups to support peacebuilding based on the Bantu
concept of **ubuntu** that incorporates the values of love, respect, reciprocity,
peacefulness, reconciliation, forgiveness, and God's vision of a shared purpose for mankind (Maphosa, 2009).

Evaluand: Peacebuilding initiative in rural Burundi undertaken by the CU in
Burundi. This program uses a bottom-up approach to develop narrative theater
in the words of community members to open up opportunities for discussion
about peace and forgiveness. It also uses radio broadcasts to disseminate messages about ubuntu values, forgiveness, and reconciliation. The CU engaged
in direct service operations by supporting the local construction of schools and
income-generating projects such as goat raising.

Design: Impact evaluation that used a sequential mixed methods design; it
began with a qualitatively dominant design rooted in Indigenous traditions
and transitioned to a quantitatively dominant design. The qualitative part of
the design included time to build the team by sharing their backgrounds with
each other and participating in three days of training in focus group facilitation; translation from English to Kirundi; community entry and recruitment of
participants; and issues relevant to the conflict context such as politics, security,
roads, transport, and financial resources. This fits in the Social Justice branch
of evaluation.

Sample: Three villages in rural Burundi were selected from the 17 in which
the CU had peacebuilding programs. The evaluators used the following
criteria: "(i) security of the research team; (ii) accessibility in terms of time,
money, and terrain; and (iii) the diversity of CU programming" (p. 94). An essential characteristic of participants was that they had experience with the violent
past in Burundi and the CU program. Purposive sampling was used to obtain
representation from groups such as former rebels, internally displaced persons,
demobilized soldiers, and widows. The total sample consisted of 66 adults:
30 females and 36 males.

Data collection: "Data were derived from both primary (focus group discussions, key informant in-depth interviews, and observation) and secondary
(library materials) sources" (p. 93). The qualitative data were quantitized for
statistical purposes. Entry into communities was facilitated by having local
assistants and because villagers had good relationships with the CU based
on their involvement in the program. The data collection began with phone
calls to village gatekeepers to explain the study, to obtain their permission to
conduct focus groups in their communities, and to build trust. Six focus groups
were held along with four key informant interviews.

Data analysis: The focus group transcripts were translated from Kirundi into
English for analysis. One of the evaluators collected quantitative data by
observing the focus groups and recorded the number of interactions for each
participant and the origins of ideas. The evaluation team used a narrative

(Continued)

(Continued)

data analysis strategy that included reading, coding, collaborative reflection, rereading, revision of coding, and quantitizing of qualitative data.

Results: Maphosa (2009) described the results of the peacebuilding initiative as "effective" in that teachers have an increased tolerance and charity toward learners. The students have also positively impacted adults through sharing about the peacebuilding. At the time of the study, the peacebuilding had not resulted in changes in education policy or the national curriculum. The evaluation also documented an increase in partnerships between community organizations, the CU, and multilateral organizations.

Benefits of using MM: Maphosa (2013) recognized the benefits of using mixed methods in that it afforded the opportunity to engage with all important stakeholders; this resulted in increased support for the peacebuilding and reconciliation process. It allowed for the assessment of the impact of the peacebuilding at individual and community levels. Quantitative and qualitative data were available about the process of the intervention as well as the outputs and outcomes. Mixed methods allowed for triangulation through the use of multiple data sources and methods. Bush and Duggan (2013) provide this statement on mixed methods benefits: "Conventional, linear approaches to evaluation are often insufficient in conflict zones. The introduction and growing practice of creative, flexible, and adaptive evaluation approaches rooted in systems and complexity thinking would help generate robust, useful findings" (p. 21).

Guidance for Designing a Mixed Methods Study in a Conflict Zone

The Organisation for Economic Co-operation and Development (OECD, 2012) Development Assistance Committee (DAC) published guidance on conducting evaluations for peacebuilding initiatives in conflict settings that explicitly acknowledges that "the complex nature of interventions in fragile and conflict-affected situations generally makes it necessary to combine different methodologies in order to answer the evaluation questions. Many favour a mixed-method approach, using both qualitative and quantitative methods and data" (pp. 49–50). Specific guidance from the OECD and Bush and Duggan (2013) includes the following:

1. A contextual analysis (or inception phase) is necessary at the beginning of the study to identify issues that need to be addressed prior to proceeding with the actual evaluation. This can include desk study, document review, and preliminary fieldwork.

Discussions based on the inception phase can contribute to improved evaluations because they can highlight the need for modifications in approaches needed to be responsive to the context.

2. Methodologically, evaluators in conflict zones need to be aware of unintended consequences, not simply intended outcomes. In such contexts, the unintended consequences can be severe and appear in the form of mass kidnappings, increased child sex work, or assassinations.

3. Be aware that baseline data may not be available because of risks of harm, lack of trust on the part of stakeholders to interact or provide data, censorship, or political oppression. Consider including questions about how conditions were prior to the intervention in the data collection. In these contexts, it is easy to exclude important voices because of displacement, internally or externally.

4. Randomized controlled trials may not be possible, but quasi-experimental designs may be useful if it is possible to find communities in conflict that have not experienced the intervention and are similar to the targeted community. However, this needs to be combined with a contextual analysis: "The evaluator must possess an intimate understanding of the two communities—particularly the local-level dynamics of conflict—in order to rule out the possibility that the variation in levels of violence was not the result of non-project-related factors (or another project)" (p. 14). Qualitative data can be very valuable in supporting an argument about the effects of an intervention.

5. Consider the use of proxy measures as indicators of outcomes, such as satellite imaging of land under cultivation or concept mapping to reveal changes in patterns of behaviors.

6. Inclusion of gender analysis is highly recommended in conflict zone evaluations because of the differential experiences of men and women in such contexts.

7. The OECD (2012) recommend the following mixed methods data collection strategies:

> Quantitative and qualitative data can be collected through censuses, observation, household surveys, interviews, questionnaires, anthropological or ethnographic research, participatory workshops and discussion groups. National statistics systems and major NGOs will often have available demographic data,

(Continued)

(Continued)

> though these may not be suited to the required sample size or detail. . . . To ensure reliability, evaluators should use multiple sources or types of information and a mix of sound quantitative and qualitative data. They should triangulate the data they use, ensure that sources are transparent, and verify the data's validity before analysing them—by fact checking with key stakeholders and interviewees, for example. By combining multiple data sources, evaluators can offset the bias that comes from relying on a single type of information and single observers. In the evaluation report's description of methods, any issues around data (including data gaps or problems with inconsistency) should be described along with the impact these data problems had on the reliability and validity of the evaluation's conclusions. (pp. 62, 64)

Extending Your Thinking

Mixed Methods Designs in Conflict Zones

1. You have been hired to conduct an evaluation of a peacebuilding program in South Asia. How would you start your process for developing an evaluation design? Sketch a mixed methods design that incorporates the advice given in this section on designing evaluations in conflict zones. How do you see this design as being different from what you would suggest for a nonconflict zone evaluation?

2. Find an evaluation conducted in a conflict zone. Read it critically. Did the evaluators use mixed methods? Is so, what design did they use? How did this add to the quality of the evaluation? If they did not use mixed methods, propose a mixed methods design that you think would add to the quality of the evaluation.

SUMMARY AND MOVING FORWARD

In this chapter, we examined variations in mixed methods designs for specific purposes and/or stakeholder groups. Needs assessments can be part of a larger study or they can be stand-alone. Therefore, evaluators can design a mixed methods study that only looks at needs or one that incorporates the needs assessment as part of a larger mixed methods design. Mixed methods in developmental evaluations focuses on an ongoing need for systematic data collection in a dynamic context— somewhat different from a defined period of time as is common in a funded project. The purpose is to provide real-time data for adjustments as needed in a learning organization. Mixed methods designs have also been developed for gender analysis, Indigenous settings, evaluations with people with disabilities and those who are Deaf, and evaluations in conflict zones to be responsive to cultural issues and power inequities. Finally, evaluators are showing increased interest in mixed methods designs for arts-based evaluations and those that use visual spatial analysis. These are areas of growth and challenge in the mixed methods community. This brings us to the next chapter in which we explore areas of growth and challenges for the mixed methods community along with identifying additional resources available to this community.

7

Trends, Challenges, and Advances in Mixed Methods Evaluation

In This Chapter

- Identifying trends and challenges for the future

- Improving evaluation theory and practice as illuminated by the multiple mixed methods frameworks used by evaluators

- Integration and dissemination in mixed methods evaluation

TRENDS AND CHALLENGES FOR THE FUTURE OF MIXED METHODS ●

These are exciting times for evaluators expanding their repertoires to include more sophisticated mixed methods designs. As noted in Chapter 1, we are in the early stages of what it means to use mixed methods in a systematic and critically conscious way. This is a time for creativity and divergence of thought, of consideration of possibilities that have not yet been established as standard practice, while at the same time being able to build on what is known about good practice from quantitative, qualitative, and mixed methodologists. So, what are the trends and challenges in mixed methods that have potential to improve evaluation theory and practice?

In this section, I build on the work of a task force of the Mixed Methods International Research Association to identify those trends and challenges over the next 5 years (Mertens et al., 2016). The issues that arose through that activity yielded these topics of interest: advances in philosophy and methodology, innovative designs, technological advancements and big data, preparation of mixed methods researchers, and responsiveness to complex social problems. These topics have relevance for mixed methods evaluators when they are looked at in the context of evaluation instead of research.

● PHILOSOPHY AND METHODOLOGY

As is evident through the multiple philosophical and theoretical frames described in this text, the evaluation world is in the midst of growing awareness of the importance of assumptions that guides its work and implications for methodological choices. Evaluators have many options in their philosophical orientations to guide thinking about mixed methods designs, including those that represent quantitatively dominated (Methods branch), qualitatively dominated (Values branch), pragmatically oriented (Use branch), transformative oriented (Social Justice branch), and designs that bring paradigms into conversation with each other (dialectical pluralism). As we move into the future, evaluators will find fertile ground in sharing their understandings of the meanings of the philosophical assumptions and how they inform their work, as well as through efforts to cross over between the branches (as is suggested in the water metaphor presented in Chapter 1).

What will it mean to bring evaluators who were trained in different branches together to engage in conversations about the influence of philosophical assumptions and their positive and limiting influences? What mechanisms are available and appropriate for sustaining conversations across branches in evaluation in respectful ways? What kinds of evaluation questions might emerge that would be different and more sophisticated than "Does it work?" or "Does it work better than another approach?" Will mixed methods designs developed from a deeper understanding of philosophical assumptions lead to improved methodologies that have increased potential to contribute to societal improvements? How will mixed methods designs from different evaluation branches inform understandings about context, the nature of the problems, the determination of appropriate solutions, and the use of evaluation for decision making?

INNOVATIVE DESIGNS •

As is also evident throughout this text, the concept of mixed methods designs for evaluations has expanded beyond the idea that a survey can include both open- and closed-ended items or that of having a survey and a focus group. The mixed methods designs in evaluation in this text illustrate the possibility for sophisticated evaluation designs capable of informing decision making throughout the life span of an initiative, whether that is a project, a program, a policy, or an organization. The mixed methods designs for program evaluation in many of the chapters are of a cyclical nature, meaning that early evaluation activities inform next steps in the program and in the evaluation. Such designs might call for a change of the culture of thinking about evaluation as something that happens at the end of a program, instead seeing it as a way to support ongoing learning and innovation.

Advancements in design research (Philip & De Bruyn, 2013) and developmental evaluation (Patton, 2011) provide a glimpse into how mixed methods designs can be developed that are responsive to changing conditions in a context or organization. Mixed methods designs have the potential to be responsive in a dynamic way that is reflective of the complexity found in most evaluation contexts. When design research principles and complexity theory are brought into mixed methods designs, it opens up possibilities for informing the understanding of the context as it changes and applying those understandings to needed adjustments in terms of interventions, implementation strategies, and revisions of these same elements. Challenges arise related to how to integrate improved understandings about the evaluation process and findings from earlier stages of an evaluation into later stages and how to use this process to influence decision and policy making. How will the value of using more sophisticated designs be established with funders due to these requiring more time and resources? What arguments will be persuasive to funders that mixed methods designs have greater potential to address complex problems and deliver solutions that have greater potential to be effective? What will be gained and/or lost by using more creative cyclical mixed methods designs for evaluators and their stakeholders?

TECHNOLOGICAL ADVANCES AND BIG DATA •

If there is one thing we can say for certain, it is that the use of technology in the field of evaluation is ubiquitous and dynamic. The implications of technology in the design of mixed methods studies is mind-boggling. Technology comes in so many forms and can be applied in so many ways. Mixed methods designs in evaluation can include data collection strategies that are technologically based, such as video capture, audio capture, web-based data collection, blogs, tweets, and so forth. How can evaluators integrate technological advancements into mixed methods designs in ways that are productive and ethical? This question comes to the fore especially when consideration is given to integrating the use of data collected through and made available through technology that was not necessarily collected for the specific evaluation.

Such data can take the form of "big data" that is receiving so much attention (Hesse, Moser, & Riley, 2015). **Big data** is a term used to describe data that are extremely large in volume, come in a variety of forms (structured, unstructured, narrative, numeric), and come from multiple sources (e.g., health surveys, social media, real-time wearable devices such as Fitbits, electronic record keeping, and other government and nongovernment databases). Big data might allow for access to data on an entire population, rather than a selected sample. How will mixed methods designs be changed if there is access to this level of data? What questions need to be explored related to the quality of the data, the merger of data across data sets, and ethical and confidentiality issues?

Data that is not big data can also be collected via technology, sometimes incidentally, sometimes purposefully. With mobile phones equipped with cameras, data can be captured surreptitiously (or serendipitously). What are the ethical implications of including such data in evaluations? How can evaluators maximize the use of technology in appropriate and ethical ways to enhance mixed methods designs by administering surveys online or in real time, using mapping applications, or using social networking applications? How can technology be used to increase the use of visual and spatial data collection and presentation of findings? How can it be used to engage with a wider range of stakeholders? What are the implications of these issues for mixed methods design?

● PREPARATION OF MIXED METHODS EVALUATORS

When I was in graduate school, my professors taught me quantitative methods of evaluation design because that was their expertise. As I moved into the world of evaluation, I realized that I was only getting part of the story with quantitative methods, and so I engaged in extensive professional development activities to add qualitative methods to my repertoire. Like many evaluators, I intuitively came to the conclusion that evaluations in complex social contexts benefited by using both quantitative and qualitative approaches. As I tried to figure out how to bring the different perspectives about methods together, I was fortunate to be in the right places at the right times to witness and participate in the birth and early growth of the mixed methods community. I tell you this story because my experience is not unlike many of those who are preparing evaluators in universities and other professional development settings. Evaluation is a multidisciplinary profession, and hence evaluators come with a legacy of the methodologies dominant in their disciplines.

According to Scriven (2008), a **transdiscipline** is a discipline that can stand alone but can also be used as a tool in several other disciplines. Evaluators might gain insights into how to integrate methods by considering evaluation as a transdiscipline. Scriven (2008) used this term to describe evaluation because it is not only a discipline unto itself, it is also used in so many other disciplines. Evaluation shares this transdisciplinary nature with other disciplines such as ethics and statistics; each has a unique way of approaching issues but is also used in other areas of inquiry such as education, health, criminal justice, social work, and economic development.

Coryn and Hattie (2006) suggest that consideration of evaluation as a transdiscipline can serve as a model for the preparation of evaluators. Jacob (2008) strengthens the argument for transdiscipline training for evaluators because of the increased acknowledgment of complexity in the evaluation of social phenomena and public programs and policies. Training alone may not be sufficient to address this challenge; it may be necessary to rethink the composition of evaluation teams to be more transdisciplinary. A parallel strand of action about preparing evaluators arises from the attention being given to defining competencies for evaluators and the process of credentialing evaluators (King & Stevahn, 2015). Whereas it is beyond the scope of this text to examine those competencies and processes, considerable activity has been and is occurring on this front, including the specification of Essential Skills Series by the Canadian Evaluation Society (2017) in 1999, followed by a voluntary credentialing process in 2003, as well as the creation of competency statements in South Africa, Aotearoa New Zealand, Japan, and Thailand. The American Evaluation Association is also taking action on this front. How will the awareness of the importance of mixed methods in evaluation influence discussions about competencies? This is a question that I do not have an answer for, but I suggest it is an important question for the evaluation community to consider.

This brief contextual analysis of the preparation of evaluators serves to highlight the challenges present in the evaluation world. What are the best ways to prepare faculty who can teach about mixed methods, new evaluators, and practicing professionals? What are the strategies that support a transdisciplinary approach to mixed methods design in evaluation? What can be done to facilitate respectful and productive conversations across disciplines to enhance mixed methods designs in evaluation? How can course sequences be developed that lead to an understanding of how to include the methodological rigor developed within specific branches of evaluation with an integrated approach to yield mixed methods designs? What should be included in undergraduate, graduate, and professional training in methods to support development of mixed methods skills?

● RESPONSIVENESS TO COMPLEX SOCIAL PROBLEMS

Many of the evaluation examples in this text serve to illustrate the application of complex mixed methods designs to address wicked problems such as poverty, violence, and climate change. Mixed methods designs in evaluation provide a sophisticated and creative means for the evaluation community to contribute to the solutions to what have heretofore been considered intransigent conditions that impact people's lives and the health of the planet. This characterization of the role of the evaluator in these terms is not without controversy. Evaluators who situate themselves on one or another of the evaluation branches (or currents) might reject or endorse this role depending on their philosophical assumptions. Should the evaluator be engaged in strategies designed to support social and environmental transformation? What are the methodological implications of explicitly addressing issues of human rights, power inequities, and oppression? What are the ethical issues of adopting (or not adopting) such a stance, and how will this be viewed by ethics review boards?

The use of mixed methods designs can lead to asking different kinds of questions reflective of the systemic structures that allow for an oppressive status quo to continue or to stimulate the kind of systemic change needed to transform society. According to *The Program Evaluation*

Standards: A Guide for Evaluators and Evaluation Users, evaluators have a professional responsibility to ensure the rigor of their work and the usefulness of their processes and results (Yarbrough, Shulha, Hopson, & Caruthers, 2011). The American Evaluation Association's (AEA; 2004) *Guiding Principles for Evaluators* reinforces the importance of the need for rigorous evaluations conducted in a culturally competent manner with inclusion of stakeholders on the basis of race/ethnicity, sex/ gender, economics, and other relevant factors. Mixed methods designs allow evaluators the flexibility they need to be inclusive in culturally responsive ways by modifying approaches to support the appropriate needs of diverse stakeholder groups. AEA's guidelines also instruct evaluators to work for the general and public welfare, meaning they are to go beyond the interests of any particular stakeholder to con- sider the welfare of society as a whole. Mixed methods designs pro- vide the needed sophistication to include not only diverse stakeholders but also phases of data collection about context, history, legacy, legis- lations, and other conditions that can influence the effectiveness of interventions.

INTEGRATION AND DISSEMINATION IN MIXED METHODS EVALUATION

Mixed methods designs also bring the possibility of creative avenues for sharing and disseminating findings from evaluations by building in dissemination as part of the design process. Evaluators can find advice about how to publish in mixed methods journals (Archibald et al., 2015; Fetters & Freshwater, 2015; Mertens, 2011; O'Cathain, Murphy, & Nicholl, 2007). It is important to share our methodological advances. Evaluators can provide leadership by publishing their work in evalu- ation journals and in mixed methods journals, as well as in method- ological journals and discipline-specific journals that might have traditionally only published quantitative or qualitative studies.

The power of mixed methods lies in the added value of having both quantitative and qualitative data and the insights that can be gained when these data are integrated in a single study or a series of studies. When multiphased, cyclical mixed methods designs are used; these present opportunities to integrate the data at several points dur- ing the evaluation. Strategies for integration and dissemination can be changed to be responsive to the phase of the evaluation as well as to the stakeholder's needs. As seen in the examples in this text, mixed methods designs have included multiple strategies for integration and dissemination of findings such as use of focus groups, web-based presentations, visual spatial depictions, and videos. Use of such methods built into the design of the evaluation allows for greater engagement with a wider range of stakeholders and has the potential to increase the usefulness of the findings at each stage of the evaluations.

● CONCLUSIONS AND MOVING FORWARD

Evaluators interested in exploring designs that are innovative and responsive to the complexity in their evaluation contexts are standing on fertile ground. A journey into the critically conscious development of mixed methods designs has begun, and it offers a myriad of opportunities to increase the impact that evaluation can have on important societal and environmental problems and solutions. The complexity involved in understanding contexts and cultures is enhanced by the use of mixed methods designs that focus on collection of data about history and diversity. Much remains to be done; the members of the evaluation community who are willing to take risks and share their experiences can lead to changes of great importance for the current population as well as for generations to come.

Appendix

Key Resources for Additional Examples and Insights Into Mixed Methods Design in Evaluation

- Mixed Methods International Research Association is an international organization working to advance mixed methods; it contains resources about mixed methods and sponsors a biannual conference (www.mmira.org).

- National Institutes of Health: Best Practices for Mixed Methods Research in the Health Sciences (https://obssr.od.nih.gov/training/mixed-methods-research). At this site, two items may be of particular interest: a mixed methods checklist and a section on review criteria for mixed methods proposals.

- World Health Organization guidance for conducting health research involving Indigenous people (http://www.who.int/ethics/indigenous_peoples/en/index6.html).

- UNICEF and UN Women's evaluation portal provides examples of over 400 evaluations using a gender equity lens (http://genderevaluation.unwomen.org).

- National Congress of American Indians provides resources for researchers working in Native communities (http://genetics.ncai.org/tips-for-researchers.cfm).

- Abdul Latif Jameel Poverty Action Lab, affiliated with the Massachusetts Institute of Technology, has a website through which you can locate more than 800 international evaluations (https://www.povertyactionlab.org/evaluations).

- The Department for International Development (DFID) in the United Kingdom (https://www.gov.uk/government/organisations/department-for-international-development), the Swedish International

Development Agency (http://www.sida.se/English), the Danish International Development Agency (http://um.dk/en/danida-en), and the Norwegian Agency for Development Cooperation (https://www.norad.no/en/front) websites can be searched for examples of mixed methods evaluations.

- Evidence for Policy and Practice Information and Co-ordination Centre (EPPI-Centre): This center is funded by the UK Department for Education and Employment to support evaluators who wish to use systematic reviews in the field of education (https://eppi.ioe .ac.uk/cms).

- University of York Centre for Reviews and Dissemination (http:// www.york.ac.uk/crd/publications).

- The Organisation for Economic Co-operation and Development (OECD) Development Assistance Committee (DAC), *Evaluating Peacebuilding Activities in Settings of Conflict and Fragility* (http://www .oecd-ilibrary.org/development/evaluating-donor-engagement-in-situations-of-conflict-and-fragility_9789264106802-en); the Learning Portal for Design, Monitoring and Evaluation for Peacebuilding (http://dmeforpeace.org); and Alliance for Peacebuilding (http:// www.allianceforpeacebuilding.org/?page).

- The U.S. International Council on Disabilities (USICD) maintains a website that contains examples of evaluations with people with disabilities that can be searched for examples of mixed methods designs (http://www.usicd.org/template/index.cfm).

- American Evaluation Association (www.eval.org) has a library with many resources in the form of guidance and examples of evaluations.

References

Ackerly, B. (2012). *Breakthrough evaluation: An external rights-based evaluation of grantmaking for gender equality.* Amsterdam: Netherlands Ministry of Foreign Affairs.

Alkin, M. (2013). *Evaluation roots* (2nd ed.). Thousand Oaks, CA: Sage.

American Evaluation Association. (2004). *Guiding principles for evaluators.* Washington, DC: Author.

American Evaluation Association. (2013). *An evaluation roadmap for a more effective government.* Washington, DC: Author.

Archibald, M. M., Radil, A. I., Zhang, X., & Hanson, W. E. (2015). Current mixed methods practices in qualitative research: A content analysis of leading journals. *International Journal of Qualitative Methods, 14*(2), 6–33.

Bamberger, M., Tarsilla, M., & Hesse-Biber, S. (2016). Why so many "rigorous" evaluations fail to identify unintended consequences of development programs: How mixed methods can contribute. *Evaluation and Program Planning, 55,* 155–162.

Bamberger, M., Vaessen, J., & Raimondo, E. (Eds.). (2016). *Dealing with complexity in development evaluation.* Thousand Oaks, CA: Sage.

Basu, K. (2013). *The method of randomization, economic policy, and reasoned intuition.* Washington, DC: World Bank.

Beletsky, L., Wagner, K. D., Arredondo, J., Palinkas, L., Rodriguez, C. M., Kalic, N., et al. (2015). Implementing Mexico's "Narcomenudeo" drug law reform: A mixed methods assessment of early experiences among people who inject drugs. *Journal of Mixed Methods Research, 10*(4), 1–18.

Boaz, A., Ashby, D., & Young, K. (2002). *Systematic reviews: What have they got to offer evidence based policy and practice?* Working Paper 2. London: ESRC UK Centre for Evidence Based Policy and Practice.

Bowman, N. R., & Francis, C. D. (2015). Culturally responsive Indigenous evaluation. In S. Hood, R. Hopson, H. Frierson, & K. Obeidat (Eds.), *Continuing the journey to reposition culture and cultural context in evaluation theory and practice* (pp. 335–359). Charlotte, NC: Information Age.

Brisolara, S. (2014). Feminist theory: Its domains and application. In S. Brisolara, D. Seigart, & S. SenGupta (Eds.), *Feminist evaluation and research* (pp. 3–41). New York, NY: Guilford Press.

Bush, K., & Duggan, C. (2013). Evaluation in conflict zones: Methodological and ethical challenges. *Journal of Peacebuilding & Development, 8*(2), 5–25. doi:10.1080/15423166.2013.812891

Bush, K., Duggan, C., McCandless, E., & Abu-Nimer, M. (2013). Evaluation in violently divided societies: Politics, ethics and methods. *Journal of Peacebuilding & Development, 8*(2), 1–4. doi:10.1080/15423166.2013.825403

Camillus, J. C. (2008). Strategy as a wicked problem. *Harvard Business Review, 86,* 98–101.

Campbell, D. T., & Fiske, D. W. (1959). Convergent and discriminant validation by the multitrait-multimethod matrix. *Psychological Bulletin, 56,* 81–105.

Canadian Evaluation Society. (2017). *Essential skills.* Retrieved from http://evaluationcanada.ca/essential-skills-series-evaluation.

Caracelli, V. J., & Cooksy, L. J. (2013). Incorporating qualitative evidence in systematic reviews: Strategies and challenges. In D. M. Mertens & S. Hess-Biber (Eds.), *Mixed methods and credibility of evidence in evaluation. New Directions for Evaluation, 138,* 97–108.

Catallo, C., Jack, S. M., Ciliska, D., & MacMillan, H. L. (2013). Mixing a grounded theory approach with a randomized controlled trial related to intimate partner violence: What challenges arise for mixed methods research? *Nursing Research and Practice.* Article ID 798213, 1–12. doi:10.1155/2013/798213

Centre for Reviews and Dissemination. (2009). *Systematic reviews.* York, UK: York Publishing Services, University of York.

Charmatz, K. (2014). *Constructing grounded theory.* Thousand Oaks, CA: Sage.

Chilisa, B. (2012). *Indigenous research methodologies.* Thousand Oaks, CA: Sage.

Christie, C. A., & Alkin, M. C. (2013). An evaluation theory tree. In M. C. Akin & C. A. Christie (Eds.), *Evaluation roots* (2nd ed., pp. 11–57). Thousand Oaks, CA: Sage.

Clarke, A., Friede, T., Putz, R., Ashdown, J., Martin, S., Blake, A., et al. (2011). Warwick-Edinburgh Mental Well-being Scale (WEMWBS): Validated for teenage school students in England and Scotland. A mixed methods assessment. *BMC Public Health, 11*(487), 1–9.

Corbin, J., & Strauss, A. (2008). *Basics of qualitative research* (3rd ed.). Thousand Oaks, CA: Sage.

Coryn, C. L. S., & Hattie, J. A. (2006). The transdisciplinary model of evaluation. *Journal of Multidisciplinary Evaluation, 4,* 107–114.

Cousins, J. B., & Whitmore, E. (1998). Framing participatory evaluation. *New Directions for Evaluation, 1998*(80), 5–23.

Cram, F. (2009). Maintaining indigenous voices. In D. Mertens & P. Ginsberg (Eds.), *SAGE handbook of social science research ethics* (pp. 308–322). Thousand Oaks, CA: Sage.

Cram, F. (2016). Lessons on decolonizing evaluation from Kaupapa Māori evaluation. *Canadian Journal of Program Evaluation, 30.3* (Special Issue), 296–312.

Cram, F. (in press). Kaupapa Maori health research. In P. Liamputtong (Ed.), *Handbook of research methods in health and social sciences.* Basel, Switzerland: Springer International.

Cram, F., & Mertens, D. M. (2015). Transformative and indigenous frameworks for multimethod and mixed methods research. In S. Hesse-Biber & B. Johnson (Eds.), *The Oxford handbook of multimethods and mixed methods research inquiry* (pp. 91–110). New York, NY: Oxford University Press.

Cram, F., & Phillips, H. (2012). Reclaiming a culturally safe place for Māori researchers within multi-cultural, transdisciplinary research groups. *International Journal of Critical Indigenous Studies, 5*(2), 36–49.

Cram, F., Sauni, P., Kennedy, V., Field, A., McKegg, A., & Pipi-Takoko, M. (2015). *InZone Project evaluation: Evaluation report.* Auckland, New Zealand: Centre for Social Impact.

Crede, I., & Borrego, M. (2013). From ethnography to items: A mixed methods approach to developing a survey to examine graduate engineering student retention. *Journal of Mixed Methods Research, 7*(1), 62–80.

Creswell, J. W., Klassen, A. C., Plano Clark, V. L., & Smith, K. C. (2011). *Best practices for mixed methods research in the health sciences.* Retrieved from https://obssr.od.nih.gov/training/mixed-methods-research.

Creswell, J. W., & Plano Clark, V. L. (2007). *Designing and conducting mixed methods research.* Thousand Oaks, CA: Sage.

Daigneault, P. M., & Jacob, S. (2014). Unexpected but most welcome: Mixed methods for the validation and revision of the participatory evaluation instrument. *Journal of Mixed Methods Research, 8*(1), 6–24.

David, S. L., Hitchcock, J. H., Ragan, B., Brooks, G., & Starkey, C. (2016). Mixing interviews and Rasch modeling: Demonstrating a procedure used to develop an instrument that measures trust. *Journal of Mixed Methods Research,* 1–20. doi:10.1177/1558689815624586

De-la-Cueva-Ariza, L., Romero-Garcia, M., Delgado-Hito, P., Acosta-Mejuto, B., Jover-Sancho, C., Ricart-Basagana, M. T., et al. (2014). Development of an instrument to measure the degree of critical patient's satisfaction with nursing care: Research protocol. *Journal of Advanced Nursing, 70*(1), 201–210.

Denscombe, M. (2008). Communities of practice: A research paradigm for the mixed methods approach. *Journal of Mixed Methods Research, 2*(3), 270–283.

Denzin, N. (2012). Triangulation 2.0. *Journal of Mixed Methods Research, 6*(2), 80–88.

Dewey, J. (1920). *Reconstruction in philosophy.* New York, NY: Henry Holt.

Dewey, J. (1938). *Logic: The theory of inquiry.* New York, NY: Henry Holt.

Dobbins, M., Hanna, S. E., Ciliska, D., Manske, S., Cameron, R., Mercer, S. L., et al. (2009). A randomized controlled trial evaluating the impact of knowledge translation and exchange strategies. *Implementation Science, 4*(61).

Du Bois, W. E. B. (1899). *The Philadelphia Negro.* Philadelphia: University of Pennsylvania Press.

Dures, E., Morris, M., Gleeson, K., & Rumsey, N. (2010). "You're whatever the patient needs at the time": The impact on health and social caregiving professional of support in people with epidermolysis bullosa. *Chronic Illness, 6*(3), 215–227.

Edwards, D., Noyes, J., Lowes, L., Spencer, L. H., & Gregory, J. W. (2014). An ongoing struggle: A mixed-methods systematic review of interventions, barriers and facilitators to achieving optimal self-care by children and young people with Type 1 Diabetes in educational settings. *BMC Pediatrics, 14,* 1–27.

Everson-Hock, E. S., Johnson, M., Jones, R., Woods, H. B., Goyder, E., Payne, N., & Chilcott, J. (2013). Community-based dietary and physical activity interventions in low socioeconomic groups in the UK: A mixed methods systematic review. *Preventive Medicine, 56,* 265–272.

Fetters, M., & Freshwater, D. (2015). Publishing a methodological mixed methods research article. *Journal of Mixed Methods Research, 9*(3), 203–213.

Fielding, N., & Cisneros-Puebla, C. A. (2009). CAQDAS-GIS convergence. *Journal of Mixed Methods Research, 3*(4), 349–370.

Frechtling, J., & Sharp, L. (Eds.). (1997). *User-friendly handbook for mixed method evaluations.* Arlington, VA: National Science Foundation.

Giddings, L. S. (2006). Mixed methods research: Positivism dressed in drag? *Journal of Research in Nursing, 11*(3), 195–203.

Gomez, A. (2014). New developments in mixed methods with vulnerable groups. *Journal of Mixed Methods Research, 8*(3), 317–320.

Gothberg, J. (2015, April). *Unintentionally excluded: How universal design for evaluation (UDE) can improve participation of marginalized groups.* Presentation at the meeting of the Center for Culturally Responsive Evaluation and Assessment, Chicago, IL.

Gough, D., Oliver, S., & Thomas, J. (2012). *An introduction to systematic reviews.* London: Sage.

Greene, J. (2007). *Mixed methods in social inquiry.* San Francisco, CA: Jossey Bass.

Greene, J., & Caracelli, V. (1997). Advances in mixed methods evaluation. *New Directions in Evaluation, 74,* San Francisco, CA: Jossey-Bass.

Greene, J. C., & Hall, J. N. (2010). Dialectics and pragmatism: Being of consequence. In A. Tashakkori & C. Teddlie (Eds.), *SAGE handbook of mixed methods in social and behavioral research* (2nd ed., pp. 119–143). Thousand Oaks, CA: Sage.

Guba, E., & Lincoln, Y. S. (1989). *Fourth generation evaluation.* Newbury Park, CA: Sage.

Guba, E., & Lincoln, Y. S. (2005). Paradigmatic controversies, contradictions, and emerging confluences. In N. Denzin & Y. S. Lincoln (Eds.), *SAGE handbook of qualitative research* (pp. 191–216). Thousand Oaks, CA: Sage.

Guillemin, M., & Westall, C. (2008). Gaining insight into women's knowing of postnatal depression using drawings. In P. Liamputtong & J. Rumbold (Eds.), *Knowing differently: Arts-based and collaborative research* (pp. 121–139). New York, NY: Nova Science.

Hall, B., & Howard, K. (2008). A synergistic approach: Conducting mixed methods research with typological and systemic design considerations. *Journal of Mixed Methods Research, 2*(3), 248–269.

Hall, J. N. (2013). Pragmatism, evidence, and mixed methods evaluation. In D. M. Mertens & S. Hesse-Biber (Eds.), *Mixed methods and credibility of evidence in evaluation. New Directions for Evaluation, 138,* 15–26.

Han, C. S., & Oliffe, J. L. (2016). Photovoice in mental illness research: A review and recommendations. *Health, 20*(2), 110–126.

Hargreaves, M. B., Honeycutt, T., Orfield, C., Vine, M., Cabili, C., Morzuch, M., et al. (2013). The Healthy Weight Collaborative: Using learning collaboratives to enhance community-based prevention initiatives addressing childhood obesity. *Journal of Health Care for the Poor and Underserved, 24,* 103–115.

Hesse, B. W., Moser, R. P., & Riley, W. T. (2015). From big data to knowledge in the social sciences. *Annals of the American Academy of Political and Social Science, 659*(1), 16–32.

Hesse-Biber, S. (2010). *Mixed methods research.* New York, NY: Guilford Press.

Hesse-Biber, S. (2013). Thinking outside the randomized controlled trials experimental box: Strategies for enhancing credibility and social justice. In D. M. Mertens & S. Hesse-Biber (Eds.), *New directions for evaluation, 138,* 49–60.

Hesse-Biber, S., & Johnson, B. (Eds.). (2015). *The Oxford handbook of multimethods and mixed methods research inquiry.* London, UK: Oxford University Press.

Hoddinott, P., Britten, J., & Pill, R. (2010). Why do interventions work in some places and not in others: A breastfeeding support group trial. *Social Science & Medicine, 70,* 769–778.

Howell, K. E. (2013). *An introduction to the philosophy of methodology.* Thousand Oaks, CA: Sage.

Hunt, G., Moloney, M., & Fazio, A. (2011). Embarking on large-scale qualitative research: Reaping the benefits of mixed methods in studying youth, clubs and drugs. *Nordic Studies on Alcohol and Drugs, 28,* 433–452.

Improve Group. (2013). *Minnesota Community Services Input Study.* Minneapolis: Minnesota Department of Human Services.

Institute of Medicine of the National Academies. (2014). *Evaluation design for complex global initiatives.* Washington, DC: The National Academies Press.

Iregbu, C. (2008). *Lead paint disclosure policy: Implications for eliminating childhood lead exposure in Baltimore City.* Dissertation. Walden University, College of Health Sciences. UMI Microform 3307541.

Jacklin, K., & Kinoshameg, P. (2008). Developing a participatory aboriginal health research project: "Only if it's going to mean something." *Journal of Empirical Research on Human Research Ethics, 3*(2), 53–67. doi:10.1525/jer.2008.3.2.53

Jacob, S. (2008). Cross-disciplinarization: A new talisman for evaluation? *American Journal of Evaluation, 29*(2), 175–194.

Jaskiewicz, L., Block, D., & Chavez, N. (2016). Finding food deserts: A comparison of methods measuring spatial access to food stores. *Health Promotion Practice, 17*(3), 400–407.

Jenson, R. (2015, April). *Unspoken voices: Supporting participation in evaluation with trauma-informed practice.* Presentation at the meeting of the Center for Culturally Responsive Evaluation and Assessment, Chicago, IL.

Johnson, R. B. (2012). Guest editor's editorial: Dialectical pluralism and mixed research. *American Behavioral Scientist, 56,* 751–754.

Johnson, R. B. (2015). Dialectical pluralism: A metaparadigm whose time has come. *Journal of Mixed Methods Research,* 1–18. doi:10.1177/1558689815607692

Johnson, R. B., & Onwuegbuzie, A. J. (2004). Mixed methods research: A research paradigm whose time has come. *Educational Researcher, 33*(7), 14–26. doi:10.3102/0013189X033007014

Johnson, R. B., Onwuegbuzie, A., & Turner, L. A. (2007). Toward a definition of mixed methods research. *Journal of Mixed Methods Research, 1*(2), 112–133.

Johnson, R. B., & Schoonenboom, J. (2015). Adding qualitative and mixed methods research to health intervention studies: Interacting with differences. *Qualitative Health Research,* 1–16. doi:10.1177/1049732315617479

Johnson, R. B., & Stefurak, T. (2013). Considering the evidence-and-credibility discussion in evaluation through the lens of dialectical pluralism. In D. M. Mertens & S. Hesse-Biber (Eds.), *Mixed methods and credibility of evidence in evaluation. New directions in evaluation, 138,* 37–48.

Jones, H. E., Kirtadze, I., Otiashvili, D., O'Grady, K. E., Murphy, K., Zule, W., et al. (2014). Process and product in cross-cultural treatment research: Development of a culturally sensitive women-centered substance use intervention in Georgia. *Journal of Addiction, 2014,* 1–12. doi:10.1155/2014/163603

Kelly, K. (2015). Evaluation of the influence of research on policy and practice in a post-conflict society: HIV/AIDS research in South Africa. In K. Bush & C. Duggan (Eds.), *Evaluation in the extreme* (pp. 189–212). Thousand Oaks, CA: Sage.

King, J. A., & Stevahn, L. (2015). Competencies for program evaluators in light of adaptive action: What? So what? Now what? In J. W. Altschuld & M. Engle (Eds.), *Accreditation, certification, and credentialing: Relevant concerns for U.S. evaluators. New Directions for Evaluation, 145,* 21–37.

Knigge, L., & Cope, M. (2006). Grounded visualization: Integrating the analysis of qualitative and quantitative data through grounded theory and visualization. *Environment and Planning, 38,* 2021–2037.

Kohler, P. D., Gothberg, J., & Coyle, J. L. (2012). *Evaluation toolkit* (2nd ed.) Kalamazoo: Western Michigan University, National Secondary Transition Technical Assistance Center.

Koskey, K. L. K., Sondergeld, T. A., Stewart, V. C., & Pugh, K. J. (2016). Applying mixed methods instrument development and construct validation process: The Transformative Experience Questionnaire. *Journal of Mixed Methods Research,* 1–28. doi:10.1177/1558689816633310

Kuehne, A., Huschke, S., & Bullinger, M. (2015). Subjective health of undocumented migrants in Germany. *BMC Public Health, 5,* 926–938.

Kuhn, T. (1962). *The structure of scientific revolutions.* Chicago, IL: University of Chicago Press.

Le Play, F. (1855). *European workers*. Tours, France: Alfred Mame.

Levin, K., Cashore, B., Bernstein, S., & Auld, G. (2012). Overcoming the tragedy of super wicked problems: Constraining our future selves to ameliorate global climate change. *Policy Sciences, 45,* 123–152. doi:10.1007/s11077-012-9151-0

Lincoln, Y. S., & Guba, E. G. (1985). *Naturalistic inquiry*. Beverly Hills, CA: Sage.

Longwe, S. (1995). Supporting women's development in the third world: Distinguishing between intervention and interference. In *Gender and Development, 3*(1). Oxford, UK: Oxfam.

Maphosa, S. B. (2009). Building peace from below: The Centre Ubuntu in Burundi. *African Peace and Conflict Journal, 2*(2), 58–71.

Maphosa, S. B. (2013). Thinking creatively about methodological issues in conflict-affected societies: A primer from the field. *Journal of Peacebuilding & Development, 8*(2), 91–104. doi:10.1080/15423166.2013.823058

March, C., Smyth, I., & Mukhopadhyay, M. (1999). A guide to gender-analysis frameworks. Oxford, UK: Oxfam.

Marra, M. (2015). Cooperating for a more egalitarian society: Complexity theory to evaluate gender equity. *Evaluation, 21*(1), 32–46.

Mathison, S. (2014). Research and evaluation: Intersections and divergence. In S. Brisolera, D. Seigart, & S. SenGupta (Eds.), *Feminist evaluation and practice* (pp. 42–58). New York, NY: Guilford Press.

Maxcy, S. J. (2003). Pragmatic threads in mixed methods research in the social sciences: The search for multiple modes of inquiry and the end of the philosophy of formalism. In A. Tashakkori & C. Teddlie (Eds.), *Handbook of mixed methods in social & behavioral research* (pp. 51–89). Thousand Oaks, CA: Sage.

Maxwell, J. A. (2012). The importance of qualitative research for causal explanation in education. *Qualitative Inquiry, 18*(8), 655–661.

Maxwell, J. A. (2015). Expanding the history and range of mixed methods research. *Journal of Mixed Methods Research,* 1–16. doi:10.1177/1558689815571132

Merriam, S. B., & Tisdell, E. J. (2016). *Qualitative research* (4th ed.). Thousand Oaks, CA: Sage.

Mertens, D. M. (2011). Publishing mixed methods research. *Journal of Mixed Methods Research, 5*(1), 3–6. doi:10.1177/1558689810390217

Mertens, D. M. (2015a). Mixed methods and wicked problems. *Journal of Mixed Methods Research, 9*(1), 3–6.

Mertens, D. M. (2015b). *Research methods in education and psychology: Integrating diversity with quantitative, qualitative, and mixed methods* (4th ed.). Thousand Oaks, CA: Sage.

Mertens, D. M., Bazeley, P., Bowleg, L., Fielding, N., Maxwell, J., Molina-Azorin, J. F., & Niglas, K. (2016). Expanding thinking through a kaleidoscopic look into the future: Implications of the Mixed Methods International Research Association's Task Force Report on the Future of Mixed Methods. *Journal of Mixed Methods Research, 10*(3), 221–227.

Mertens, D. M., Fraser, J., & Heimlich, J. E. (2008). M or F? Gender, identity, and the transformative paradigm. *Museums & Social Issues, 3*(1), 93–106.

Mertens, D. M., & Hesse-Biber, S. (Eds.). (2013). Mixed methods and credibility of evidence in evaluation. *New Directions in Evaluation, 138.*

Mertens, D. M., & Tarsilla, M. (2015). Mixed methods evaluation. In S. Hesse-Biber & B. Johnson (Eds.), *The Oxford handbook of multimethod and mixed methods research inquiry* (pp. 426–446). Oxford, UK: Oxford University Press.

Mertens, D. M., & Wilson, A. T. (2012). *Program evaluation theory and practice: A comprehensive guide.* New York, NY: Guilford Press.

Midgley, N., Ansaldo, F., & Target, M. (2014). The meaningful assessment of therapy outcomes: Incorporating a qualitative study into a randomized controlled trial evaluating the treatment of adolescent depression. *Psychotherapy, 51*(1), 128–137.

Morgan, D. L. (2007). Paradigms lost and pragmatism regained. *Journal of Mixed Methods Research, 1*(1), 48–76.

Morse, J. (1999). The armchair walkthrough [Editorial]. *Qualitative Health Research, 9*(4), 435–436.

Moser, C. (2005). An introduction to gender audit methodology: Its design and implementation in DFID Malawi. London, UK: Overseas Development Institute. Retrieved from http://www.odi.org.uk/PPPG/publications/ papers_reports/ODI_Moser_gender_audit_methodology.pdf? itemprcd= gender.

National Institute for Health and Excellence. (2009). *Annual report 2008/2009.* London, UK: Author.

National Oceanic and Atmospheric Administration. (2015). *Currents: The Global Conveyor Belt.* Retrieved from http://oceanservice.noaa.gov/education/ kits/currents/06conveyor2.html.

Noyes, J. (2010). Never mind the qualitative, feel the depth! The evolving role of qualitative research in Cochrane intervention reviews. *Journal of Research in Nursing, 15*(6), 525–534.

Noyes, J., & Lewin, S. (2011). Extracting qualitative evidence. In J. Noyes, K. Hannes, A. Booth, J. Harris, A. Harden, J. Popay, et al. (Eds.), *Supplementary guidance for inclusion of qualitative research in Cochrane Systematic Reviews of interventions.* Version 1 (updated August 2011). London, UK: Cochrane Collaboration Qualitative Methods Group. Retrieved from http://cqrmg .cochrane.org/supplemental-handbook-guidance.

Noyes, J., Popay, J., Pearson, A., Hannes, K. and Booth, A. (2008). Qualitative Research and Cochrane Reviews. In In Julian P. T. Higgins & Sally Green (Eds.), *Cochrane Handbook for Systematic Reviews of Interventions: Cochrane Book Series.* John Wiley & Sons, Ltd, Chichester, UK. doi: 10.1002/ 9780470712184.ch20

Noyes, J., Popay, J., Pearson, A., Hannes, K., & Booth, A. (2011). Qualitative research and Cochrane reviews. In Julian P. T. Higgins & Sally Green (Eds.), *Cochrane handbook for scientific reviews of interventions*, version 5.1.0.

Cochrane Collaboration. Retrieved from http://handbook.cochrane.org/front_page.htm.

Nutley, S., Davies, H., & Walter, I. (2002). *Evidence based policy and practice: Cross sector lessons from the UK.* Working Paper 9. London, UK: ESRC UK Centre for Evidence Based Policy and Practice.

Nyanzi, S., Manneh, H., & Walraven, G. (2007). Traditional birth attendants in rural Gambia: Beyond health to social cohesion. *African Journal of Reproductive Health, 11,* 43–56.

O'Cathain, A., Murphy, E., & Nicholl, J. (2007). Integration and publications as indicators of "yield" from mixed methods studies. *Journal of Mixed Methods Research, 1*(2), 147–163.

Oliver, K., Innvar, S., Lorenc, T., Woodman, J., & Thomas, J. (2014). A systematic review of barriers to and facilitators of the use of evidence by policymakers. *BMC Health Services Research, 14,* 2–12.

Onwuegbuzie, A., Bustamante, R. M., & Nelson, J. A. (2010). Mixed research as a tool for developing quantitative instruments. *Journal of Mixed Methods Research, 4*(1), 56–78.

Organisation for Economic Co-operation and Development. (2012). *Evaluating peacebuilding activities in settings of conflict and fragility: Improving learning for results.* Paris, France: Author. doi:10.1787/9789264106802-en

Overholt, C., Anderson, M., Cloud, K., & Austin, J. E. (1985). *Gender roles in development projects: A case book.* West Hartford, CT: Kumarian Press.

Patton, M. (2011). *Developmental evaluation.* New York, NY: Guilford Press.

Patton, M., McKegg, K., & Wehipeihana, N. (2016). *Developmental evaluation exemplars.* New York, NY: Guilford Press.

Peterson, J. C., Czajkowski, S., Charlson, M. E., Link, A. R., Wells, M. T., Isen, A. M., et al. (2013). Translating basic behavioral and social science research to clinical application: The EVOLVE mixed methods approach. *Journal of Counseling and Clinical Psychology, 81*(2), 217–230.

Petrosino, A., Turpin-Petrosino, C., Hollis-Peel, M., & Lavenberg, J. G. (2013). Scared Straight and other juvenile awareness programs for preventing juvenile delinquency: A systematic review. *Campbell Systematic Reviews, 2013, 5.* doi:10.4073/csr.so13.5

Pham, M. T., Rajic, A., Greig, J. D., Sargeant, J. M., Papdopoulous, A., & McEwen, S. A. (2014). A scoping review of scoping reviews: Advancing the approach and enhancing the consistency. *Research Synthesis Methods, 5,* 371–385.

Philip, H., & De Bruyn, P. (2013, June). *A mixed methods approach to combining behavioral and design research methods in information systems research.* Paper presented at the 21st European Conference on Information Systems, Utrecht, Netherlands.

Phillips, C. B., Dwan, K., Hepworth, J., Pearce, C., & Hall, S. (2014). Using qualitative mixed method to study small health care organizations while maximizing trustworthiness and authenticity. *BMC Health Services Research, 14,* 559–578.

Pluye, P., & Hong, Q. N. (2014). Combining the power of stories and the power of numbers: Mixed methods research and mixed studies reviews. *Annual Review of Public Health, 2014, 35*, 29–45.

Raimondo, E., Bamberger, M., & Vaessen, J. (2016). Introduction. In M. Bamberger, J. Vaessen, & E. Raimondo (Eds.), *Dealing with complexity in development evaluation* (pp. xxxv–xliv). Thousand Oaks, CA: Sage.

Rao, A., Sandler, J., Kelleher, D., & Miller, C. (2016). *Gender at work: Theory and practice for 21st century organizations.* New York, NY: Routledge.

Rittel, H. W. J., & Webber, M. M. (1973). Dilemmas in a general theory of planning. *Policy Sciences, 4*, 155–169.

Rucks-Ahidiana, Z., & Bierbaum, A. H. (2015). Qualitative spaces: Integrating spatial analysis for a mixed methods approach. *International Journal of Qualitative Methods, 14*(2), 92–103.

Scriven, M. (1980). *The logic of evaluation.* Inverness, CA: Edgepress.

Scriven, M. (2008). The concept of transdiscipline: And of evaluation as a transdiscipline. *Journal of Multidisciplinary Evaluation, 5*(10), 65–66.

Segone, M. (Ed.). (2015). *National evaluation policies for sustainable and equitable development.* New York, NY: UN Evaluation Group.

Shadish, W. (1998). Evaluation theory is who we are. *American Journal of Evaluation, 19*, 1–19.

Shadish, W., & Luellen, J. K. (2005). History of evaluation. In S. Mathison (Ed.), *Encyclopedia of Evaluation* (pp. 183–186). Thousand Oaks, CA: Sage.

Shannon-Baker, P. (2015a). "But I wanted to appear happy": How using arts-informed and mixed methods approaches complicate qualitatively driven research on culture shock. *International Journal of Qualitative Methods, 14*, 34–52.

Shannon-Baker, P. (2015b). Making paradigms meaningful in mixed methods research. *Journal of Mixed Methods Research*, 1–16.

Simons, H., & McCormack, B. (2007). Integrating arts-based inquiry in evaluation methodology. *Qualitative Inquiry, 13*(2), 292–311.

Sleeper, R. W. (1986). *The necessity of pragmatism: John Dewey's conception of philosophy.* New Haven, CT: Yale University Press.

Smith, L. T. (2012). *Decolonizing methodologies: Research and indigenous peoples* (2nd ed.). London, UK & New York, NY: Zed Books.

Stake, R. E. (1995). *The art of case study research.* London, UK: Sage.

Stufflebeam, D., Madaus, G. F., & Kellaghan, T. (2000). *Evaluation models.* Boston, MA: Kluwer Academic.

Suleweski, J., & Gothberg, J. (2013). Universal design checklist for evaluation (4th ed.). Available at http://comm.eval.org/communities/community-home/librarydocuments/viewdocument?DocumentKey=62107753-a359-40d1-96d7-2fc113ae9ba8.

Tashakkori, A., & Teddlie, C. (Eds.). (2003). *SAGE handbook of mixed methods in social and behavioral research.* Thousand Oaks, CA: Sage.

Tashakkori, A., & Teddlie, C. (Eds.). (2010). *SAGE handbook of mixed methods in social and behavioral research* (2nd ed.). Thousand Oaks, CA: Sage.

Teddlie, C., & Tashakkori, A. (2009). *Foundations of mixed methods research.* Thousand Oaks, CA: Sage.

Teddlie, C., & Tashakkori, A. (2010). Overview of contemporary issues in mixed methods research. In A. Tashakkori & C. Teddlie (Eds.), *SAGE handbook of mixed methods in social and behavioral research* (pp. 1–44). Thousand Oaks, CA: Sage.

Thomas, J., Harden, A., Oakley, A., Oliver, S., Sutcliffe, K., Rees, R., et al. (2004). Integrating qualitative research with trials in systematic reviews. *British Medical Journal, 238*(7446), 1010–1012.

Toal, S. A. (2009). The validation of the evaluation involvement scale for use in multisite settings. *American Journal of Evaluation, 30,* 349–362.

Todrys, K. W., Amon, J. J., Malembeka, G., & Clayton, M. (2011). Imprisoned and imperiled: Access to HIV and TB prevention and treatment, and denial of human rights, in Zambian prisons. *Journal of the International AIDS Society, 14,* 1–8.

Trochim, W., & Kane, M. (2005). Concept mapping. *International Journal for Quality in Health Care, 17*(3), 187–191.

Tsushima, R. (2015). Methodological diversity in language assessment research: The role of mixed methods in classroom-based language assessment studies. *International Journal of Qualitative Methods, 14*(2), 104–121.

UN Women. (2015). *How to manage gender-responsive evaluation: Evaluation handbook.* New York, NY: Author.

Ungar, M., & Liebenberg, L. (2011). Assessing resilience across cultures using mixed methods: Construction of the Child and Youth Resilience Measure. *Journal of Mixed Methods Research, 5*(2), 126–149.

U.S. Department of Health and Human Services, Centers for Disease Control and Prevention. (2011). *Introduction to program evaluation for public health programs.* Atlanta, GA: Author.

Veitch, C., Lincoln, M., Bundy, A., Gallego, G., Dew, A., Bulkeley, K., et al. (2012). Integrating evidence into policy and sustainable disability services delivery in western New South Wales, Australia: The "wobbly hub and the double spokes" project. *BMC Health Services Research, 12,* 1–8.

White, H. (2013a). An introduction to the use of randomized control trials to evaluate development interventions. *Journal of Development Effectiveness, 5*(1), 30–49.

White, H. (2013b). The use of mixed methods in randomized control trials. In D. M. Mertens & S. Hesse-Biber (Eds.), *Mixed methods and credibility of evidence in evaluation: New directions for evaluation,* (no. 138), pp. 61–73.

Wilson, J. (2013). *Exploring the past, present and future of cultural competency research: The revision and expansion of the sociocultural adaptation construct.* Unpublished doctoral dissertation. Victoria University of Wellington.

Wilson, S. (2008). *Research as ceremony: Indigenous research methods.* Black Point, Nova Scotia: Fernwood.

World Bank. (2012). Poverty and social impact analysis (PSIA). Washington, DC: Author.

Yarbrough, D. B., Shulha, L. M., Hopson, R. K., & Caruthers, F. A. (2011). *The program evaluation standards: A guide for evaluators and evaluation users* (3rd ed.). Thousand Oaks, CA: Sage.

Index